Rebuilding
Post-War Britain

For Latvians, Lithuanians and Estonians all over the world

Rebuilding Post-War Britain

Latvian, Lithuanian and Estonian refugees in Britain, 1946–51

EMILY GILBERT

PEN & SWORD
HISTORY

First published in Great Britain in 2017 by
Pen & Sword History
an imprint of
Pen & Sword Books Ltd
47 Church Street
Barnsley
South Yorkshire
S70 2AS

ISBN 978 147386 057 5

A CIP catalogue record for this book is
available from the British Library.

Printed and bound in Malta
by Gutenberg Press Ltd

Pen & Sword Books Ltd incorporates the Imprints of Pen & Sword Books
Archaeology, Atlas, Aviation, Battleground, Discovery, Family History,
History, Maritime, Military, Naval, Politics, Railways, Select, Transport,
True Crime, Fiction, Frontline Books, Leo Cooper, Praetorian Press,
Seaforth Publishing, Wharncliffe and White Owl.

For a complete list of Pen & Sword titles please contact
PEN & SWORD BOOKS LIMITED
47 Church Street, Barnsley, South Yorkshire, S70 2AS, England
E-mail: enquiries@pen-and-sword.co.uk

Contents

Acknowledgements

Thank you to Pen and Sword Publishers for seeing the potential in this book, particularly Eloise Hansen, Carol Trow and Heather Williams who provided excellent advice and support throughout the project.

I would also like to thank all the Latvians, Lithuanians and Estonians in Britain, and across the globe, who helped with this book. I am particularly grateful to everyone at the Latvian clubs in Leeds and Nottingham, the Lithuanian clubs in Manchester and Nottingham, and the Estonian club in Bradford. I would like to thank all the original questionnaire and interview participants and their families, and all those who generously contributed a range of community documents, including rare books, personal memoirs, newspapers and journals, which formed extremely useful source materials for this study. I am particularly grateful to Heino Poopuu for allowing me to use his fascinating unpublished memoir *Remembering Pussa* about his childhood on the Estonian island of Saaremaa which forms the backbone for Chapter 1 (*'A Wonderful Life': Growing up in the Interwar Homelands*). Vida Gasperas provided multiple contacts and links for the project and arranged a visit to *Židinys* in Nottingham. Inese Auziņa-Smita (Smith) was very helpful and took me on a tour around the Latvian retirement home *Straumēni*, including the amazing library housed there. Vladas Dargis arranged accommodation in Vilnius and Bruno Rullis and Jānis Šmits from Leeds were extremely helpful in so many ways, as were many other individuals and their families. There are too many to list individually here; some of them have sadly passed away, while others have wished to remain anonymous.

I am also extremely grateful to the many second generation Latvians, Lithuanians and Estonians who have supported this project in recent years. I am indebted to Alexandra Māzers who has enthusiastically shared her experiences as a second generation Latvian in Britain, and allowed me to use treasured family photographs on the cover of the book.

ACKNOWLEDGEMENTS

I would like to thank Anita Woronycz, a second generation Lithuanian, who has been an amazing proof-reader of this book, and provided useful comments and feedback. Anita's help in the final stages of the book was invaluable and I could not have finished it without her. Any mistakes are, however, my own! I am very grateful to Susanna Brazauskas who has also shared family photographs used on the spine of this book and also to Astrid Radze-Constable and her two sisters, Martina and Anne-Marie, who have shared stories and enthusiasm for the project.

Karen Mitchell kindly shared the amazing story of her Lithuanian grandparents, which forms the start of the Prologue *A Brief History of Latvians, Lithuanians and Estonians in Britain before the Second World War*. Irene Adickas, Glynis Harrison, Angela Wall, Pauline Szelewski, Sarah Dauksta and Andrew Rimaitis all shared family histories and/or photographs used in this book an Paul Lucas provided useful information about Scottish Lithuanians. I would also like to thank Luke Māzers, Mark Māzers, Reet Järvik, and the many others who have helped in so many ways with this project, but who I am unable to name individually due to lack of space.

I would like to thank my PhD supervisor, Professor Colin Holmes, who provided the initial idea for the research and oversaw its completion with support and enthusiasm. Colin has also continued to provide moral and practical support throughout this project. Thank you to the Department of History at the University of Sheffield, where the original research was undertaken and the Economic and Social Research Council, which funded the research.

Last but not least, a big thank you to John, my partner, who has supported me throughout and my sons, Isaac and Seth, as well as my wider family and friends who have been very supportive and kept me on an even keel.

Emily Gilbert 2017

Introduction

'Some carried all their belongings in a grey army blanket; others wore fur coats and smart hats.'
(News Chronicle, *reporting on the arrival of eighty-seven Baltic women in Britain, 22 October 1946)*

Between 1946 and 1950, twenty-five thousand Latvian, Lithuania and Estonian men, women and children arrived on Britain's eastern shores via the ports of Hull, Tilbury and Harwich. They travelled on cruise liners and British Navy ships, and disembarked with a mix of excitement and trepidation at their new lives ahead. This was the final stage of long and arduous displacement journeys, which had begun years earlier at the start of the Second World War, with the occupation of their homelands by Soviet Russia and Nazi Germany.

Many of the newcomers arrived via the Port of Hull, sailing down the River Humber before docking at Hull's historic docks, long used as a transit point for European migrants. Often arriving in the morning after a night-time crossing, their view of Hull was a very different scene to the vistas of the pre-war, often rural, landscapes of their homelands. Early morning sea mists lifted from the brown muddy waters of the Humber estuary, to reveal a war-ravaged scene. Collapsed shells of buildings lined the shore and smoke rose from chimneys standing tall on the skyline. The grey-brown palette submerged all colour and was a stark contrast to the lush green fields and natural panoramas of home. However, the refugees had seen worse in Germany, and were grateful finally to be given the opportunity to start a new life in a safe country.

Having accepted work placements on the European Volunteer Workers schemes, the arriving refugees would be working in a variety of jobs in Britain's undermanned industries, and their dependents who arrived

INTRODUCTION

later, would have the chance to recreate some semblance of family life in a new country. Representatives from the Women's Royal Voluntary Service greeted the new arrivals and chatted to them about the next stage of their journeys while they drank mugs of tea. One Latvian EVW noted that he was given fish and chips after arriving at Hull, which made him feel very sick after years of meagre rations. From the ports, they boarded buses and trains to the hostels and camps, where they would be registered and settled into their temporary accommodation, until they were assigned work and longer term accommodation.

This was a typical first twenty-four hours in the lives of the Baltic refugees as they arrived in Britain. Between 1946 and 1950, 13,000 Latvians, and over 6,000 Lithuanian and 5,000 Estonian Displaced Persons (DPs) came to Britain in this way. They came as part of two organised 'European Volunteer Worker' schemes – 'Balt Cygnet' and 'Westward Ho!' – to fill critical labour shortages in British industry and help rebuild Britain's fragile post-war economy. In total, over 80,000 DPs of Baltic and Eastern European nationalities participated in these schemes and were known collectively as European Volunteer Workers or 'EVWs'.

The newcomers arrived in a post-war Britain, that was not as 'Great' as they had anticipated. At the close of the Second World War in 1945, Great Britain was in a precarious state. Heavily bombed and having suffered mass deaths and casualties during the war, the country was on its knees. Bombed out towns and cities created huge housing problems, returning soldiers and mass infection overwhelmed hospitals, and the country was struggling to feed, clothe and fuel the nation. The task facing the new Atlee Labour government elected in July 1945 was immense. Not only was the country in serious debt, it relied heavily on imports to provide for the nations' basic needs. Exports were at a critical low, and the country was unable to lift itself out of this mess, as it did not have enough workers to man the factories, to nurse the sick or to harvest the crops. The population had suffered a serious decline due to the war, women who had worked during the war, returned to family duties, and the number of healthy, working age men and women willing to work in certain sectors of the economy, was now insufficient.

As well as domestic problems at home, Britain also had responsibility for millions of refugees in the British zones of Germany and Austria. The Second World War had led to a severe refugee crisis in Europe, with unprecedented numbers of people now displaced from their homelands and stranded in Displaced Persons' camps. Among these millions, were several hundred thousand refugees from the Baltic countries of Latvia, Lithuania and Estonia, who had been displaced due to the Soviet and Nazi invasions and occupations of these three, small, north-eastern European countries, beginning in 1939. These occupations had brought about the end of independence for the three states of Latvia, Lithuania and Estonia, and the beginning of a long period of incorporation into the Soviet Union. After years of conflict, and difficult journeys and experiences, Latvian, Lithuanian and Estonian refugees found themselves marooned in Displaced Persons' Camps in Germany and Austria. Designated as 'Displaced Persons' or 'DPs', and without a safe homeland to return to, they faced the prospect of an uncertain future, in limbo, in the middle of Europe. The huge numbers of Prisoners of War from all across Europe, tens of thousands of whom were accommodated in camps both in Britain and the British zones of Germany and Austria, posed an additional issue for the British Government to solve.

With no homelands to return to, these refugees posed a significant challenge for the Allied Governments after the war, not only in terms of the high costs to look after them, but also the political challenges posed by their existence in Europe and the necessity of finding a longer-term solution to address the situation. Housed in inadequate accommodation in the DP Camps, the sheer numbers of men, women and children from a variety of Baltic and mainly Eastern European countries, presented a major problem for western governments, already swamped by domestic difficulties.

In seeking to address the dual problems at home and in Europe, the Attlee government came up with the solution of recruiting some of the millions of refugees in Europe for labour in Britain. Several schemes were implemented, the largest of which was the 'European Volunteer Workers' (EVW) scheme which recruited 80,000 refugees from the Baltic and East European DP nationalities in Europe, for work in Britain's hospitals, coalmines, brickworks, iron and steel works, textile factories and agriculture.

By providing manpower in critical industries and economic sectors, the 25,000 Latvian, Lithuanian and Estonian refugees who came to Britain as part of these EVW schemes between 1946 and 1950, were significant participants in the rebuilding of Britain. Their contribution, alongside that of the other nationalities in the EVW schemes, as well as

INTRODUCTION

that of the Polish Resettlement Corps, and the other European refugees who came to Britain on smaller scale schemes, and individual work permits, needs to be recognised. The vital contribution of these refugees to the rebuilding of the British economy has been seriously neglected. Only a small number of largely academic works have presented the stories of the EVWs, yet these nationalities remain overlooked in both immigration and general histories of Britain.[1]

Although there have been some studies that have looked at the EVW schemes in Britain, few have described in any detail, the specific experiences of Latvians, Lithuanians or Estonians. Using life stories gained from interviews with Latvians, Lithuanians and Estonians in Britain, and information from government documents relating to the schemes, this book tracks the refugees' experiences from their lives in the pre-war homelands to the present day. Despite believing that their stay in Britain would be temporary and that they would return home once the occupying Soviet powers had been defeated, many of the original refugees remained in Britain for the remainder of their lives.

To set the post-war migration of Latvians, Lithuanians and Estonians in Britain into its relevant context, I have included brief comparative chapters on the two other significant migrations of these nationalities to Britain, specifically at the end of the nineteenth century and early twentieth century, and the more recent migration to Britain since Latvia, Lithuania and Estonia joined the European Union in 2004.

PROLOGUE

A Brief History of Latvians, Lithuanians and Estonians in Britain before the Second World War

In January 1903, a fifteen-year-old Lithuanian, Kazimieras Roškas, arrived at the port of Grimsby on the north east coast of England on the steamship SS *Nottingham*, which had sailed from Hamburg in Germany the previous day. Kazimieras and his older brother who had accompanied him, had been hoping to travel on by train to Liverpool and board another ship to America – a popular route for emigrants from Europe. Unfortunately, their belongings and money were stolen on board the vessel and they were unable to continue with their journey.

Forced to stay in Britain for the foreseeable future, they both found jobs in Scotland, a popular destination for Lithuanians during this period, working in the coalmines in the greater Glasgow area. Kazimieras's brother eventually re-emigrated to Argentina, while Kazimieras settled down to his new life in Scotland. Like many other Lithuanians who emigrated to Britain at the time, they were escaping conscription into the Russian army and hoping to find a better life and future.

In 1911, Agota, an eleven-year-old Lithuanian girl, came to Britain with her older brother to join three aunts already in Scotland. She was hoping to find an improved quality of life and her brother to avoid conscription. Her family had bought her some new boots for the journey, but they hurt so much that she spent most of the journey barefoot, holding her boots in her hands. After arriving in Scotland, they were looked after by an aunt and uncle in Auchinleck in Ayrshire, where Agota attended school and learned to read and write English. After leaving school, she went to work in a rope factory near Dundee before moving nearer to another aunt in the Carfin area and working as a shop assistant. It was here that she met Kazimieras Roškas at the Carfin Grotto, a pilgrimage site for Catholics across Scotland. At Carfin, still a popular pilgrimage site today, masses were held in Lithuanian for the growing congregation in this area.

Agota and Kazimieras were married in 1922 at the Roman Catholic Church at Addiwell, West Calder, and went to live in Stoneyburn, where many other Lithuanian families also resided. They went on to have five children and Kazimieras was eventually naturalised as a British citizen at the age of sixty.

Agota and Kazimieras's story has been researched by their granddaughter, Karen Mitchell, and reflects the experiences of many Lithuanians who emigrated to Britain during this period, along with a much smaller number of Latvians and Estonians.

These Latvians, Lithuanians and Estonians migrated to Britain in the late nineteenth and early twentieth centuries to escape repression by the Tsarist regime (which at that time ruled over the three countries known collectively today as the Baltic States), as well as to start a new life and take a chance on a brighter future. In addition, there was also some migration from the Baltic countries during the period of Latvian, Lithuanian and Estonian independence from 1918 to1940 and during the Second World War.

During the late Tsarist period of the late nineteenth and early twentieth century, all three present-day Baltic nations were provinces of the Russian Empire, not independent countries as they are today. Living standards were low and particularly after the assassination of Tsar Alexander II in 1881, repression of political activists and intellectuals was widespread. Intellectuals from the Baltic region had been inspired by the French revolutionary movement and the spread of romantic nationalism across Europe and they had set about constructing national identities in earnest, unifying and cementing national languages and resurrecting ancient traditions.

National awakenings grew out of an intellectual reaction to the Enlightenment that emphasized national identity and developed a romantic view of cultural self-expression through nationhood. However, it was also during this period when Russification policies were most vigorously pursued by the Tsarist State, which aimed to quell the national awakenings and homogenise the territories of the Empire. The Russian Empire also singled out Jews, of whom there were significant numbers in the Baltic provinces, particularly in Lithuania, for particularly repressive measures, as they were regarded as a threat to the Russification of the Empire and the monopoly of Russian Orthodoxy. Jews were also wrongly blamed for the assassination of Tsar Alexander II and a wave of anti-Jewish riots or pogroms swept through the Empire.

As a result, there were several types of migrants to Britain during this period: Latvians, Lithuanians and Estonians who migrated to gain a better standard of living, including young men escaping conscription; political refugees and intellectuals fleeing Tsarist oppression; and finally, Jewish refugees who had fled the pogroms. These refugees and migrants did not enter Britain in one or two waves, nor was their migration at all organised, but rather a slow trickle of refugees over the course of half a century until the First World War.

The date of the arrival in Britain of the very first immigrant from Latvia, Lithuania or Estonia is not known. Indeed, very little is known particularly about Latvian or Estonian immigration before 1918, partly due to the fact that many of the immigrants would have been recorded as Russian or Polish, and also because of their small numbers.

Latviesi Lielbritanijā, a history of Latvians in Britain edited by Jānis Andrups claims that the first sign of Latvians in Great Britain was the publication in London in 1899 of the first Latvian language monthly in Europe, *Latviešu Strādnieks* (The Latvian Worker). The number of political refugees from Latvia who headed for Britain grew after the 1905 revolution in the Russian Empire, when repressive measures against Latvian revolutionaries, social democrats and nationalists were stepped up. In the years up to the First World War, a number of Latvian sailors were also temporarily resident in British ports, especially in Cardiff and Liverpool. According to Jānis Andrups in *Latviesi Lielbritanijā*, the total number of all the above groups was, however, never more than a few hundred.

Even less is known about Estonians in Great Britain before 1918. They were probably the least numerous of the three Baltic nationalities who came to Britain during this period, since many refugees and economic migrants were attracted to Scandinavian countries.

According to Nigol Hindo, twelve Estonian tailors worked in London before the First World War, although none achieved 'any outstanding success in their craft'. There were about twenty craftsmen in total, of different trades and two Estonians in London who achieved prominence during this period. One was Georg Hackenschmidt, a world class wrestler and weightlifter who settled in London in 1903. The other, a Mr Rogenhagen, a wealthy London businessman, was born in Tallinn, and although he had lived in Britain for many years and became a naturalised British subject, still considered himself to be an Estonian.

As in Latvia, many Estonian revolutionaries escaped after the 1905 revolution, when many Estonian intellectuals were arrested, and the Russian army clamped down on protests and gatherings, in one incident in October, killing 94 people and injuring 200. Revolutionaries and intellectuals sought to further their aspirations for Estonian statehood abroad, from countries like Finland and Great Britain.

In comparison to the histories of Latvians and Estonians in Britain, the immigration of Lithuanians to Britain during this period has been documented to a far greater degree, especially those who settled in Scotland.[1] This is partly due to the larger numbers of Lithuanians who settled in Britain, and also because of the relatively concentrated patterns of settlement.

The first sizeable group of Lithuanian known to have arrived in Britain were POWs from the Crimean War, who settled in Britain in the 1860s. Other immigrants from Lithuania began arriving shortly afterwards. Research undertaken by a second generation Lithuanian in Britain, John Millar, suggests that in Scotland, where many of the immigrants headed, the trickle of Lithuanians migrating to Scotland before 1881 became a flood in the 1890s. Census data makes the task of estimating numbers extremely difficult as place of birth was noted as Poland, Russia or Russian Poland, due to historical boundary changes and pre-independence status as part of Russia and Poland. However, as many as 7,000 Lithuanians are thought to have resided in Scotland at the beginning of the twentieth century, with Scotland quickly emerging as the primary centre of Lithuanian cultural and intellectual life in Britain, during this period. The main attraction was the Scottish coalfield, which offered plentiful labour, as did the large iron and steel works in Scotland. A chain effect can also be discerned, whereby Lithuanians finding work reported back to their home village and relatives, who would then follow.

The majority of the Lithuanians who headed for Scotland during this period, were Catholics from the peasant class. However, despite originating from the countryside, they quickly became established members of the industrial working classes. Scottish Lithuanians set up political bodies, including, in 1903, a branch of the Lithuanian Social Democratic Party and the Lithuanian Working Women's Association.

The reactions of locals to the Lithuanian newcomers were mixed. Fellow workers in the coalfields were reportedly often hostile to the Lithuanians, believing that as peasants with poor English, these newcomers were not proficient to carry out these jobs. As peasants or agricultural labourers, most of the Lithuanians who arrived in Scotland had never seen a mine before, although they quickly built up experience in this sector, along with work in iron and steel, where many of them gained their first jobs in Britain. For example, at Glengarnock in Ayrshire, many Lithuanians began work as spare furnacemen in the iron and steel industries, before going on to work in the mining industry in the area.

In many cases, the reactions of fellow workers were initially negative, but over time they began to accept them more and more. Lithuanians were regarded as a threat to employment and wage levels, as well as a danger to their fellow workers, as they were unskilled, and lacked fluency in English, and it was feared that they might not be able to communicate or respond in a situation of danger. In 1887, the Ayrshire Miner's Union demanded their removal on the grounds that 'their presence is a menace to the health and morality of the place and is, besides, being used to reduce the already too low wages earned by workmen'.[2] Local newspapers carried reports of the Lithuanians' 'reckless, drunken behaviour'. *The Bellshill Speaker* reported in a long article on 20 July 1900 that the Lithuanians were a 'most barbarous people and [in this district] we seem to have the very scum of their nation'. However, over time, and as Lithuanians proved themselves to be hard, dedicated workers who also enjoyed a drink in local pubs after work, relationships improved somewhat, although there certainly remained a divide between the locals and the Lithuanians. In *John Bull's Island*, Colin Holmes provides a useful summary of the changing relationships between Lithuanians and locals, which did fluctuate during this period. However, he notes that:

> 'It is important to distinguish between short-term and long-term developments. As time progressed, Lithuanian colliers began to organise and unite with Scottish miners to defend their joint interests'.[3]

One of the Lithuanians who worked as a collier in Scotland during this period, was the father of Matt Busby, who became a prominent and highly regarded footballer and manager. Matt Busby was born in 1909 in the Bellshill area of Glasgow to a Lithuanian mother and father, who had recently migrated to Scotland in search of a better standard of living. Busby is best known for managing Manchester United for twenty-five years, winning thirteen trophies, and is regarded as one of the greatest football managers of all time.

A fellow second generation Lithuanian who also grew up in Scotland was Billy McNeill, born later in 1940, to a Lithuanian mother and Irish father. Like Busby, McNeill was a prominent footballer and manager, who is best known for leading Celtic to victory in the European Cup in 1967. Other well-known Lithuanian families who lived in Scotland during this period, include the Jupitus family who arrived in Scotland sometime after 1912. This family has gained recognition through Phill Jupitus, a well-known comedian, who was brought up by his Lithuanian stepfather and who took on the Jupitus name, which is an Anglicised version of a Lithuanian surname.

While their children and grandchildren successfully integrated into Scottish and British life, the first-generation Scottish Lithuanians clung more vigorously to their homeland cultures. Considering their relatively small numbers, they were remarkably successful at establishing community structures, especially those to maintain their Catholic faith. It is notable, that it was primarily Catholic clergymen who established many of the Lithuanian community structures and cultural activities in Scotland during this period. The Lithuanian's Catholic faith was key to maintaining their links and bonds to Lithuania during this period, and maintaining a sense of Lithuanian cultural and identity. The growing need to establish a Lithuanian parish in Scotland in the very early twentieth century led to an official request submitted for a Lithuanian church in Bellshill, their main settlement. However, the local clergy was opposed to a separate church, believing it would be a barrier to learning English and anyway did not recognise the existence of a separate Lithuanian nation, describing Lithuanians, like many locals did, as 'Poles'. As a result, the Lithuanian community organised their own priests to come over to Scotland. Masses were held in different parts of Scotland, including in the Bellshill area and nearby Carfin. As the only people in the community of high education and standing, the clergy also became leaders of the community. Therefore, the initial proliferation of Lithuanian societies and clubs in Scotland owed much of its inspiration and organisation to the chaplains.[4]

The subsequent events of the First World War and the 1917 Anglo-Russian Military Convention, brought about a significant demise of the Lithuanian community in Scotland. The 1917 Convention related to the reciprocal liability to military service of British subjects resident in Russia and Russian subjects resident in Great Britain. As Lithuanians in Scotland were regarded as 'Russians' by the British Government (even though they were 'Poles' to ordinary Scots), all men aged between eighteen and forty-one were required to carry out a period of service in the Russian army. This led to most of the Lithuanian men of working age in Scotland being sent to Russia, with estimates ranging between 1,000 to 2,000 in total. By the time most arrived back in the Russian Empire, the country was in the grip of the Bolshevik Revolution. Ironically, many of those who had originally come to Britain to escape military service now found themselves back in the Russian Empire carrying out military service at the height of war and revolution.

Due to the departure of these men, an estimated 200 dependent families were left behind in the Bellshill area of Lanarkshire, facing the threat of eviction from company-owned housing. The effect of the Convention was to split the Lithuanian community and to effectively wipe out the wide variety of political and social organisations that had been established among the Lithuanian community. The dependants of those men who returned to Russia were regarded as Bolshevik sympathisers and as a permanent financial liability, and many were later repatriated in February and March 1920. In total, at least 600 women and children were sent back to the Russian Empire.

It is important to note that although many Lithuanians fought on the side of the Russian Army during the First World War, a significant number joined the British Army and fought on the British side during the First World War, as a way of escaping conscription to the Russian army. About 1500 Lithuanians joined the British forces (about one eighth of the total population of Lithuanians in Britain), of whom sixty-five were killed during the fighting.[5] Their contribution to the British war effort during the First World War needs to be recognized.

About one third of the men who were deported to the Russian Empire were eventually allowed back to Britain and some families still do not know, even to this day, what happened to their relatives. The small number of Lithuanian families who remained in Scotland after the war, as well as the intermarriage of their children during the 1920s and 1930s, inevitably led to a weakening of their community.

PROLOGUE

Far less is known about Lithuanians in other parts of Britain during this period. There were an estimated 1,000 Lithuanians in London and 4,000 in England as a whole by 1914.[6] There were approximately fourteen Lithuanian families in Bradford in 1908, the majority of whom worked as tailors, although it is not clear if these were Lithuanian Jews or Catholic Lithuanians.[7] According to Colin Holmes, there is evidence of wider patterns of employment of Lithuanians beyond the mining and iron and steel industries. Areas of employment include Lithuanians working in the sugar works in Liverpool, the salt works in Cheshire, and railway works. However, as Holmes notes, wherever they were employed, the Lithuanians seem to have primarily 'been concentrated in heavy labouring activity'.[8]

One of the Lithuanian families living in London during this period was the family of John Gielgud, a famous actor who was born in London in 1904 to a Lithuanian-Polish father. Gielgud's surname derives from Gelgaudiškis, a village in Lithuania. The family had previously been well-off landowners, but due to their participation in a failed uprising against Russian rule in 1830–31, their estates were confiscated, and the family fled to England.

A number of Lithuanians did re-emigrate to the United States, but numbers are not known. Many of those who came to Britain had planned to stay in Britain temporarily before heading on to America, but many did not make the journey. There are also examples of Lithuanians with tickets to go to America being conned with fake tickets and unable to make the journey.

The immigrants discussed above, who were mainly Catholic peasants from the countryside, can be distinguished from a separate wave of immigration during the same period of Lithuanian Jewish refugees. Furthermore, these two groups had virtually no contact with each other. Some of these Jews came from the south-western corner of contemporary Lithuania, then part of Russian Poland, and the Pale of Settlement, an area in the north west of the Russian Empire which the Tsarist authorities had designated for Jews to live in, which included areas of present day Lithuania, Belarus, Ukraine and Poland, an area stretching from the Baltic to the Black Sea.

Jews from these areas began arriving in Britain from 1880 onwards, with numbers steadily increasing year on year, due to three main reasons: a desire to improve their economic status; to escape from an increasingly repressive Tsarist regime; and finally, a change in Jews' legal status. Although a law on residence introduced in 1865 had potentially opened the door for large numbers of Jews (approximately one-fifth of those resident in the Pale) to live outside the Pale of Settlement and be given empire-wide residence, the ambiguity of their new legal status left re-settlers at the mercy of numerous external forces. Faced with a choice between confinement to the Pale, harassment as a result of resettlement, or emigration, many of those with the necessary resources, opted for emigration.

One of the Jewish families fleeing at this time, was the family of Isaiah Berlin, a prolific and internationally recognised philosopher and polit-ical theorist. Berlin was born in 1909 in Latvia and grew up in Riga before arriving in Britain in 1920 with his family, who were escaping anti-Semitism in the Russian Empire at that time. Another Jewish ref-ugee from Lithuania who came to Britain at this time was Montague Burton (born in 1885 as Meshe David Osinsky in Kaunas), who set up Burton's Menswear, a well-known men's clothing shop which continues to thrive on Britain's high streets today. The family of Malcolm Rifkind, a conservative MP who served under Margaret Thatcher, were also famously immigrants. His grandfather arrived in Britain from Lithuania in the mid-nineteenth century to escape the pogroms, as did the families of many other well-known and influential people in Britain, including (among many others): David Suchet (actor); Henry Daniels (statistician); Andy Zaltzman (comedian); Simon Schama who grew up in Britain (his-torian); Eta Cohen (prolific violinist and teacher); Brian Epstein (man-ager of The Beatles); and the Gavron family, who include prolific writers, a film director and a Labour Life Peer (Robert Gavron).

In addition to the migrations before the First World War, there was also a trickle of Latvian, Lithuania and Estonian migrants to Britain between 1918 and 1940, during the period of Latvian, Estonian and Lithuanian independence. The British Government granted all three Baltic countries *de jure* recognition during this period, which enabled diplomatic repre-sentations to be set up in London.

One of the key figures among Britain's Latvian community during this period was Karlis Zariņš, also known as Charles Zarine, who arrived in London in 1933 to take up the post of Envoy Extraordinary and Minister Plenipotentiary. Charles Zarine subsequently became one of the key fig-ures in the establishment of a Latvian community in Britain, promoting economic links between Britain and Latvia, as well as stimulating Latvian culture in Britain. Significantly, Zariņš encouraged dialogue between the Latvian Lutheran Church and the Church of England shortly after his arrival in London. This led to the acceptance of intercommunion with the Lutheran Church of Latvia by the Church of England in 1939. Zariņš continued his activities during the Second World War and after 1945, thereby cementing his reputation as a key figure within the Latvian community in Britain.

The diplomatic representation of the Estonian Republic in London dates back to April 1918, when Professor A. Piip arrived there with a delegation. A few months previously, on 16 February 1918, an organisation, '*Londoni Eesti Ilma Parteita Sotsiaal Gruppe. Eesthonien sotcial group*' was founded, with a loosely stated aim of promoting social life among its members.[9] During the period of Estonian independence, migrants continued to arrive from Estonia: Britain was regarded as a desirable place to come to learn and practise English, and London in particular, offered a large variety of language courses both at beginner and advanced levels. An intergovernmental agreement enabled foreign students to live with local families and earn their keep by doing a certain amount of housework, which eased the financial burden for women who took up this opportunity. Estonian students also came to Britain to study at educational institutions specialising in catering, tailoring, commerce and economics. Some students were supported by grants from the Estonian government and by stipends from the British Council. By 1941, *Londoni Eesti Selts* had eighty-one members, including some sailors and people living outside the capital.

Latvians and Lithuanians also migrated to Britain during this period, primarily to London for educational purposes. Like Estonians, they took advantage of the bi-lateral arrangements with the British Government, enabling them to live with British families in return for housekeeping duties. In most cases this migration was short term, with many returning to Latvia, Lithuania and Estonia after a few years.

Before the Second World War broke out therefore, there had already been some small-scale migration of Latvians, Lithuanians and Estonians to Great Britain, resulting in the establishment of some community structures and cultural activity. However, none of this migration was anywhere near the scale of what was to come, due to the Nazi and Soviet occupations of the Baltic States and the subsequent displacement of hundreds of thousands of Latvians, Lithuanians and Estonians from their homelands.

CHAPTER 1

'A Wonderful Life' – Growing Up in the Interwar Homelands

'I suppose that initial growing up period were the formative years, well, that...sort of instils it into you...you see I had this farming background and the Estonian childhood, growing up in the country...it was very different to anything [in Britain].'

Heino Poopuu arrived in Britain in 1947, on the Westward Ho! labour recruitment scheme, aged just 21. Like many of the refugees who arrived in Britain after the Second World War, he had grown up in the countryside, in Heino's case, on the idyllic island of Saaremaa, off the western shores of Estonia. In his memoir, *Remembering Pussa*, Heino wrote about his childhood on the island:

'I was born and brought up during our political independence, the golden age, which ended with the occupation of Estonia by the Soviet Union of Stalin in 1940.'

Heino described the village he grew up in on Saaremaa – Koovi – as a stable, close-knit community of just sixty-eight residents, which sat on the shores of the Baltic Sea. This was a community in the old-fashioned sense, where people supported each other, through large extended families and strong relations with neighbours. Heino recalled that: 'I don't recall the term loneliness ever being used!'

The Poopuu's farm – Pussa – was a large farmstead on the banks of the Cove of Koovi and 'produced corn, a large variety of vegetable and fruit, flax, hemp, hops, meat, dairy products, wool, landed fish....and manufactured most of the clothing, furniture, and implements in use on the farm'. Heino lived on the farm with his large extended family, and in

1

his memoir, he recalled some of the hardships endured by his family, as well as happier times, such as playing with his cousins around the huge windmill, that was jointly owned with the neighbouring farm.

Heino went to school in a neighbouring village and despite harsh environmental conditions, the 'drudgery' involved in many of the farming and household chores, as well as the relative poverty of people, it was a happy, idyllic time, when the family and the local community provided help and support in times of need. Heino described it as a 'virtually self-sustainable life', which provided the children and young people growing up there with a strong sense of identity, industriousness and adaptability.

Heino's experiences of growing up in the countryside, captured so beautifully in his memoir *Remembering Pussa*, mirror that of many of the refugees who later came to Britain. The majority grew up on farms and in villages and recall their childhoods as idyllic, happy times. It was 'a wonderful life,' according to one interviewee, that contrasted sharply with their later lives in the dirty, smoggy towns and cities of industrial Britain. There is no doubt that memory and reminiscence have shaped their recollections and may have put a more favourable gloss over the often harsh realities of their lives in the homelands, but these were the memories that were shaped in Britain, and which played such an important part in exile cultures and identities.

Unlike the earlier refugees in the previous chapter who were escaping Tsarist rule and repression, the post-war newcomers had been lucky enough to grow up in newly independent countries; and moreover, countries which had experienced an unprecedented period of freedom, national awakening and relative prosperity.

Prior to 1918, Latvia and Estonia had never existed as independent states in the form we know them today (although Lithuania had enjoyed a brief spell of statehood prior to its submergence into the Polish-Lithuanian Commonwealth in 1387). Indeed, the word 'Estonian' only entered the vocabulary in 1860. Their unenviable geographical position sandwiched between East and West has determined Latvia, Lithuania and Estonia's history for centuries.

It is important to note that, despite neighbouring each other and common histories, the three nations of Latvia, Lithuania and Estonia were culturally distinct from each other, the result of unique paths of historical development and different foreign influences. Until the thirteenth century, all three contemporary Baltic States had been a collection of independent kingdoms, inhabited by an array of diverse nationalities. The predecessors of contemporary Latvians, Lithuanians and Estonians populated various regions in the area alongside other nationalities, many of whom have died out over the course of history. While Latvians and Lithuanians are descended from Baltic tribes in the region, Estonians are descendants of Finno-Ugric peoples, who were thought to have inhabited the region from the third millennium BC. Indo-Europeans were believed to have settled in the areas of contemporary Latvia and Lithuania around the same period, and intermingled with the local populations to form the basis of the Baltic tribes.

Between the thirteenth and eighteenth century, the Baltic region was invaded by several Western nations. The regions now composing Latvia and Estonia both succumbed to a German-led invasion, which resulted in to the imposition of Lutheran Christianity and the enserfment of the peasant populations. During subsequent centuries, different areas of present-day Latvia and Estonia were annexed by various foreign powers. In 1561, southern Estonia (Livonia) was integrated into the Polish-Lithuanian Commonwealth, while the rest of the region was brought under Swedish rule. Foreign regimes in charge of different parts of present-day Latvia during this period, included the Vatican, Denmark, Prussia, Poland-Lithuania, Sweden and Russia. Following the establishment of the Livonian State by the German Teutonic Knights in the thirteenth century, in the fifteenth century, Livonia was partitioned and south-western Latvia became the Duchy of Kurland under the suzerainty of the Polish monarchy. The rest of Livonia became a dependency of the Polish-Lithuanian Commonwealth, and from 1629 to 1721 was annexed by Sweden. Swedish rule lasted until the start of the Great Northern War in the early eighteenth century.

The area of contemporary Lithuania was able to resist the German crusading onslaught, and in 1231, Grand Duke Mindaugas united Lithuanian tribes in the region into a nation, leading to a brief period of Lithuanian statehood. Under the leadership of his successors, notably Gediminas, Algirdas and Vytautas, the Lithuanian state expanded from the Baltic to the Black Sea. In 1387, Lithuanian Grand Duke Jogaila accepted the crown of Poland and established the Polish-Lithuanian Commonwealth. This led to the permanent introduction of Latin Christianity into Lithuania between 1387 and 1413. The union with Poland became institutionalised over a number of years, and in 1569, Lithuania was merged into a single state, albeit with some autonomy, which effectively reduced ethnic Lithuania to a provincial status. The result was extensive Polonisation among nobles and gentry, who accepted the Polish language and customs in an attempt to improve and maintain their own status in the Commonwealth. The Polish influence on Lithuania's history has been one of the key defining characteristics of Lithuania's past, the influence of which lasts until today, most obviously through the status of Catholicism as the national religion.

During the eighteenth century, the territories comprising contemporary Latvia, Lithuania and Estonia became subjugated to the Russian Empire, a rule which lasted until 1918. Russian annexation transformed the different regions of contemporary Latvia, Lithuania and Estonia into constituent provinces of the Russian Empire. Until emancipation in the nineteenth century, the indigenous peasantry was ruled both by the German land-owning nobility (in Latvia and Estonia), the Polish nobles (in Lithuania), and the Russian State, which sought to Russify the local populations. Mirroring developments in the rest of Europe, Latvia, Lithuania and Estonia experienced national awakenings in the latter half of the nineteenth century, which led to the development of the concepts of national cultures and identities. Initially movements for greater cultural autonomy, and spearheaded by the German nobles and clergy in Latvia and Estonia, and by the Polish nobles and clergy in Lithuania, they soon developed into movements for greater political autonomy. Supported by the liberal intelligentsia and the new literate working classes, the latter having developed as a result of emancipation and industrialisation, these national movements demanded autonomy in the 1905 revolution. However, it was not until the collapse of Empire in both Russia and Germany that the opportunity was presented to successfully assert independence in 1918. Independent statehood was finally secured in all three countries in 1920, following the wars of independence.

During the period of independence, political, social and economic reforms were far-reaching, and aimed to remove all vestiges of Russian control, including the powers of the German and Polish land-owning nobility. Politically, all three countries became constitutional democracies, in sharp contrast to the earlier experience of Tsarist autocracy. Democratic systems based on proportional representation were introduced which promoted a proliferation of small parties. However, the democratic experience was short-lived, brought to an end by increasing economic problems and the political instability caused by the large number of political parties. Authoritarianism was established earliest in Lithuania, where in 1926, Antanas Smetona was brought to power by a military coup, overthrowing the democratic state and establishing an authoritarian regime. Smetona's regime lasted until 1938, when foreign policy failures forced the establishment of a coalition government and gradual democratisation. In Latvia, Karlis Ulmanis dissolved Parliament in 1934 and established an authoritarian regime, called the 'Government of National Unity' which he headed as President. In Estonia, from 1934 to 1938, President Konstantin Päts ruled by Presidential Decree partly in an attempt to pre-empt a far-rightist coup. A constitutional regime was re-established in Estonia in 1938.

Despite mixed political and economic fortunes, social reform during this period was significant, and included the expansion of the education system and the introduction of basic social welfare systems. Overall, there was a rise in living standards and wage levels in all three countries during the inter-war period. The inter-war period also saw the dual processes of urbanisation and industrialisation, which had begun under Russian rule, continue. Approximately one-third of the population of Latvia and Estonia lived in urban areas of over 2,000 residents, as did about one-seventh of Lithuania's inhabitants.

Inter-war Latvia, Lithuania and Estonia had small populations. In 1934, Estonia had a populace numbering just over 1.1 million, while Latvia had a more sizeable population of almost 2 million. Lithuania had the largest number of inhabitants – just under 2.4 million in 1937. Lithuania was also largest country in terms of area, although the fact that the distance from the northernmost point of Estonia to the southern tip of Lithuania is less than the length of England, gives some impression of the size of the three countries.

Despite their small geographical area, the populations were fairly widely dispersed, although growing urbanisation and industrialisation was leading to a concentration of people in a small number of urban areas. The most striking difference between urban and rural areas was that life in towns and cities was more cosmopolitan and culturally diverse than rural life. In the capital cities, architecture expressed a wide variety of foreign styles and influences, from Riga's art nouveau architecture, to Tallinn's Swedish and Danish buildings. Many aspects of culture

5

and everyday life in the cities were reminders of an occupied past and a multi-ethnic present, from the very name of Tallinn itself (meaning 'Danish castle'), to Riga's synagogues. Riga during the inter-war period was sometimes described as a 'small Paris'. Photographs of Riga from this era show well-dressed men and women walking down busy streets, full of shops and cars. A Latvian woman now in Britain, but who grew up in Riga, described the city in the inter-war period in the following terms:

> *'...it was a lovely city. ...it was a really western city, nice shops and nice cinemas and being capital of Latvia, we had opera house there. We had three theatres, and no end of cinemas and everything happened there, exhibitions... It was, very, very nice there.'*

Tallinn, Estonia's capital was also culturally diverse, with a variety of ethnic groups, and an array of cultural influences visible, particularly in its architecture, from Denmark, Sweden and Germany. As a seaport, and incredibly close to Helsinki, Tallinn like Riga enjoyed a wide variety of foreign influences from abroad.

The new capital of Lithuania during the inter-war period, Kaunas, was not as cosmopolitan or culturally diverse as Riga, although diversity could be seen particularly with Lithuania's Jewish population, as well as Polish influences, and its membership of the Hanseatic League in the seventh century, through buildings such as the Merchant's House.

Kaunas was Lithuania's capital during this period because the geographical boundaries of inter-war Estonia, Latvia and Lithuania were slightly different from the present-day. Vilnius was then part of Poland, having been captured by the Polish leader Pilsudski in 1920, during the wars of independence. As a result, Kaunas became the capital of inter-war Lithuania. Kaunas lay in the eastern interior of Lithuania while the capitals of Latvia and Estonia were ports on the Baltic Sea (Riga and Tallinn respectively).

All three countries had significant minority groups, many of whom lived in the capital cities. George Kennan, an American diplomat and historian, who was based in Riga during the early 1930s, described how Riga enjoyed a variegated and highly cosmopolitan cultural life, including newspapers and theatres in the Lettish, German, Russian and Yiddish tongues and vigorous Lutheran, Roman Catholic, Russian Orthodox and Jewish religious communities.

The proportions of the total populations belonging to ethnic minorities were approximately one-tenth in Estonia, one-fifth in Lithuania and
one-quarter in Latvia. Russians formed the largest minority in Estonia and
Latvia (eight and ten per cent of the total population in 1934), and Jews
were the largest minority group in Lithuania (seven per cent in 1923).
Jews and Germans were also sizeable groups in Latvia and Estonia, and
significant Polish and German communities existed in Lithuania.

Evidence suggest that attitudes towards Russian inhabitants during the
inter-war period were negative, but that they were regarded as less of a
threat than other groups, such as Jews or Germans, primarily because
they had less economic power. Russians were linked to the most recent
oppressors, the Tsarist Empire, and they were looked down upon,
regarded as uneducated and slovenly. The comments of a Lithuanian
woman in Britain reveal the negative attitudes towards Russia in independent Lithuania:

> 'The attitude in the inter-war period towards Russia was 'If
> you're Russian you're a communist and that was it'. Russia
> was bad. Russia was not clever. If you're a Russian you're poor,
> you're uneducated. Russian was aligned with communism.
> Communism was bad and that was it. If you were a communist
> that was the ... worst thing you could be, a communist and that
> was that.'

The interwar period saw an energetic promotion of national cultures and
identities in all three countries by the new national leaders, in an attempt
to solidify and strengthen national, rather than regional, religious or class
identities, which had proliferated previously. Earlier strategies to promote national identities begun in the nineteenth century were intensified.

As in the national awakenings, language played a vital role as a means
to solidify and unify the nation. One of the earliest reforms was the recognition of Latvian, Lithuanian and Estonian as the official language of the
state. Latvian, Lithuanian and Estonian language schools were organised,
and national literature was promoted. A curriculum was introduced educating pupils about the history and culture of their nation, and nineteenth
century Latvian, Lithuanian and Estonian poems and novels were read.
As the school system was expanded, the classroom became one of the
key forums for the consolidation of national identities. Folk songs were

printed in school textbooks, which in Latvia were standardised throughout the country from the 1920s onwards. History textbooks linked the child's own life with that of his or her predecessors, and constructed an identity, which was deeply rooted in the countryside. The different parts of the country were linked together in textbooks, to promote a sense of national unity. The young Latvians, Lithuanians and Estonians were not only taught about their own nation, but also about other countries in the world, including their previous oppressors and more respected nations, including Great Britain and Sweden. The Latvian, Lithuanian and Estonian states were clearly situated in the world, with charts and statistics comparing their nation's progress with that of other nations.

In addition to school reforms, arts, education and other cultural endeavours were promoted. Folk traditions, national literature, music, theatre and dance were vigorously supported by the State. The new states were embellished with a variety of symbols and motifs, denoting national identities and imprinting on the mind of every citizen, a series of identifiable national images. Flags, coats of arms and national anthems were introduced as symbols of the independent nations.

A series of festivals, celebrations and religious days punctuated the routine in both town and country and formed a significant component of the culture and annual cycle of life in each nation. These included days marking events in the farming calendar, weddings, births, funerals, national days and name days. Some of these had been marked for centuries, some were new days introduced during independence, and others were old traditions now celebrated freely, having been repressed during the Tsarist years.

Some of the national festivals in the three Baltic States were based on the countries' ancient pagan past, when celebrations were held marking important dates in the farming calendar. One of the most important of the old traditions which was celebrated freely and with renewed vigour in the independence period was St. John's Day, an important fertility festival held at midsummer. St. John's Day was celebrated in all three Baltic countries, but was perhaps most important in Latvia. Jānis, a Latvian man, living in Leeds described the celebrations in Latvia:

'St John's Day – that was the most...important thing for everybody in the countryside. Nobody went to sleep that night, until sunrise of course. That's allowed. That's allowed by the Latvian

tradition. Well of course, where [there] was somebody called name Jānis...they had to stay at home and wait for somebody to call to, you know, they used to come singing in the neighbourhood. And then when that was done they spend about half an hour or so eating and drinking and what have you, and playing music and dancing or whatever and then you go to the next house where there is John...where there is a John in the family, they're just waiting. They have to provide the beer and the eating and so on.'

New days marking national independence were introduced in all three countries to instil a sense of national pride and nationhood. Latvian Independence Day was celebrated on 18 November, Estonian Independence Day on 24 February and Lithuanian Independence Day on 16 February. However, the significance of these days was initially muted. Heino Poopuu described the celebration of the new National Independence Day in Estonia:

'February the 24th was declared an annual public holiday to commemorate the Declaration of Estonian National Independence in 1918. This event lacked tradition and had some way to go before being accepted as a proper by the older generation in our community.'

However, in later correspondence he stressed that while 'older generations in my village certainly did not attend any of the annual Independence Day official ceremonies on 24 February but as a pupil of our local school I was expected to and did take part in these on several occasions.' He attributed the lack of enthusiasm to the immaturity of independence and the 'conservatism of the country folk'. Only later, during the Soviet period and in exile, did the National Independence Days attain major significance as symbols of national identity.

In Estonia, St. John's Day assumed a dual significance in the new independent Republic. Heino Poopuu explained:

'... St John's Day, the traditional mid-summer celebration with dancing by the bonfires at night. This shortest night of the year was imbued with magical connotations of eternal youth and purity in Estonian folklore. The young Republic had adopted

9

this festival for the purpose of commemorating a decisive battle in the War of Independence against the Germans and renamed it Victory Day. So, in addition to a pagan and Christian tradition, it had become an important patriotic occasion too, with brass band-led processions and rather lengthy speeches.'

According to Heino Poopuu, Victory Day which commemorated 'a victorious battle in the war of independence against a Baltic German force on 23 June 1920, celebrated on the eve of St. John's Day with procession and bonfires, was quite popular'.

In Lithuania, where the Tsarist attacks on religion had been viewed as direct attacks on the Lithuanian nation, the celebration of religious festivals began to attain significance during the independence period as representations of Lithuanian independence. Although the Tsarist government had not attempted to circumvent religious activity to the same degree as the later Soviet governments, celebration of religious festivals also became celebrations of nationhood. The celebration of religious days was also popular in Latvia and Estonia, although the link to national identity was far weaker than in Lithuania. Heino Poopuu described the lavish festivities associated with Christmas and New Year's Eve in Estonia, while Easter and Whitsuntide in contrast 'passed quietly as days of rest and relaxation.' He also remarked that in Estonia, somewhat ironically, despite the Lutheranism of the population, Catholic Saints' name days were 'still very much part of traditions'.

Another important 'national cultural event' in the new independent states was the Song Festival. In Estonia, the Song Festival was held in Tallinn at four-five yearly intervals during the inter-war period. Heino Poopuu noted that since many people in outlying regions could not afford to travel to Tallinn for these events, smaller scale versions of it were held in the regions. For example, on the island of Saaremaa, where he lived, a smaller version was held in Kuressaare.

The construction of national monuments, buildings and the establishment and modification of exhibits in national museums served to express independent nationhood further. In Latvia, it was during the independence period that the Monument of Freedom in Riga was first erected as a symbol of liberty.

Historically, the Baltic States were farming nations, and despite growing urbanisation, the rural/urban ratio of the population remained high, with the majority of the populations continuing to live in the countryside. As a result, the farmstead became one of the most important symbols of independent Latvian, Lithuanian and Estonian nations. In Latvia, the Ethnographic Open-Air Museum of Latvia was opened in Riga in 1924, to depict the life of the Latvian peasant, and to encapsulate the history and characteristics of the Latvian nation.

During the 1920s and 1930s, most of the refugees in this study were children growing up on the farm, going to school and also helping out with work on the farm, and in the home. Among those who grew up in the countryside, the refugees who came to Britain derived from a wide variety of farming backgrounds; some grew up in small self-sufficient farmsteads which grew barely enough to feed the family, while others lived on larger, profit-making farms. One Latvian in Britain, born in 1926, grew up on a large farmstead, which had 300 acres of farmland and 100 acres of forest. Many of the farms undertook mixed farming, while others concentrated on one or two crops. Others undertook fishing as an important component of the farm's functions.

Life on the farmstead was described by most interview participants as a happy time. However, some of the interviewees stressed that despite being a happy time, there were many hardships. Life in the countryside was a fairly isolated, parochial existence. Some of the Latvians who came to Britain told me that they had only been to Riga once or twice as children and could not even remember it. A Latvian man, now living in Leeds described how as a child he saw Riga only three times:

> *'I haven't seen Latvia...when I left home I was 16. I was 16 when I left and at that time well, I was going to school, I was living in country. I've even been a couple of times in Riga, that's all, about three times, including the one when I was a right little one.'*

Some of the participants stressed that life in the country was a hard, ascetic life. As young children, they had few toys or luxuries, and had to work hard on the farm. One Lithuanian woman who was only a young child during the 1930's described life on the farm as a 'hard life'. Since her mother died in 1932, she had lived with her aunt and grandmother, and described how 'from early morning till...night they were working. I remember they [were] working really hard you know, my aunty, my

11

grandmother and … well I had to help, like I said early mornings and night. Way of life.' When I asked her if she remembered her childhood as a happy time, she replied: 'In a way I was happy. We had nothing like you know. You had nothing, but that was the way you know in Lithuania'. She described how as children they played with sticks and 'whatever we could find, [we did not have] many toys.'

For one Latvian man who grew up on a farm in Latvia, the relationship with nature gained from growing up on the farm was perhaps the most important aspect of his childhood in Latvia. The close relationship to the land gave him a firm sense of belonging in Latvia, and increased his bond to the country. He left his homeland at the age of sixteen. He commented:

> *'I was with it all the time. I was picking mushrooms and watching birds and all the time I was with nature you know … swimming in river and so on you know. I learnt to swim … I was very close to the earth. I did all the work what there was – ploughing and mowing and everything, you know. Of course I did it with horses … there weren't many tractors then. But I could do it and I did it. And I worked with the earth, with it. And that's where it came from, from the earth, that's where everywhere came from, the food and everything.'*

Similar sentiments can be found in other testimonies. Heino Poopuu, author of *Remembering Pussa* also described in an interview, how the childhood on the farm gave him a strong rural identity, which later formed a significant component of his Estonian identity. He commented on the huge differences between his Estonian childhood and his later life in Britain:

> *'I suppose that initial growing up period were the formative years, well, that…sort of instils it into you.*
> *'… you see I had this farming background and the Estonian childhood, growing up in the country … it was very different to anything [in Britain]. Apart from the language differences and religion, the whole erm, the whole gist of life is quite different … that very basics you can't – much the same as your accent, you can't do much about it, even if you wanted to, it's still there, so, so perhaps I'm still a countryman to some extent.'*

12

The characteristics of family life in Latvia, Lithuania and Estonia originated from the rural way of life, and there were many similarities with
traditional peasant families of other pre-industrial nations. Despite industrialisation, family life in towns and cities was still largely based on the
rural family structure. The family was a very strong, close knit unit,
often with a large extended family living close by, in the same village or
region. Typically, in Estonia and Latvia, a married couple had three or
four children, in Lithuania, about four or five. Traditional gender relations persisted.

The cuisine of the inter-war Baltic States was another aspect of culture with roots firmly in the countryside. Since most farms were largely
self-sufficient, cuisine reflected seasonal growing patterns. In addition to
arable land growing a variety of crops including rye, barley, buckwheat
and oats, a typical farmstead included a threshing barn, pigsty, orchard,
granary, kitchen garden, potato bunker and smokehouse. Most farms
kept at least one cow, several pigs and some poultry. A wide variety of
fruits and vegetables were grown, including potatoes, cabbage, beetroot,
onions, carrots, cucumbers, apples and various fruit bushes, including
cranberries, blackberries and raspberries. Eggs were produced and a variety of milk products were made including sour cream, curd and cottage
cheese. Some farms had beehives and produced large supplies of honey.
The farmstead also made use of the surrounding landscape. Fishing in
the sea, lakes and rivers was commonplace and berries and mushrooms
were collected in wooded areas.

In urban areas, the cuisine was similar to that in the countryside – it
still reflected the seasons, since much of the food was produced locally,
but was a little more sophisticated and contained an increasing amount of
imported foodstuffs. Urban diets also reflected the greater degree of foreign influences in the towns and cities and the multi-ethnic composition
of urban populations.

In both towns and the countryside, 'workaday menus' were plain,
simple, one-course affairs. The diet relied heavily on thick meat or, less
frequently, fish soups or broths with permutations of added lentils, vegetables or cereals. These soups, eaten with rye bread, constituted the main
meal of the day. According to Poopuu, in Estonia, common main meals
without meat or fish included porridge with butter and flour enriched
mashed potatoes with bacon dripping. Bacon dripping was used in many
recipes in all three Baltic Republics, to add flavour and nourishment.

In Latvia for example, grey peas with bacon dripping was (and still is) a national favourite (Latvian name: *zirņi ar speķi*). Puddings and desserts were usually eaten only on special occasions. A Latvian in Britain also noted that during the inter-war period: '... we didn't have ... such things as sweets and chocolates and things.' Each nation had its own national specialities, for example, one of the Lithuania's national dishes – potato pancakes (*bulviniai blynai*) – used two of the nation's most readily available foods, potatoes and eggs, together.

As in Britain, there was a great tradition of beer drinking among men in all three countries. All beer was home-brewed, and enjoyed on social and special occasions. Heino Poopuu discussed the significance of beer among the communities on Saaremaa:

> *'There is no doubt that our home-brew was a vital ingredient of what might be termed our culture or the way of life we led, for it wasn't only the completion of certain essential jobs at the farm that depended on its availability, but more important – our social life without beer would have been very dull and arid indeed. To say that some of our men would have been absolutely lost without it would not be an exaggeration.'*

Rural traditions, such as cuisine and celebrations in the farming calendar, later formed the mainstay of cultures and identities in exile; rural traditions brought refugees from different regions together in the DP camps and later in Britain, through song, food, dance and festivals. The contrast with the noisy urban environments the refugees ended up in, in industrial Britain, served further to emphasize their rural pasts and identities, and solidify the rural-national link as a central tenet of national and ethnic identities in exile.

It is also important to stress that due to the varied historical pasts of different regions in the inter-war Baltic States, there were wide cultural differences between areas. The Latgale region, in eastern Latvia, which had been part of the Polish-Lithuanian Commonwealth, was perhaps the most extreme example of this. Unlike the rest of Latvia, which was mainly Lutheran, Latgale had a significant Catholic population even among the local Latvian majority, as well as a distinctive dialect.

In Lithuania, the Memelland area around the port of Klaipėda, was also culturally different from the rest of the country. The area had

14

previously been part of East Prussia but was annexed to Lithuania in 1923 and had a largely German population. There were also significant numbers of 'Prussian Lithuanians' and 'Memellanders' who were largely Lutherans, unlike the rest of the population in Lithuania who were mainly Catholics. Lithuanians from this area regarded themselves as culturally and ethnically distinct from the rest of the Lithuanian population. The new Lithuanian state however, regarded them as Germanised Lithuanians who must be Lithuanised; again, efforts were made in schools and through national days and celebrations to culturally integrate this area into Lithuania, and to unify the nation. The authoritarian regime of A. Smetona enforced a policy of discrimination and Lithuanisation, but by 1939, efforts to Lithuanise Memelland were only partially successful, and the area retained a strong regional identity.

The Baltic refugees who came to Britain lived all over the geographical areas that constitute present-day Latvia, Lithuania and Estonia, although the majority originated from the western areas of Latvia, Lithuania and Estonia, from where they could escape the advancing Russian armies with greater ease, and from where the German army recruited first. Those who lived in the east had less success in escaping the Russian occupiers. There were thus few refugees from the Latgale region in Latvia, compared to central and western areas, since this region fell to the Russians swiftly. Likewise, there were fewer refugees from the north-eastern areas of Lithuania, in comparison with southern and western areas.

There was a revival of religion during the inter-war period, after decades of suppression by the Russian State. Latvia and Estonia were primarily Lutheran countries, due to the German introduction of Lutheran Christianity in the Middle Ages (although Latgale in Latvia was Catholic), and Lithuania was overwhelmingly Catholic, due to the introduction of Latin Christianity by the Polish-Lithuanian Commonwealth.

Catholics made up a majority of the ethnic Lithuanian nationality, which composed some 80 per cent of the population and the numbers were increased by the significant Polish Catholic minority in Lithuania. In 1939, 85.5 per cent of the population were Catholic, 4.5 per cent were Protestant, 7 per cent Jewish, 2.5 per cent Orthodox and 0.5 per cent other religions. The numbers of active believers were significantly higher than among the Lutheran population in either Estonia or Latvia, and Catholicism formed an important component of everyday life. After the declaration of independence, the Catholic Church gained full freedoms and privileges.

The overwhelming majority of Estonians and Latvians who came to Britain were Lutheran, although as already mentioned, a few Latvians were Catholics from the Latgale region of Latvia. Most of the Lutheran Latvians in Britain stressed to me that religion was important mainly for social reasons and that Lutheranism was not a particularly significant component of Latvian national identity during the inter-war period. This was partly due to the religious heterogeneity in Latvia, and also because of its link with the oppressive Baltic German nobility.

I asked a Latvian woman, now living in Britain who was born in 1923, and grew up on a farm if she was religious as a child, and if she went to church. She replied:

> *'Erm, not terribly religious no. Yes, I suppose more than I am now. I was at school and I used to have a prayer in the morning and we used to go to church. I was never really overly religious, no, never really devoted. Never really religious really.'*

When assessing narratives relating to life in the homeland, but told in the present, it is important to remember that they may have been reconstructed as a result of later experiences, for example, life in exile, recent return visits, and the reminiscence process associated with ageing. This is illustrated by the comments of a Latvian, now living in Rochdale:

> *'I just think about it [the homeland] only ... when I was twenty ... eighteen, nineteen ... oh, there were beautiful fields, all everything's nice, all meadows, all flowers, everything's nice. Nice farms.'*

I asked a Lithuanian woman in Manchester, whether she recalled her life in Lithuania as an idyllic time. She replied: 'Yes. I remember independence...yeah. That time I always remember, the life, because it was very good. Very good life. Everything we got'. This particular woman came to England in 1948 accompanied by her young daughter, who was not yet ten years old. Although she spent only her first few years in Lithuania, the daughter described how the Lithuanian community remembered independence as an idyllic period, and how the younger generations were taught about the 'wonderful' life there. She stated:

'I was taught that it was a wonderful life there. I was brought up in this dream – wonderful life, wonderful country. Everything was absolutely terrific. I was brought up in that spirit. We all were in fact. Everyone reminisced.'

In collective memory, the period of inter-war independence was regarded as 'a golden age'. Just as during the independence period, history was reinterpreted to legitimise independence, so too the histories written during the Soviet period by Latvian, Lithuanian and Estonian émigré and dissident historians stress the achievements of the inter-war republics. The participants in this project frequently voiced the opinion that without the Soviet and German occupations, the Baltic States would now be on a par economically, socially and politically with the countries of Western Europe. They stressed the economic successes, and the return to democracy just as the war in Europe was breaking out. According to many exiles, the drift to authoritarianism which occurred in Lithuania from 1926 onwards, and in Latvia and Estonia during the mid to late thirties, was only brief and caused primarily by the economic problems brought about by the world recession and the immaturity of the democratic political systems.

Participants and historians have also stressed the cultural vitality of the inter-war period. However, despite a collective memory of the homeland as idyllic and happy years, it would be a mistake to suggest that all individual memories of childhood were remembered as happy. A Latvian man, now living in Leeds, grew up in Liepaja in Latvia, and left his home aged sixteen. His mother died when he was five, and with ten children in the family, the children were separated. Some of his brothers and sisters were placed in orphanages. He described his unhappy childhood:

'I was [a] tough kid. I was bullied ... expelled three times, expelled from school for fighting. I came from [a] town. I wasn't brought up you know, in country on a farm, so they took the mickey out of you when you came from town, so [you had to] stand up and fight for yourself.'

In interviews, memories of childhood and of the homeland were described as very fresh in the memory. Many of the participants in this study voiced the same opinion as one Latvian man who stated that 'I remember everything from childhood more than I remember what happened yester-day'. As a natural process of time and the ageing process, the clarity of homeland memories may have been intensified by the diasporic experi-ence. Although not all the memories of life in the homeland during the inter-war period were positive, the overwhelming sense that this period was a 'wonderful' 'carefree' and 'happy' time, is important in the cre-ation of exile identities and cultures after displacement. In short, exile identities and cultures in exile were based in part on a remembered and mythologised past.

CHAPTER 2

'Life was nothing then. Life meant for nothing' – War and Displacement, 1939–1945

'We didn't really have a lot of things, but my father said that if you were a refugee, if you try to carry too much with you, you'd in the end lose everything, so take essentials.'

In 1939, most Latvians, Lithuanians and Estonians who later became refugees, were still children or young adults living in their homelands, attending school, higher education or starting their first jobs. Just seven years later, they were refugees living in Displaced Persons camps. It was during these years that Latvian, Lithuanian and Estonian independence came to an abrupt end and tens of thousands of Baltic citizens were uprooted from their homelands. In 1940–41, the Baltic States endured the first Soviet occupation, which was rapidly followed by a German occupation from 1941 to 1944. In the autumn of 1944, a second Russian offensive began.

The developments leading to the first Russian occupation of the Baltic States are infamous. On 23 August 1939, the so-called 'Molotov-Ribbentrop' or 'Nazi-Soviet Pact' was signed by German and Russian Foreign Ministers, a non-aggression pact within which a 'secret protocol' assigned Latvia and Estonia to the Soviet sphere of influence and Lithuania to the German sphere. On 23 September, following the fall of Poland to Germany, a second secret protocol amended the pact, allocating Lithuania to the Soviet Union in return for German concessions in Poland. These protocols laid the way open for Soviet occupation of the Baltic States, bringing to an end their independence which had been gained for the first time only twenty-one years earlier in 1918.

Some population displacement took place shortly after the Nazi-Soviet Pact had been signed, when Hitler carried out the mass resettlement of Baltic Germans from Latvia and Estonia, to Polish territories incorporated into the Reich. The secret German-Soviet agreement in September 1939 had made provision for German nationals and ethnic Germans to migrate from areas under Soviet jurisdiction to those under German control. As a result, nearly fourteen thousand Germans were evacuated from Estonia and over fifty thousand from Latvia. They were to be employed to assist in the correction of Germany's wartime labour shortage. In this way, Baltic German labourers helped to provide the economic and technical basis for the German armies.

Earlier, in March 1939, Germany had also signed a pact with Lithuania, thereby forcing the handover of the Klaipėda region, known by Germans as Memelland, to Germany. This meant that many Lithuanians in the area were forced to work for the German authorities, and others escaped to other areas of Lithuania to avoid this.

This was the experience of Dalia's family, described in the opening to her memoir *God Give Us Wings* by Felicia (Dalia) Prekeris Brown. Dalia and her family lived in this area of Lithuania and her father had a good job as principal of a local elementary school, but they were forced to move to another part of Lithuania as a result of the pact. They did not know it at the time, but this would be the first in a series of displacements that eventually saw Dalia and her family arrive in England in the late 1940s.

Later on in the war, 'Memelland' was occupied by Russia as it pushed westwards, and Germany was forced to retreat. 'Memelland' then became an integral part of the new Lithuanian Soviet Socialist Republic and was renamed Klaipėda.

Russia began occupying other parts of Latvia, Lithuania and Estonia almost as soon as the Nazi-Soviet Pact was signed. Initially, the occupations were not bloody, and as one Latvian stated, 'there was no war'. 'The Russians just came in ... they just occupied, without any war'. All three Baltic countries received ultimatums demanding the establishment of Russian military bases on their soil. In Lithuania, the return of Vilnius was offered as an inducement, but the reality was that none of the Baltic countries had any choice but to concede to Russia, to avoid full-blown military occupation.

Under the agreements, the Baltic countries were forced to agree to the reconstruction of Baltic governments under Soviet supervision. Rigged elections were held in all three Baltic States in which candidates were chosen by the USSR, producing 'People's Assemblies', which 'requested' annexation to the Soviet Union in July 1940. According to a Latvian woman in Great Britain, the Soviet regime claimed that 'the Latvians had voted that they wanted the Soviet System.' She described the rigged elections:

> *'Well of course we voted because they were already in, with the army and all your passport was stamped, whether you went to vote or not and there's only one thing to vote on...no choice, just the one. The passport was stamped so you could see who didn't go to vote. It was stamped and then as soon as this government was elected they went to Moscow and asked to join. So it was all a put-up job.'*

These elections brought about the formal Soviet occupation of Latvia, Lithuania and Estonia, which led to major changes to the lives of the inhabitants of the Baltic States.

Transformations of the political elite took place, including the expansion and consolidation of the tiny local communist parties, through local support and Russian cadres, and the expulsion of non-communist left-wingers unwilling to convert to communism. Many members of the political elite from the independence period were deported, including Latvian President Karlis Ulmanis, who was deported to Russia, where he died in prison two years later. President Konstantin Päts of Estonia was also deported and later died in an NKVD 'psychiatric clinic' in 1956. By the end of 1940, arrests and deportations of those deemed to be enemies of the new regime were at the rate of 200–300 a month.

Deportations culminated on the terrible night of 13–14 June 1941, when an estimated 100,000 Latvian, Lithuanian and Estonian men, women and children, including many civil servants and professionals, were deported to Siberia in cattle trucks. Those selected for deportation included the twenty-three categories of 'enemies of the people' and their families. These categories included government officials, businessmen, trade unionists and clergymen. Milosz states that almost one per cent of the total population of the Baltic States was deported during this one night. A substantial proportion spent the rest of their lives in Siberia, unable to return to Soviet-occupied homelands.

In 1955, Plensers described the deportations in Latvia when:

'Over 15,000 Latvians, regardless of sex or age were dragged from their sleep to lorries and transported to railway "loading stations", where the male heads of families were separated from their wives and children. The deportees were crammed into freight cars. For sanitary purposes, the cars had holes cut into the floor, which also served as the only opening for air. Thus the victims were subjected to unbearable physical and mental torture in the stifling cars, scorched by the summer heat, without food and water. Their journey which ultimately took them to slave labour camps in remote districts of Arctic Russia and Siberia, lasted for several weeks.'[1]

The night of 13–14 June became a symbol of the barbarism of Russia for the Baltic States and the Baltic diaspora. Every year on the night of the 13–14 June, or as close to that date as possible, special remembrance gatherings are held in Latvian, Lithuanian and Estonian clubs across Great Britain, commemorating the deportations. Almost every Latvian, Lithuanian and Estonian knew a relative, friend or neighbour who was deported on that night. Deportations brought home to even the youngest Latvians, Lithuanians and Estonians the brutality of the Russian occupation. The experiences of a Latvian woman now living in Nottingham are not untypical:

My grandmother died in Siberia. My cousins grew up in Siberia. My aunty was there and my mother's cousin was there with his family.

Another Latvian woman also lost her aunt, uncle and grandmother in the deportations. She describes what happened to those who were deported to Siberia:

'I think it may not be true to say that every family had a family member deported but at least every family…at least knew someone either a friend or whatever, but a lot of people lost relatives and that was in '41, just before German army came in, two weeks before … it was war. They had little to eat in Russia

22

and of course they wouldn't save any for people like this, I mean they were split off immediately ... went to labour camps. The women, children were sent out to Kolkhoz. They didn't really want them ... but whatever the women managed to ... get from begging I suppose they'd give to children, and then ... within a year they were all dead because of malnutrition and the children were picked up and put in homes.'

Some of the Baltic refugees who ended up in Britain after the war were just children or teenagers when the Russians first occupied the Baltic States in 1940–41. A Latvian woman from Riga who now lives in Nottingham was just fourteen when the Russian occupation began:

'Well, of course they robbed the country, everything ... everything was sent to [the] Soviet Union, and ... you couldn't get anything in the shops anymore, and ... what I can remember they had a lot of what they call the "Demonstrations and Manifestations". On certain days, you had to walk in these demonstrations ... and you had to carry the placards, and ... "Long live the Soviet Union", "Long live the October Revolution", and all that. And, all I can remember, that year in my memory, is sort of very drab, very grey. I can remember, especially in the autumn and winter, it seemed the skies were grey, and you weren't happy at all, and ... just the red flags everywhere.'

Still at school when the first occupation took place, she described how the occupation affected her schooling:

'We were learning Middle Ages. Well, that was all right, but also we were still on the History of Latvia...that was cancelled, but instead of that you had to learn the Party, the Short Course of the Communist Party. That was the first thing you learned at school.'

While the Soviet regime was able to undertake some Sovietisation of culture, including changes in school syllabi, restrictions on religious worship and the disbanding of community organisations, it was unable to achieve complete cultural assimilation, due to the relatively short period of occupation. However, significant changes did take place rapidly, leaving populations in no doubt about the Soviet regime's long term goals. In all three nations, all non-Communist-controlled public activity was proscribed. Political, social, religious and ideological groups which could not be assimilated within Communist fronts were disbanded. The curricula saw drastic revisions, including the deletion of some writers in the native literary tradition. For example, Vincas Kudirka, the author of Lithuania's national anthem, was removed from the curriculum. Press control was introduced early. Printing houses and shops were taken over and lists of banned books and brochures were issued.

In Lithuania, the Soviet regime began implementing its goals for the annihilation of Catholicism. Soviet law had always proclaimed that religious practice should be confined to worship within the four walls of a church. Thus, all Catholic societies and organisations were annihilated, their assets confiscated, and all specialised activities were abolished, including chaplaincy work in hospitals and schools. Priests were forced to sign an oath of loyalty to the Soviet Union and all monastic and seminary land was confiscated. Wayside crosses and shrines were desecrated and demolished and several religious holidays were abolished. Intimidation of priests and believers brought fear to many Lithuanian Catholics, who comprised over 85 per cent of the population in 1939.

Similar developments also took place in Latvia and Estonia, where the Lutheran Church was targeted in the Soviet regime's drive towards atheism. In Estonia, for example, church property was nationalised, the theology faculty of Tartu University was closed and church publishing and chaplaincy work with children and youth were banned. Only Sunday church services and the celebration of key religious events, such as funerals were tolerated.

Many of the participants in this study from all three Baltic States described the fear engendered by the Soviet occupation and how they were forced to live from day to day, able only to make few plans for the future. In terms of the economic downturn, people who lived in towns and cities were more severely affected than those living in the countryside, who were often largely self-sufficient. One woman who lived in Riga noted that 'In a month all [the] shops were empty.' In contrast, another Latvian woman who was just a teenager during the first Russian occupation and who lived on a farmstead in the countryside, remembers not missing much in the way of food, since the farm was almost completely self-sufficient. The most important shortage as she recalls, was sugar. For her, the main effect of the occupation was fear – fear of talking to anyone about the Russians for fear of reprisals, and fear for the future. Another Latvian from Leeds also described the fear engendered by the Russian occupation:

> *'I'm sorry to say, unless you've been occupied you can't...under-stand what it's like to be occupied by a foreign power. It's impos-sible to explain, so the people in Britain don't know...when you can't speak, when you...have three of four people and you can't have a discussion, because you don't know who's listening or maybe the third or the fourth person might be a collaborator or...whatever...you're living in fear all the time.'*

The Russian occupation of the Baltic States in 1940–41 produced wide-spread hatred towards the Soviet regime among the Baltic populations. In Latvia, the year 1940–41 is known as the 'Year of Horrors' (*Baigais Gads*), and remained etched in their memories throughout exile. Estimates for the numbers killed or deported during the first Soviet occupation are 34,250 in Latvia, almost 60,000 in Estonia and 75,000 in Lithuania. Animosity towards Russia and Russians quickly intensified as a result of the occupation, with the Soviet regime now deemed to be the primary enemy of the Latvian, Lithuanian and Estonian nations.

A Latvian who was only about ten years old when the Russian occupa-tion began described his attitude towards the Russians:

> *'Well, as I say the Russians were very, very, very evil. They didn't...respect anybody or anybody's privileges or privacy or anything. They used to go around you know, robbing, raping and all the rest of it ...'*

An Estonian man in Britain drew attention to the more potent anti-Russian element in the Estonian identity as a result of the Russian occupation, which became more significant than the traditional anti-German feeling:

> *'Traditionally, Estonians [and Russians] are ... historically, they were enemies. I don't know in what order, but probably Germans*

first, greatest, greatest [enemy]. To my grandfather...of course Germans were the enemy number one then, then Russians, Poles, Swedes, Danes and so on, but up to this Russian – the Communist period, the Germans were considered to be enemy number one. Estonians, on the whole, didn't like Germans. They respected them, but they didn't like them. The Russians, they didn't like them either very much, but they didn't particularly hate them, they tended to sort of look down on them a little bit, but communism changed all that, so enemy number one is Russia now and Russians.'

It was not only the oppressive measures unleashed by the Soviet regime which engendered opposition. Most importantly perhaps, it was the loss of a hard-fought-for independence which had solidified the previously embryonic national identities. Whereas before, concern had been about little other than the farmstead, the village, family and friends, the survival of the nation was now in threat. While outward displays of patriotism risked life and limb, the Russian occupation and, particularly the deportations, instilled a deep sense of nationhood and patriotism into the young Latvians, Lithuanians and Estonians. During this period, the home became the main arena for cultural expressions of national identity, where Latvian, Lithuanian and Estonian authors were read, national foods prepared and the fate of the homeland discussed in earnest.

As well as engendering shifts in national identities, the initial Russian occupation led to the first displacement of some of the Latvians, Lithuanians and Estonians who later migrated to Great Britain. A number was recruited into the Russian army in order to shore up Russian efforts against the encroaching German invaders and subsequently were displaced in Europe. However, this was the route of only a small minority of men who came to Britain, mainly Estonians.

Recruitment was most extensive among the Estonian population due to the length of time taken by Germany to invade and occupy Estonia during their summer offensive of the Baltic countries in 1941. As a result, Estonia suffered considerably more destruction and casualties. It also enabled mobilisation into the Soviet army, leading about 10,000 young Estonian men to their deaths in Russian lumber camps. According to Misiūnas and Taagapera, most of the Baltic Red Army recruits were considered unreliable, and for this reason were sent to die in labour camps.

They estimate that the peak number of ethnic Latvians, Lithuanians and Estonians in Red Army combat units may have been 18,000 Estonians (of whom 800 surrendered to the Germans at Velikie Luki in December 1941), 10,000 Latvians and 5,000 Lithuanians.[2]

Some of those who were captured by the Germans at Velikie Luki and held as POWs were later able to escape when the Western front advanced, reaching safety in the DP camps. This was the experience of one Estonian man I interviewed in West Yorkshire:

> '... the war started, Russia started mobilising people you know, men from Estonia to take to Russia and I was waiting with the first mobilisation from Tallinn, our capital ... I was called up on 2 June 1941. So I was the first lot, but they had more after that.
>
> '... first of all they sent us all in the labour camps, and [at] that time there were terrible conditions – lack of food, cold ...
>
> 'And in 1942, early on anyway, February I think ... they started forming the national units, Estonian first, which consisted eventually of two divisions, called Estonian Riflecorps, and first time after training and all that, first time I were in battle of Velikie Luki, which ... started back end of '42, which were encircled by Russians before, and Germans were still encircled and Estonian units were put in to fight the Germans in that circle. Only one unit went to open front.
>
> 'I was in battle 6 January. We set off from Siberia just 23 December and we arrived just the night before the Velikie Luki by train, and then the following morning we were sent to battle. And [laughs] I was squadron leader and they all just vanished. We were made to storm a strong building and the Germans were in them ... we didn't have anybody left. I got wounded and I, well I fell down in an old crater ....
>
> 'I was long enough in that crater. It was snow covered and well I didn't know what to do. I got wounded in the back with a splinter. I could feel blood running and I didn't know how bad it was ...'

He managed eventually to get out of the crater and find help for his wound. He was sent back to battle at Velikie Luki a fortnight later, where he managed to survive another battle when, by his estimates, about 2,250 men out of a regiment of 3,000 were killed. After attempting to cross Lake Peipsi, which divides Estonia from Russia, he was captured by the Germans and held as a prisoner of war. He was taken to a POW camp in Germany, near Essen, thus describing the conditions:

> *'We were woken up at five o'clock in the morning, and then we stood in the yard till eight o'clock. Dinner was sort of bits of potatoes and like a pig swill with blood and ... [we] had a pint of that in the evenings. I was only there three months and I only weighed 48 kilos. I'm 80 now ...'*

When the Western front began to advance, the Germans took their POWs back behind the lines and he managed to escape to the Allied side, where he worked in a German village for a year. He then moved into a DP camp, before being recruited for work in a textile mill near Halifax. After six years of war and displacement, he finally landed in the port of Harwich, England, on 7 September 1947.

Although like all the EVW stories, this man's experiences are unique, they give an impression of some of the ordeals endured by those recruited by the Russians and the hazardous journey from the homeland to Britain. Very few recruits to the Russian army found safety, and indeed the Estonian man interviewed above informed me that he was the only member of the active Estonian community in his locality in Britain who had fought on the Russian side.

The German occupation of the Baltic States began just one week after the Russian deportations on 22 June 1941. Within days, the Wehrmacht had cut a swathe into the Baltic and the Red Army fled westwards.

Promising to liberate the Latvians, Lithuanians and Estonians from Russian tyranny and arbitrary rule, the Germans were initially welcomed. As one commentator suggested, Latvians, like Lithuanians and Estonians, 'had lived through a year so horrible that they bedecked their age-old enemies, the advancing Germans, with flowers'.[3] A Latvian woman in Nottingham explained that before the mass deportations, Latvians 'hated the Germans as well because they were the rulers of Latvians for 700 years. But in this instance, we were really pleased that they came'.

The welcome was not wholehearted, however, since most Latvians, Lithuanians and Estonians regarded the Germans merely as the lesser of two evils. Andrejs Plakans stated that many Latvians 'believed that, under the circumstances, this "traditional enemy" (Germans) would be an improvement over the "traditional enemy" (Russians) whose brief rule had just been concluded'.[4] A Latvian woman stressed that the Latvians would have 'welcomed Ghenghis Khan if he had saved us from Russians', and a Latvian man noted that while the Germans did liberate Latvia, 'of course the Germans weren't any friends really. We knew that they were occupiers just like the Russians were, but they were not as nasty as Russians were'.

Nevertheless, the welcoming of the German occupation, initially tinged with cynicism, soon turned to disillusionment when German promises of autonomy came to naught. A Latvian woman described the feelings of disappointment. Initially, 'there was all Latvian flags out...but, they soon ordered them to be taken down you know. They (the Latvians) felt very much disappointed. Well, it was sort of get rid of one devil, and another one comes in'.

Some of the interviewees were more positive about their experience of German rule, claiming that there was a return to a normality of sorts and that they were left alone by the Germans to get on with their daily lives. One Latvian woman, now living in Nottingham, talked about how life returned to some sort of normality under the Germans:

> 'We enjoyed the German films, and as I went to school again, we had dances, we could go to theatres. At least we, you know, we were free, from my opinion, because I was only a youngster then, we were free to do what we liked, but under the Russians you know, you couldn't. You were told you had to do this and you had to do that. Now you are going here ...'

Another woman agreed that German rule was preferable to rule by Russia:

> 'Well, maybe they [the Germans] were a bit better than Russians, but no, not that good. [They] still occupied the nation, but to me, Germans were better than Russians.'

One of the reasons why German rule was initially perceived as being more tolerable than Soviet rule was that Germanisation was less of an urgent priority to the Germans than Sovietisation had been to the Soviets. Certain changes relating to cultural life were implemented, including censorship, and the Nazification of history and biology curricula in schools. However, the Germans offered some concessions in terms of the toleration of national culture. The Catholic religion of many Lithuanians was largely left alone and the performing arts, such as theatre and opera, continued to function. In Latvia, the Latvian flag and national anthem were permitted and in 1943, a song festival was held.

However, whilst successful in appeasing the Baltic populations initially, cultural concessions were insufficient to stem opposition to German rule in the longer term. In the economic sphere, the Germans sought to utilise Baltic territory as an exploitative resource to aid the war effort. Although some token restoration of private property took place in 1943, initial promises of full re-privatisation did not materialise. The currency was re-valued, leaving the Baltic peoples, already fleeced by Soviet fiscal re-evaluations, virtually penniless. Rationing in towns and cities continued to leave the self-sufficient farmers in a better position than urban dwellers, and, as under the first Soviet occupation, the black market flourished. Harsh economic policies fuelled the rising tide of resentment towards German rule during 1943. Other policies which furthered opposition to German rule included the enforced recruitment for labour in Germany and conscription into the German military forces, which also led to the second and third displacement routes of Latvians, Lithuanians and Estonians to Britain.

The second major route of displacement for Latvians, Lithuanians and Estonians, was conscription for labour in Germany. The use of Baltic labour for manpower began almost immediately and continued throughout the German occupation. Men and women from all three countries were recruited for labour. Approximately three per cent of the Lithuanian population, two per cent of the Estonian population and one per cent of Latvians were recruited for labour in Germany.

Recruitment for labour was stepped up at the end of 1941, when Germany began to requisition tens of thousands of Baltic workers for its factories. On 19 December 1941, Rosenberg decreed a general work obligation for those aged 18–45. Failure to register was to be punished by three months' imprisonment and a 1,000 mark fine. In 1942, university students were first required to serve a year in the German youth labour force (*Reicharbeitsdienst*). Labour decrees continued throughout the German occupation. The Baltic populations were relatively successful in evading labour obligations by using a variety of avoidance tactics.

Some fled to the woods, while for others, methods such as bribery of local officials were often enough to avoid labour conscription. However, as resistance increased, conscription methods grew harsher. By the end of July 1944, a total of 126,000 Baltic workers had been sent to Germany, including 75,000 Lithuanians, 35,000 from Latvia and 15,000 from Estonia. Baltic workers were employed in a wide variety of areas of labour. Many, including thousands of women, were engaged in military construction work or work in the militarised industries.

A Latvian woman in Britain described her experiences as a labourer in Germany:

> *'I was sent to Germany to work. We probably would have tried to go anyway because I was absolutely terrified of the Russians ... it was quite heartbreaking really. It wasn't a happy time for us.'*

A Lithuanian man in Bolton was also recruited for labour in Germany. He faced the choice of labour in Germany or digging trenches on the Eastern Front:

> *'I left Lithuania in 1943. I was 18 years of age. The war was going on in the east, and the Germans wanted workers and I had no choice. Actually, no, I had a choice. They said you want to go and dig trenches in the Eastern Front or you want to go to Germany and work in Germany? There at least there will be no lice. So I went to Germany and I worked. I worked on an air-field, and that's why I always have a great respect to the Royal Air Force because we used to...they used to bomb the flaming place and we used to fill the holes up you see [laughs]. And [they] used to come and bomb us while we were still there. Can you imagine on an airfield, flat as a pancake, nowhere to hide, no? So that was the experience. That was how I got to Germany.'*

At the end of the war, most of those who had been employed as labourers in Germany were able to find their way to DP camps dotted across Germany, and from there were recruited for labour in Britain.

German recruitment of Latvians, Lithuanians and Estonians for labour rapidly extended to the military sphere. Thousands of Latvian, Lithuanian and Estonian men were recruited into the German war machine from

1941 to 1943, later being captured by the Allies as POWs. Many were subsequently able to acquire DP status and migrate to Britain.

Milosz estimates that six, seven and two per cent of the total populations of Estonia, Latvia and Lithuania respectively were recruited into German military forces by July 1944.[5] The greatest recruitment occurred in Latvia, where according to some calculations, a total of approximately 140,000 men served the German military in 1944. According to Misiūnas and Taagapera, during the whole period of the German occupation, at least 70,000 Estonians joined the German army and more than 10,000 may have died in action.[6] Far smaller numbers were recruited in Lithuania, where the Germans met with the stiffest opposition and resistance.

The enrolment of the Baltic populations for German military purposes began as early as 1941. Over the next three years, a variety of military and paramilitary groups were established in the Baltic States. The recruitment of Latvians, Lithuanians and Estonians into the German military during this period is extremely controversial and it is beyond the scope of this book to discuss this issue in depth. The following overview will, however, present an introduction to the main issues.

The major focus of controversy is whether some Latvians, Lithuanians and Estonians in Britain committed war crimes, either while they were in the German military, or during some of the more sporadic killings of Jews during the initial months of the German invasion. During the German occupation of the Baltic States, tens of thousands of Baltic Jews were killed, most systematically, and some as part of German-led and German-promoted sporadic pogroms. During this period, the Jewish population of the Baltic States was decimated. Latvia, Lithuania and Estonia were major sites of the Holocaust, and local involvement in these actions has become a major issue of debate in the historical analysis of the Second World War in the Baltic States.

These issues are significant in relation to Latvians, Lithuanians and Estonians in Britain because it is claimed that the British Government's screening of DPs prior to recruitment as EVWs, was inadequate, and that it enabled war criminals and collaborators to enter Britain. This point has been argued by David Cesarani in his book *Justice Delayed: How Britain became a refuge for Nazi War Criminals*. The issues were raised by the Simon Wiesenthal Centre in 1986 and subsequently led to the passing of the War Crimes Act in Britain in 1991. This act allowed prosecution for murders in German-occupied territories before 1945 even if the accused were not British citizens at the time of the alleged offences. The Act marked an about-turn in government policy towards suspected East European war criminals in Britain.

400 cases were investigated under the Act. However, only two cases were brought to court, mainly due to lack of evidence, as well as the advanced age and ill health of potential defendants. One of the suspects, Harry Svikeris (Latvian), died in 1995 before a case could be brought against him. The case of Mr. Svikeris had allegedly been one of the strongest on Scotland Yard's list at that time.

It was not only Latvians and Estonians who were alleged to have slipped through British screening policies. DPs of other nationalities such as Ukrainians and Belarusians were also accused of war crimes while fighting for the German military during the Second World War. In 1999, the first full trial of a suspected war criminal was held when 78-year-old Belarusian Anthony Sawoniuk was found guilty of murdering Jews while serving as a police officer in Nazi-occupied Belarus, and was given a life sentence. Sawoniuk was the last suspect on the Home Office's list and no further suspects were brought to trial under this Act. Sawoniuk was given two life sentences and died in prison in 2005, age eighty-four.

In December 1999, Konrad Kalejs, a suspected Latvian war criminal and Australian citizen, was found to be living in the Latvian retirement home "Straumēni" in Britain after being deported from America and Canada. Jewish groups called for charges to be brought against Kalejs, who was alleged to have been a member of the Arājs Commando, which carried out atrocities during the Second World War. British newspapers carried the story on front pages.

Cases such as those of Konrads Kalejs and Harry Svikeris brought negative media attention to the Baltic communities in Britain, even though only a tiny minority of members of these communities was ever suspected of involvement in atrocities during the Second World War.

In recent years, there has been a great deal of ongoing research on the subject of Latvian, Lithuanian and Estonian involvement in the Holocaust, as historians seek to analyse recently opened archives and oral testimonies. However, a high degree of disagreement continues to exist among historians about the issues, with Jewish, German, Latvian, Lithuanian, Estonian and other historians, having wildly different interpretations of this period of history. As Alfred Senn, a highly respected historian of Lithuania, notes:

> *'The subject of the Holocaust in Lithuania exemplifies the arguments of those who insist there is such thing as 'objective history.' Historians can establish that something took place in a certain place on a certain date, but this, by historical standards, constitutes only chronology or, as East Europeans call it, 'faktologija' ('factology'). The moment a historian begins to analyse the larger context, his findings become unacceptable to one or another group of readers. As in any murder trial, one side calls for indictment and punishment, while the other tries to mitigate or deny the guilt of the defendant by presenting a variety of extenuating circumstances. Survivors and victims of the Holocaust demand condemnation and punishment. Anything else seems tantamount to rationalisation or sympathising.'[7]*

The first phase of Latvian, Lithuanian and Estonian involvement in the Holocaust began during the early phase of the German occupation in June 1941, as the German *Einsatzgruppen*, mobile killing units *(*full name, *Einsatzgruppen der Sicherheitspolizei und des SD)*, swept into the Baltic States. As Raul Hilberg makes clear in his groundbreaking book *The Destruction of the European Jews*, it was German policy from the start to encourage local involvement in the 'Final Solution' so that it could be argued that the local populations had resorted to the 'most severe measures' against the Jewish 'enemy' on their 'own initiative and without instructions from German authorities'. Many of the operations were filmed and documented by the German authorities to act as 'evidence 'for later times' of the 'severity of native treatment of the Jews.' However, as Hilberg notes, it was not always easy to encourage local involvement and in many areas, there was stiff local resistance.[8]

Einsatzgruppen A, headed by the infamous commander Franz Stahlecker, operated in the Baltic States one of four such units, and according to Hilberg, its numbers were supplemented by 87 members of the local auxiliary police from Latvia, Lithuania and Estonia. The unit dispersed throughout the Jewish areas of the Baltic States, with the *Kommandos* led mainly by German commanders. Maps in Hilberg's book show the spread of the units throughout towns and villages with

Jewish populations, as well as the devastating massacres in these areas. *Einsatzgruppen* A killed almost 140,000 people in the five months following the invasion, including 136,421 Jews. The *Kommandos* encouraged sporadic pogroms in local areas in addition to the more organised massacres.[9]

One of the most notorious units of the *Einsatzgruppen* was the Arājs Commando, which carried out significant Nazi atrocities in Latvia. Unlike some of the other German-led Commandos, this was headed by a Latvian, Viktors Arājs, a police officer. Soon after its formation, on 6–7 July, the *Einsatzgruppen A* with the help of the *Arājs Kommando,* killed 2,300 Jews in Riga. The *Arājs Kommando* went on to kill tens of thousands of Jews in other parts of Latvia and later moved on to Belarus, where it continued its killing activities.

Part of Germany's strategy to recruit local volunteers was to persuade locals that the massacre of the Jews was necessary to wipe out these purportedly 'pro-Soviet collaborators' and ensure the full restoration of national independence of the Baltic States. The perception that all Jews were pro-Soviet was furthered by German propaganda, even though thousands of Jews had been deported alongside ethnic Latvians, Lithuanians and Estonians during the first Soviet occupation.

It is important also to note that Jews were not the only targets of the German military authorities, and that thousands of Roma, mental patients and Soviet collaborators were also killed during this period.

In addition to the *Einsatzgruppen* or *SD* units, the German military also established police battalions in all three Baltic States in the late summer of 1941. They were composed of former police, militia and some civilian volunteers. Their primary purported purpose was to keep order and facilitate the implementation of Nazi power in the Baltic States. Misiūnas and Taagapera note that Germany's larger scale recruitment of Latvians, Lithuanians and Estonians into the Police Battalions was the result of the earlier failure to gain enough volunteers from among anti-Soviet resistance groups for its own military ends. In Lithuania, they recruited from prisoners captured and held in POW camps, many of whom believed that they would be joining units of a re-born Lithuanian army. The first Police Battalion was formed in September 1941. According to Misiūnas and Taagapera, others were presented with the choice of recruitment or POW Camp. Police Battalions were also created in Latvia and Estonia, during the same period. In Latvia, approximately 15,000 men participated in the

Battalions. Misiūnas and Taagapera have cited several motivations for joining:

> 'A few were genuinely pro-Nazi, while others sought revenge against Bolshevism for the deportations or murders of dear ones and the indignities inflicted on their homelands. Some tried to cover up their earlier collaboration with the Soviets or to escape false accusations to that effect.'[10]

There were multiple different police battalion units, with various geographical remits. Some of the battalions played a role alongside the *Einsatzgruppen* in the killing of Jews, while others supported the troops fighting on the Eastern Front.

In addition to making up the Police Battalions, Latvians. Lithuanians and Estonians were also recruited for Wehrmacht auxiliaries (HiWi – Hilfswillige der Wehrmacht, roughly translated as 'volunteer units'), which recruited about 12,000 men from Latvia. Many of these were recruited from Russian POW Camps. Plensners (who puts the figure of Latvian draftees much higher at 27,000 based on statistics from the Chief of the SS-Ersatzkommando) describes the situation of Latvian draftees into Wehrmacht auxiliaries:

> 'In small groups these unfortunate and unprotected Latvians were thrown from one place to another as the German units moved. They made persistent appeals to the Latvian authorities, especially to the Inspector General of the Legion, whose determined efforts later resulted in many transfers to Latvian units. A large number resorted to desertion but were frequently caught and court-martialled. Other deserters reported to the Legion hoping for protection, and it was possible to arrange their unofficial transfer.'[11]

A variety of other units were also organised. For example, in Latvia, eight border guard battalions were formed, and large numbers of men 'were assigned to special units, such as motorised, transport, anti-aircraft constructions etc.'[12]

As Germany began to weaken during 1942 and 1943, plans got underway for a larger and more organised local military force in the Baltic States in order to strengthen the German war effort. The result was the formation of the Legions. Orders for the creation of Estonian, Latvian and Lithuanian Legions (national units of the Waffen-SS) were given out by Hitler on 10 February 1943.

In Latvia and Estonia, the plans to establish Legions were largely successful. Despite forming part of the German army, the Legions were nominally under local command. Some sections of the population supported the idea of national units, believing that they would be fighting for the freedom of their country. However, Sinka argues that they were in effect offered a 'Hobson's Choice', this being either conscription and dispersal among the German forces or enlistment in "voluntary" units officered by Latvians and Estonians. A Latvian in Britain noted the motivations for choosing the latter option:

'Well, you see we didn't want to be...integrated into the German army at all. We wanted to stay Latvians separately, because we wanted to be Latvians. We're not Germans. We just didn't want the Germans as we didn't want the Russians. So what we wanted – we wanted a Latvian unit and it was called Latvian Voluntary SS [Legion]...they were all Latvians you see and there were Latvian Officers and everything you see, because we didn't want to be Germans. That's why we were a different unit separately you see ...'

The Germans conceded to one point upon which the Latvians and Estonians insisted – that they Latvians and Estonians) would not fight against the Western Allies, but only against the Soviet forces on the Eastern Front.

Recruitment was initially theoretically voluntary, but rapidly became enforced, even though the units continued to bear the name – Latvian and Estonian 'Voluntary' Waffen-SS Legions, to give legitimacy to their formation. Ezergailis noted that in Latvia, although a call for volunteers went out, during the same month (February 1943), 'the Germans also organised a draft'.[13] Misiūnas and Taagapera claim that in both Latvia and Estonia, while initially 'in theory, individuals had a choice, but the widely-known poor conditions in the Labour Battalions, combined with various pressures exerted by local recruitment officers, induced over half the "volunteers" to choose Legion service.'[14]

The basis of the drafts was Rosenberg's labour law of 19 December 1941. Although The Hague Convention prohibited the induction of men and women in occupied territories for military purposes, it allowed their use for labour. Thus, the Nazis twisted the Rosenberg law in order to conscript Baltic citizens for military purposes and the 'voluntary' tag became a way of bypassing international law.

Many Latvians and Estonians in Britain were keen to emphasise the enforced nature of recruitment, with one noting that: 'They were wrong to call them in the army you see, so what they did…they called it a voluntary unit… I remember it clearly in papers. They set the call up dates and everything to report to join the Latvian Voluntary SS Legion…' Another pointed out that they had little choice but to 'volunteer': 'if I hadn't gone to Latvian Legion, they would have either…maybe not shot [me], but concentration camp definitely.'

Others pointed out that while most recruits were conscripted, some did volunteer. An Estonian man who fought in the Russian army gave me his opinion about his fellow Estonians who were recruited into the German army:

> 'Germans mobilised some Estonians, but some went voluntarily. They say they fought for Estonia. I don't believe them. I didn't volunteer. I was forced. I had no choice. But they volunteered for it. Some, not all. Some. Later on, Germans mobilised, but there were some [who] went voluntarily. I'm not supposed to tell you that.'

There is no doubt that in a state of war, some did not know what they might be expected to do while in the Legion, whereas others misguidedly believed they were fighting to save their homeland and were prepared to go to any lengths necessary to defend their beloved country. Germany manipulated locals into believing they were fighting to regain national independence and fend off the Soviet invaders. One Latvian who volunteered for the German forces was well aware that the Latvians were in a no-win situation: 'If Germany won, we would have maybe ended up same as the rest of them, ended up in concentration camps or something like that. Because they will always find something to accuse you of and that's it'. Another Latvian stated that while he saw the Germans as Latvia's liberators:

> 'Afterwards we don't know what would have happened if Germany had won the war, we don't know that. Nobody knows, and going back to…Hitler's ideas because he wanted a pure

38

German nation, so I don't see how we would have fitted into that. So perhaps we would have been as badly off under the Russian occupation I dare say. I don't know. Nobody knows that.'

The first draft of February 1943 called up men born between 1919 and 1924. Following the initial conscription, a new draft was called in Latvia and Estonia in October–November 1943. Later on, the call up extended to men born between 1906 and 1926. On 10 October 1944, even men born between 1900 and 1905 were called into service, although only for digging fortifications.

At its peak, the Estonian Legion was one division numbering 11,000 men. The Latvian Legion comprised two divisions: the 19th Division and the 15th Division, which, according to Ezergailis, initially numbered 12,298 and 14,446 men respectively.[15] Gradually, other units such as construction and border guard battalions were added. Members of the Legions primarily engaged in front line battles on the Eastern Front. The 15th Division was engaged in battles initially in the Volkhov swamps near St. Petersburg. It undertook most of its fighting in 1944, covering the German retreat in the Northern sector of the Russian front and later, within Latvia. In late 1944, the 15th Division was transferred to Pomerania, North Germany, to convalesce, re-organise and replenish its ranks. It then covered the retreat from Pomerania during the winter and spring of 1945. Most of the men in the 15th Division were captured by British and American forces in northern Germany and held as prisoners of war. The 19th Division was organised after the 15th Division, in January 1944. The 19th Division undertook most of its activity in Kurzeme, Latvia, holding the line against the Red Army in late 1944 and early 1945. The 19th Division was one of the last military units in the Second World War to lay down its arms. Its members became Russian POWs and most were deported to Siberia.

Despite their name, the Latvian and Estonian Waffen SS Legions, there is now agreement among historians that they were frontline troops and cannot be compared in any way to German Waffen-SS units. This point was stressed by a Latvian in Britain who stated:

'You see there were quite a lot of SS and in the west they think that all SS is the same. Well [Latvian] Waffen SS were just units that were fighting in the front. That's all. We were SS units in the front.

'We were fighting Russians on the front along with anybody else...but because Latvians had this SS on they were warmongers and god knows what, they were Nazis ...'

Juris Sinka, author of *Latvia and Latvians* also stressed the point that the Latvian Legion was distinct from the German Waffen SS units:

'In the light of recent slanderous allegations, circulating in the west and originating largely from the Soviet Union, about the role of the Latvian and Estonian forces in the Second World War, it must be stated that these forces – whatever the label, and the label was not of the Baltic people's choosing – were ordinary conscript armed forces which received ordinary training and were used exclusively for fighting against Soviet armed forces. They had nothing whatever to do with the political SS units which received special training in German SS schools and carried out special assignments. The only special assignments the men of the Latvian Legion were ever required to carry out were concerned with military operations in particularly difficult sectors of the front line ...'[16]

These facts were later used by Baltic representatives in the case made to Allied governments to transfer former Legionaries into DP camps. In November 1944, the Latvian Legion gained permission to remove the SS initials from the uniforms of the Legion and substitute the former National Army emblem – the sun in the 15th division and the National Fire Cross (reversed swastika) in the 19th division. In 1950, the Displaced Persons Commission reversed the classification of the Legions as 'Waffen SS'.

One of the main controversies relating to Latvians in Britain is that approximately half of Latvian SD members (Ezergailis estimates 600 out of a total of 12,000), including members of the *Arājs Kommando*, were transferred to the Latvian Legion in late 1944 after Germany lost most of its eastern territories. As a result of the transfer, these SD men ended their criminal activities. However, the transfer created complications and embarrassment for the Latvian Legion when attempting to claim that its members had merely been front-line troops. Many SD members used the

Legion as an alibi, which made the allied search for war criminals confusing. Ezergailis outlined the problem:

> *'The transfer of SD men into the Legion gave them an opportunity to mask their past, and, ultimately, on the basis of the DP quota, for some of the Latvian war criminals the chance to enter the United States and other Allied countries.'*[17]

In Lithuania, plans to establish a Legion were unsuccessful due to stiff local resistance to recruitment. On 17 March 1943, induction was halted and the Lithuanians were declared unworthy of joining the SS. A subsequent attempt to raise forces in Lithuania also failed. Initially, a revised plan for a Territorial Force of 10,000 men led by Lithuanian officers under the command of General Plechavičius to fight Soviet partisans on Lithuanian territory proved to be hugely successful. The Lithuanian resistance saw an opportunity to establish a nucleus national army and supported the General. Recruitment was a huge success and volunteers exceeded the quota. However, in May, the Germans demanded the transfer of the newly recruited troops to the direct command of the SS. The General refused, however, and his troops followed suit. The General was arrested and sent to the Salaspils concentration camp near Riga. A number of the resisting troops were executed, the SS was disarmed and about 3500 men were arrested and sent to the Luftwaffe in Germany. The remainder escaped capture and fled to the forests.

In assessing the role of Latvians, Lithuanians and Estonians in the German military during the Second World War, while some historians have emphasised that a small number of Latvians, Lithuanians and Estonians were collaborators and instigators of war crimes, others have pointed out that those recruited to the German military were primarily victims of war and not perpetrators.

In *A History of the Baltic States*, Andres Kasekamp has stressed that historical context must be taken into account, when assessing why some Baltic civilians participated in the atrocities against the Jewish population, most significantly that they had only recently experienced the mass murders and deportations by the Soviet Union, with many losing family members, friends and neighbours.

Kasekamp stresses that the term 'collaborator' is 'inaccurate for those individuals who co-operated with the Nazis in the Baltic countries, since the state to which they owed allegiance had already been destroyed'. He highlights that many local Baltic families sheltered Jews during this period and that: 'The Baltic people endured three brutal occupations by the two totalitarian powers. They had little opportunity to make morally untainted choices between two evils'.[18]

Some historians have also argued that while there was undoubtedly some anti-semitism among local populations, this was undoubtedly whipped up by the Germans, and according to Milosz, 'fanned by the erroneous impression that Jews suffered less than others from Soviet repression and by the unfortunately correct impression that Jews were relatively over-represented among the few pro-Soviet quislings'. According to Hiden and Salmon:

> 'The record of Baltic collaboration in the murder of their Jewish fellow citizens is a shameful one. Yet there is little in their previous record to suggest that it would have taken place without German instigation. All three Baltic governments had a good record for their treatment of Jews between the wars.'[19]

Kasekamp reiterates this point noting that it would be 'misleading to ascribe participation in genocide to "ancient hatreds", and that the causal explanation for the local involvement in the Holocaust, 'is linked to the preceding year of brutal Soviet rule when Jews for the first time rose to positions of power, which created resentment because many Estonians, Latvians and Lithuanians perceived them as having being complicit in the destruction of their statehood'.[20]

Research on these topics has continued apace during the last few decades as archives have been opened and former participants have been interviewed. Nonetheless, the controversies remain. It must be reiterated that whatever the conclusions, the overwhelming majority of participants in this study were victims of the war, and the actions of a minority must not be allowed to blur or become the overriding or central narrative of Latvians, Lithuanians or Estonians who were displaced during the war.

While many young Baltic men were fighting on the German front or employed as labourers in Germany, other Latvians, Lithuanians and Estonians were still living under the German occupation between 1941 and 1943, hoping for an end to the war. Some younger men had been lucky and missed the German drafts due to their age. As the Germans began to suffer heavy defeats during 1944 and their position in the Baltics weakened, the threat of a second Russian invasion loomed. When rumours spread that an invasion was imminent, many Baltic citizens decided to flee. Having lived through the horrors of the first occupation, those who left their homeland during this period were not prepared to stay and risk deportation or murder. Memories of the harsh deportations and treatment by the Russian occupiers made the decision to leave a quick one for many families, many of whom had already made some preparations in the event that this situation might come about.

Large numbers of educated and professional people left in this wave of emigration. These types of people had figured disproportionately in the 1941 deportations, having been categorised as enemies of the people by the Soviet regime. Those fleeing included large numbers of academics, clergymen, actors, musicians, writers and artists. For example, 145 of the 241 Lutheran ministers who still had congregations in Latvia in 1944 fled during this period. A large percentage of Latvians, Lithuanians and Estonians in Britain were displaced in this manner, especially women, children, older refugees and Lithuanian men.

One Lithuanian woman fled Lithuania on 9 October 1944, as the Russian army had already made significant incursions into Lithuanian territory. Her parents had been deported to Siberia during the first Russian occupation and, as she and her husband were civil servants, they decided to leave. She was accompanied by her family, including her daughter, who explained what happened and why her parents decided to flee:

> *'We flew from Lithuania because we saw the saw the Russians taking away all the intelligentsia [in 1941]. When the Russians came, my mother had information given to her that her parents were deported to Siberia. They saw what was happening when the Russians came. They were arresting people. They actually saw all this around them and they were afraid ... because my mother worked for the local government and my father had been in the police force ... and he was also employed by the local authority. They were civil servants. That is why they were afraid for themselves and they saw what was happening to people around them. Because of their position and what they saw, they decided to leave.*
>
> *'They saw people that had been murdered by Russians, drowned, murdered, hung.*

They actually saw that. Life was nothing then. Life meant for nothing.
'Because they [the Russians] came the second time, they didn't want to stay anymore. They didn't want to stay anymore.'

The Russian army began to regain territory in Latvia during the summer and autumn of 1944 and Riga fell on 13 October. One Latvian woman from Riga explains why her family decided to leave their homeland:

'We had Germans stationed in our cottage in the country as well for a short while and they were very friendly from Rhineland, and this one chap, I couldn't speak much German but my parents could and my auntie could and he said, "Well, be prepared because well, we can't defend any longer your country, and we will be withdrawing, so get ready to move out if you don't want to stay", so we knew that was it. We left on 27 September and the Russians occupied Riga on 13 October [1944].'

As the Russian armies overran parts of Eastern Latvia, many Latvian refugees settled initially in Kurzeme, in the west of Latvia, which remained under German control for some months. Even the journey from their homes to Kurzeme was hazardous. One Latvian reported that:

'When we were refugees in 1944, before we reached the docks of a place called Liepāja, which is on the Baltic coast the Russian planes came over at treetop heights, and they shot indiscriminately at the people, horses whatever, because they knew that we were refugees ... maybe hundreds and women and children, men, who didn't escape, didn't get under the wagons or in the ditches deep enough.'

The German surrender in the spring of 1945 was unexpectedly sudden for the refugees in Kurzeme and they were forced to flee to Germany. Another Latvian woman had fled to Kurzeme with her family in 1944, before being obliged to leave Latvia altogether by the German surrender. She described her journey:

'We went through Latvia, to Liepāja, to that port and it was getting so congested with refugees ... but the [Latvian] army

was still fighting in that corner of Latvia. They never lost. They had to surrender, when the armistice was signed, and they said, "You can't stay here. You've got to move to Germany". It was getting too full, what with the military and everything. So people were loaded onto boats and then they went to one of the two Polish ports. I think the Germans call them Danzig and Gottenhaven, and the Poles call them Gdansk and Gdynia. And from then on you got put on trains and you got pulled back and pulled around Germany and then we ended up in Mecklenburg and then the Germans retreated, the Russians came in there as well, because they came into Germany. Eventually we ended back in Schleswig and that stayed British.'

Given that anti-German sentiment persisted among the refugees, the decision to go to Germany was extremely difficult. However, as the alternative was life under the Soviet regime, most did not find the decision too hard to make. Germany, interested in the Baltic peoples as workers, 'opened her doors and provided transportation for the fleeing refugees'.[21]

Estimates of the numbers fleeing their homelands during the autumn of 1944 and early 1945 vary from as few as 50,000 to as high as 150,000 for Lithuanians fleeing to Germany, and between 60–80,000 Estonians to Germany and Sweden and Evacuation to Germany was possible from Latvia for a longer time than Estonia or Lithuania because the Germans were entrenched in Western Latvia until the end of the war in May 1945.

Estonians fled to Sweden in large numbers across the Baltic Sea, partly because it was neutral during the war, and relatively near to Estonia compared to Germany. Some historians feel that more Estonians would have fled Estonia had it been easier to do. As it was, people used any boats they could get their hands on and risked the rough seas.[22]

For Latvians, emigration to Sweden was particularly hazardous due to the Soviet blockade of the eastern end of the Baltic Sea, and many escaping vessels vanished in transit, destroyed by mines or Soviet torpedoes. Although they were hampered by an insufficient number of ships, a majority of Latvians were able to enter Germany through East Prussian harbours. A few entered overland by train.

Lithuanians also fled by boat to East Prussia, and considerable numbers travelled overland to Germany through Poland. Those fleeing included men, women and children of all ages; some fled as a family unit, others with neighbours or friends. Photographs of the refugees in museums in the Baltic States depict long lines of refugees with horses and carts and sacks of belongings.

The journey from homeland to DP camp was long and treacherous and often took many months, sometimes even one or two years. The refugees stopped at many places along the way to find temporary work or shelter. During this period, they did not know where they were heading. Their main concern was to avoid danger. The refugees experienced a great sense of disorientation in that many felt that they were deserting their homelands and had no idea what their fate would be.

Many families were separated as a result of this dislocation. Some family members refused to leave their homeland and were left behind. Others had to leave so quickly that there was no hope of finding family members first. Bronė, a Lithuanian woman, was forced to flee Lithuania with her cousin, but without the rest of her family. She was living and working in a town, about twenty kilometres from the family home and was unable to return 'because [the] Russians were already there'. She never heard what had happened to her family and did not write to them until she had retired at the age of sixty, for fear of possible consequences for her family.

Experiences once in Germany were mixed. Some of the refugees who entered Germany prior to the end of the war were placed in a variety of jobs, for example in German industry. Others worked on German farms. Some of the refugees also faced the necessity of a second escape when, in the spring of 1945, the Soviet Union extended the military front and occupation into the heart of Germany. While most of the respondents recall the years in Germany as an unhappy, uncertain time, one Latvian who was just 17 when she left Latvia describes it as 'an adventure'. She stated that although she liked Germany:

> 'It was rather strange to me, leaving Latvia. I was sorry. I think I cried for a few months every night because you know I missed it. But I liked Germany as well. It was like, sort of an adventure for me. It wasn't "Oh you've left Latvia and that's it now", but of course at that time we hoped we would get back soon.'

When in the spring of 1945, the Soviet Union extended the military front and occupation into the heart of Germany, Latvian, Lithuanian and

Estonian members of various German military units were among those who attempted to avoid falling into the hands of the Soviet Union at this time, and made their way to the Allied lines, where they were made prisoners of war. POWs were placed in a variety of camps in Western Europe. Many former legionaries were housed in a large POW camp in Belgium.

As the war ended and the German armistice was signed in May 1945, the Allies began to liberate concentration camp survivors, prisoners of war and forced labourers. The thousands of Baltic refugees who had flooded Europe during the last months of the war were joined by liberated Baltic POWs, labourers and camp survivors. Kulischer estimates a number of over 200,000 non-returning Balts in Europe at the end of the war, while other historians estimate even higher numbers.[23]

It was on 28 December 1945, while members of the Latvian Legion were in a prisoner of war camp in Belgium, that the organisation *Daugavas Vanagi* was formed. *Daugavas Vanagi* began as a welfare organisation for disabled servicemen and their families, war widows and orphans, but it soon became a national body concerned with the material and spiritual welfare of all Latvians in the West. Translated, *Daugavas Vanagi* means 'Falcons of the Daugava', this being the main river in Latvia flowing through Riga into the Baltic Sea. According to one interviewee, the DVF:

> '*was mainly for the ex-servicemen themselves, a welfare Fund, but it grew, it included women later on ... and young people who wanted to join and so on after the years.*'

Many Latvians, Lithuanians and Estonians were keen to enter the safe havens of the DP camps, and tens of thousands headed for Allied-run camps dotted across Germany and Austria. However, some were initially unsure, as they feared repatriation to the Soviet Union once in the camps, particularly those who had fought in the German armies.

At the close of war, the position of the Baltic refugees in Europe was precarious. The British Government continued to withhold *de jure* recognition of the incorporation of the Baltic States into the Soviet Union, but stalled on its long-term stand on the issue. At this stage, the refugees viewed entering DP camps as a risk, since from there, they could easily be repatriated and these fears were not unfounded. The enforced repatriation of 150 Latvians, ten Lithuanians and seven Estonians by the Swedish Government in January 1946 concerned Baltic refugees in the British zone, since they felt they could not trust assurances from the British Government that they would not be sent back to what was now the Soviet Union.

The Allied forces were, in principle, loath to refuse DP status to Baltic citizens, since by doing so they exposed them to the threat of repatriation. The British Government was alarmed by rumours in July 1945 that the French were repatriating Baltic refugees and stressed that a definitive policy on Baltic nationals must be formulated quickly in order to prevent this happening. Although the rumours about the French actions proved to be largely unfounded, the incident had prompted the British authorities to treat the problem as an urgent issue, in need of early resolution. In January 1946, the Swedish Government repatriated a number of Latvians, Lithuanians and Estonians, which also concerned both the DPs and the British Government.

However, by the end of 1945, the Allies had gained sufficient trust among the refugees that they began moving in far greater numbers to the DP camps. Lithuanian publications, previously cautious on the subject, were now advising their countrymen to take advantage of the camp facilities since moving in was no longer regarded as dangerous.

The position of former recruits in the German forces remained unclear, however. There were known to be around 50,000 Latvians, Lithuanians and Estonians in the British zone of Germany in September 1945, over 20,000 of whom had served in the German armed forces. Latvians constituted by far the largest contingent of former soldiers who had served in the German armed forces. The situation of former Germany army recruits was exacerbated by rumours in the press of many of the Western Allied powers, charging former legionaries with collaboration with the Nazis. Soviet propaganda fuelled these rumours.

At this time, Germany and Austria were divided into four occupation zones: British, American, French and Soviet. Most of the Baltic refugees who had the misfortune to end up in the Soviet zone were forcibly repatriated and many of those who had served the German military forces suffered terrible fates under the Soviet regime. In western occupation zones, responsibility for refugees and DPs was divided between the military authorities and UNRRA, with each having different policies towards refugees and DPs, giving rise to considerable confusion.

UNRRA's policies towards former soldiers were outlined in UNRRA Council's resolution No. 71 of February 1946, which specified that all those who could be identified as war criminals, collaborators, quislings and traitors must be excluded from DP status. Also excluded were ex-Wehrmacht (German Army) personnel who were of non-German nationality or stateless, although non-German ex-Wehrmacht were able to secure aid either if they could show discharge papers and passed a military screening to determine if they had been collaborators, war criminals or volunteers, or if they were actually Volksdeutsche. UNRRA eligibility screening began in early 1946. Some former soldiers refrained from registering with UNRRA in fear of repatriation and settled in the German countryside.

Latvian, Lithuanian and Estonian exile organisations and diplomatic representatives began pressuring the Allied authorities to reconsider the status of former soldiers and submitted evidence to show that they had not been involved in any criminal or treacherous activities. The Baltic representatives emphasised that the Legions were forcibly conscripted by the German military and labelled "voluntary" only in order to circumvent international law which forbids the recruiting of soldiers from occupied populations'. Representatives further argued that the legionaries were front line troops and had committed no war crimes.

Policy was gradually worked out as a result of appeals from Baltic representatives, discussions in Parliament and information received by the Foreign Office. The main area of concern was distinguishing those who had volunteered for service from those who had been forcibly conscripted, a task which Thomas Brimelow of the Foreign Office described in October 1945 as 'impossible'. However, British policy was clarified after December 1945, when the Russians demanded that Baltic citizens either be returned to their homelands or disbanded and discharged immediately. According to the findings of the All-Party Parliamentary War Crimes Group, this demand led to a swift change in the direction of British policy and the decision to discharge former legionaries into British administered DP camps, together with the necessary screening procedures to filter out war criminals.

According to the All-Party War Crimes Group, British policy towards the Balts was 'less stringent' than that of the US or UNRRA. While the US and the UNRRA insisted that they prove their collaboration with Germany before being allowed to acquire DP status, British authorities on the other hand, 'assigned Balts this privileged category unless the authorities themselves had possession of evidence as to why they ought not do so'.

Foreign Office policy made it clear that while they could not 'regard Baltic nationals as war criminals or traitors when the only charge against them is that they fought against the Soviet armed forces', they had 'no wish to withhold them from justice if they are war criminals in the accepted sense'. For suspected war criminals in each case, 'the production of satisfactory prima facie evidence that the person concerned has been guilty of a war crime in the ordinary sense' was required. The approach of the British authorities towards war criminals and collaborators, which considered that a person be regarded as innocent until proved guilty, contrasted with that of the UNRRA, which decreed that a person must prove their innocence in order to acquire DP status.[24]

As they entered the DP camps, the majority of Baltic refugees held high hopes for an imminent return to the homeland. The fact that the Western powers refused to recognise the incorporation of the Baltic States into the Soviet Union gave them hope that the Soviet Union would soon be ousted. While the first half of 1946 can be described as a period of hope among Baltic refugees, there were contradictory messages coming from Western Governments about their ultimate fate.

As a result of the Second World War and the German and Russian occupations of Latvia, Lithuania and Estonia from the late autumn of 1939 until the end of 1945, Estonia lost twenty-five per cent of its pre-war population, Latvia lost thirty per cent and Lithuania lost fifteen per cent (a lower percentage due to regaining the Klaipėda area and east of Vilnius), through death, deportation and migration. War and occupation deaths during the same period were eight per cent in Estonia and nine per cent in Latvia and Lithuania.

By the close of the war, the Soviet Union had consolidated its hold over Latvia, Lithuania and Estonia, bringing the final death throes to these small nations as independent states. Among the refugees in Germany about to enter the DP camps, many of whom had lost family and friends, and above all, their homelands, a sense of disorientation and anger set in. In six years, the lives of the Latvians, Lithuanians and Estonians whom we discussed in the previous chapter were irrevocably altered. Many were just teenagers, going to school and helping on the farmstead, or young adults with promising lives ahead of them, forced to grow up rapidly. Some fought in armies, others trekked across Europe, while a smaller number worked as labourers in Germany. For many, the ramifications of individual ordeals during this period were to be felt for a lifetime.

CHAPTER 3

'We were in heaven!' – Life in the Displaced Persons' Camps

'The DP camps were like little states in the middle of somebody's country.'

During 1945, tens of thousands of Latvian, Lithuanian and Estonian refugees entered Displaced Persons' Camps in Germany and Austria. By 30 September 1945, over 178,904 Baltic refugees had gained DP status, over fifty thousand of whom were in camps in the British zone of Germany. Numbers rose over subsequent months, reaching a peak in the summer of 1946.

The DP Camps were inhabited by men, women and children of all ages and many different nationalities, including Latvians, Lithuanians and Estonians, Poles, Yugoslavs, Hungarians, Ukrainians, Byelorussians – all victims of Soviet Russia and Nazi Germany's war aims. Here, undernourished and living in frequently overcrowded conditions, the Baltic refugees spent up to five years of their lives.

It was in the relatively safe haven of the camps that the uprooted Latvians, Lithuanians and Estonians began to assess their situation and when hopes for an imminent return to the homeland gradually faded. It was also in the DP Camps that exile identities and cultures began to take shape: 'Little Latvias, Lithuanias and Estonias' literally sprang up, where the cultures and traditions of the homelands were replicated as far as was possible in the ascetic and often harsh conditions of the camps.

While life as a Displaced Person was undoubtedly a very difficult experience, there were some positives to be gained from this period of the refugees' lives. Some were lucky enough to go to school, university, gain skills, work, meet future partners, be reunited with family and fellow countrymen, and, at the very least, were safe, with shelter and basic food rations.

In July 1945, following the termination of SHAEF (the Supreme Headquarters Allied Expeditionary Force), the body previously jointly responsible with UNRRA (United Nations Relief and Rehabilitation Administration) for DPs and refugees in Germany during the war, Western Germany was divided into three military zonal authorities: British, French and American, with each zone able to make independent decisions regarding its displaced persons. Eastern Germany remained under Soviet command. The British military authorities controlled five regions in their zone (North Rhine, Westphalia, Hannover, Hansestadt Hamburg and Schleswig Holstein), with headquarters at Lemgo. The British authorities also controlled part of western Austria, which was divided into French, British, American and Soviet zones, and organised under similar lines to Germany.

New agreements negotiated at the end of 1945 and the beginning of 1946, specified that UNRRA was to remain subordinate to the British, French and American military authorities who were to exercise sovereign authority in Western Germany. Different responsibilities were allocated to UNRRA and the military authorities in the DP camps. The military authorities had responsibility for laws controlling the conduct of DPs, the procurement, storage and distribution of food, clothing and medicine, final permission for voluntary relief agencies to operate, transportation facilities, conditions of employment for DPs, distribution of radio and newspapers, with the rights to censorship, and the co-ordination of all resettlement movements. The UNRRA was responsible among other matters for the maintenance of Central Headquarters for Germany together with the appropriate zonal and other subordinate headquarters to supervise the UNRRA operations, the procurement and operation of surplus military vehicles, the procurement of amenity supplies such as tobacco, razors, cigarettes, recreational and educational equipment, and finally, the operation of a Central Tracing Bureau to locate missing DPs.

By the autumn of 1945, it had become increasingly clear that a new international agency would be required to oversee the resettlement of those refugees, who for one reason or another, were unable or unwilling to return to their homelands. The joint operations of UNRRA and the military authorities had only been envisaged as a short-term solution, and a long term organisation was required. Thus, a new international agency, the IRO (International Refugee Organisation), was established, with the specific task of resettling non-repatriable refugees. The IRO constitution was approved on 15 December 1946, and from 1 July 1947 acquired full responsibility for the care and maintenance of 712,675 refugees and displaced persons. By doing so, IRO replaced UNRRA in the task of care and maintenance of DPs after July 1947.

As Elin Toona Gottschalk describes in her evocative memoir of her experiences as an Estonian refugee, *Into Exile*, the landscape of Europe at the end of the war was dotted with refugees, criss-crossing in different directions, in a desperate bid to find safety and shelter.

> *'In the months after the war's end, all of Europe was crawling with disorientated people, moving in all directions, most of them crossing in and out of Central Europe.'*

In many cases, they found safety in the DP camps, hundreds of them by now established across the Western zones of Europe, primarily in Germany and Austria. As refugees from all over war-ravaged Europe began to flood the camps, the immense task faced by the UNRRA and the military authorities became clear. In the British zone of Western Germany alone, by 30 September 1945, there were a total of 50,572 Baltic refugees out of a total DP population of 648,784 DPs of many nationalities, including Poles, Ukrainians, Byelorussians, Hungarians, Yugoslavs, Bulgarians and Romanians.

Numbers rose over the following months. In September 1945, there were 21,453 Estonian, 64,979 Latvian and 47,269 Lithuanian DPs in Western Germany. By June 1946, the numbers were 32,000 Estonians, 80,000 Latvians and 59,000 Lithuanians. There were far fewer Baltic DPs in the western zones of Austria. On 30 September 1945, there were 5,130 Baltic DPs in the US, French and British zones of Austria combined, including only 979 in the British zone.

To cater for the needs of the vast number of DPs, suitable living accommodation had to be found. The DPs were accommodated in a wide variety of locations and dwellings all over West Germany and Austria, ranging from former munitions factories, deserted houses in villages, bombed out army barracks, air raid shelters and even castles and a zoo – Hamburg Zoo was taken over by the British authorities in 1945 to house a camp for Displaced Persons.

Some of these buildings were revamped and prepared to fit the needs of the DPs. In his 1957 study, *European Refugees: 1939–52, A Study in Forced Population Movement*, Malcolm Proudfoot explained:

> *'Extensive repairs were made to damaged buildings to make them fit for winter. Thousands of sheet-metal stoves were installed in rooms, with connecting stove pipes, more often than not, inserted through the windows. Central heating units were put in working order. Indoor toilets and wash rooms were repaired or installed. Thousands of double-decked bunks were replaced by cots, and many straw ticks were discarded for cotton felt mattresses. Many large rooms were partitioned to provide for desirable segregation. Indoor recreation halls and chapels were improvised.'*

However, the sheer number of DPs arriving in the camps meant that preparations were in many cases minimal and conditions varied widely, from the extremely squalid to the reasonably clean and comfortable.

The range of nationalities within the camps was also variable. While most of the camps contained several different nationalities, some were single-nationality camps. Although some of the refugees were relatively lucky in that they stayed in the same camp until their recruitment for labour in Britain, most moved from one location to another, often several times. As the post-war organisation of the refugees gained momentum, and refugees were either repatriated or recruited by western nations for labour, the system was re-ordered and re-organised. As soon as was possible, the smaller and less comfortable camps were closed and the refugees moved to larger, more habitable bases. A re-ordering towards single nationality camps also took place.

There were enormous differences in the individual experiences of Baltic DPs not only because of varying living conditions, but also due to the mechanics of displacement. While some Baltic refugees came to the DP camps alone, including most of the men who had fought in military units, others arrived as family units or with at least one family member or spouse.

A Latvian woman, now living in Nottingham, fled from Riga with her parents in 1944 and eventually entered Spakenburg, a large DP camp at Geesthacht. Spakenburg accommodated about 3,000 Latvians and a much smaller number of Lithuanians and Estonians. She described the conditions as follows:

> *'Oh we were lucky. It used to be a munitions factory before and during the war and they had the worker's houses and we were housed in these sort of family houses and we had a room each which was very good, we had a room and we had a kitchen. There were three rooms upstairs ... there was probably just one person in a room, or you were in a larger room, if you were brothers. We had two brothers above us and then two single persons in the other two rooms. And we were downstairs, three of us and the kitchen was a communal kitchen, but I think the others, they must have had an electrical stove or something. They didn't come into the kitchen at all, so we had two rooms really.'*

There was another camp in Geestacht called Saule which accommodated an estimated 3–4,000 Latvians. But there the conditions were not so good. The same witness described the conditions in Spakenburg as luxurious:

> ... *'because in the other camp [Saule] they were in barracks and there were about fourteen people in a room or something like that. They were separated just with curtains or blankets even. They hung up an old blanket so you didn't see the other person's bed. But we were really well off.'*

Some of the larger camps, which housed up to as many as 10,000 DPs were complete communities, with their own police and fire departments, schools and churches, entertainment and sports centres, print media and medical facilities.

For example, the conditions at Gottorf castle DP camp in Schleswig, Northern Germany, were described by two Latvians in Britain who stayed there as 'fairly good'. It was described as 'a lovely modern castle', with 'lovely water [all] round', where:

> ... *'from smaller camps from other towns, the Latvians were all brought together to this castle ... because we had a school there as well – there were two, an ordinary school and a secondary school, so the lot of them who were coming for the school,*

they came over as well, so there was a lot of Latvians there ... I might be exaggerating but I think there was nearly one thousand [Latvians there].'

The castle was four storeys high, and 'then there were some stables ... and all them were full as well.' The other Latvian described Gottorf 'as a big castle there were plenty of rooms. Some of them were divided of course, provisionally. Ours were. No, it was fairly, fairly good.'

Some of these larger, well-organised camps formed a stark contrast with smaller ones, where facilities and conditions proved to be more makeshift and spartan. Many were crammed in small spaces with their families, and were often forced to stay in temporary shelters while longer term accommodation could be found. For example, some had no alternative but to sleep under concrete air raid shelters or even in the open during the summer months.

A Latvian woman in West Yorkshire fled Riga in January 1945 and reached the safety of Braunau-on-the-Inn DP camp in Austria in 1946. Here she stayed for two years until she came to England in 1948. The camp was housed in former army barracks, and initially everyone had to live together, with families being segregated only later on. The conditions were described as poor – there was no social life, the food was inadequate, and the barracks were 'full of bugs'.

DP camps in Austria were rumoured to be even less comfortable than those in Germany, with Charles Zarine from the Latvian Legation in London, writing to Mr. Hankey (Head of the Northern Department in the Foreign Office, London) in July 1946, that '... from the point of view of material welfare ... [Austria] is the worst region for Baltic refugees.'

The food in the camps was generally meagre and of poor quality because provisions in Germany both during and after the war were scarce. Generally, there was just enough to live on, but no more, and the necessary calorie requirements to maintain a stable weight were often not met, especially as time went on. During the summer of 1945, food supplies for DPs in western Germany ranged from 2300 to 2600 calories per day. However, during the autumn and winter, food supplies dwindled. Rations in the British zone were cut to 2170 calories and then to 1850 by March 1946. In July, the ration was decreased further to 1550 calories. Again, the volume of provisions varied enormously from camp to camp. A Latvian in Britain described the food in her camp:

'We had it handed out. In some camps you had a kitchen, and you had soups and you had bread. You were given the bread and something to put on. But even the bread ... was maize bread. I went to school and I was in a different camp for about three months, and that was winter '45–'46, right after the war, and we had this very coarse black bread and at one time we got some, we were given a little lard as well, and some onions and I know, all I had to eat, I didn't like soups very much and they weren't nice soups either and I had this black bread, a little bit of lard and onion on it. And I know one Christmas Eve, when I went home, my parents were in the camp, and all we had on that Christmas Eve – because I think they saved the nicer things for Christmas Day – we had boiled swede and sort of fresh herrings cooked in water. We didn't even have fat. I will always remember that. But then on Christmas Day, I'm sure we had something much nicer. Not enough, no.'

Most of the DPs talked about the insufficient food rations. Even basic foods became luxury items. A Lithuanian woman now living in Nottingham was a child at the time she stayed in Meerbeck DP camp. She recalled that, '... in Meerbeck, Father Christmas would bring us an orange. Now for me an orange was fantastic. It was absolutely fantastic.'

In most of the camps, a black market operated where belongings such as jewellery would be sold for food or other items, such as cigarettes. A Latvian in Leeds explained the system:

'You probably heard there used to be a lot of black market selling. If you had a bit of money ... Well, we were lucky. We had some of the Latvian money. Well of course the price of silver alone, the people in black market, they take it in exchange for whatever we wanted ... so that eased things.'

One Lithuanian woman in Oldenburg camp in the British zone traded her knitting for more food. Although wool was practically unobtainable, it was possible to unravel old socks or sweaters.

'Anyone who could sew or who could repair shoes could earn cigarettes, especially since the clothing handed out by the Red Cross and other charitable organisations rarely fitted properly.'

The skills that the DPs had acquired living on the farmsteads in the home-lands came in very useful, and they were able to identify edible plants and mushrooms in the forests nearby, as well as to craft tools by hand and other items they could trade, with very few materials. Some of the DPs who lived in houses kept some animals such as pigs or chickens despite this being officially forbidden. In many cases, however, the authorities turned a blind eye. Elin Toona Gottschalk recalls how her father kept pigs in the house in the DP camp where they lived. The pigs were 'an open secret. They were going to be slaughtered for Christmas and everybody was going to get some meat.'

Despite the poor conditions in many of the DP camps, to the refugees they provided an enormous relief after months or years of war and dis-placement – at least they were safe. An Estonian now in West Yorkshire spent two years in Oldenburg DP camp from 1945 to 1947, after a period spent fighting in the war on the German side. He described how to have been through the war and then to have one's own bed, bedroom, three meals a day and pocket money, was 'marvellous'. Oldenburg DP Camp was a lively camp with singing, dancing and sports for the young. He met people from many different nationalities and had some casual girlfriends in the camp. Describing the experience, this Estonian stated that at the time, 'We were in heaven.'

Many of the younger refugees formed relationships in the camps. There were many thousands of young, single men and women with time on their hands and with a rich social calendar in many of the camps, it was inevitable that many DPs formed close friendships and relationships with each other. Some DPs even married in the camps. An Estonian man from Halifax was married in Stolzenau DP camp by a German Bürgermeister in 1947, just months before coming to England with his new wife in September 1947.

Although the prospects for finding paid work whilst living in the camps were poor, there were many opportunities to learn different skills and trades, such as motor mechanics, tailoring or shoemaking. Some of the DPs taught English or worked in the canteen or post office. Creative types wrote, painted or practised music. Children and teenagers were able to continue their studies in DP schools. However, despite these opportu-nities and the many cultural and sporting activities available, many DPs emphasised the day-to-day boredom in the camps, the long hours chat-ting about current events in the homeland and their future, playing cards

58

to pass the time and feelings of impatience and frustration. They were in limbo, unable to make concrete plans or provision for their futures.

A Latvian witness, living in West Yorkshire, described, however, how the refugees did not just sit back and wait for events to impact on them, but made a proactive effort to make the best of their present situation. From her experiences in Feldburg DP camp in Western Germany, which accommodated only Latvians, she made the following observations:

> 'There's one thing about Latvians we make things do ... I mean we're active. We actually try to help ourselves. We don't expect help from other people and first of all we try. In this camp, we sort of did it up a bit and try to make the most of things. We weren't just sitting down and just waiting for someone to do something for us. We tried to improve things, shall we say.'

Some of the DPs were able to work and earn a wage in the camps, although many posts were unpaid, voluntary positions. From the outset it had been military policy to provide employment for displaced persons, and to encourage able-bodied men and women among them to volunteer for useful work. A majority were employed in an administrative capacity, although there was a variety of work, both in and outside the camps. In December 1946, it was calculated that 60 per cent of all employable males of the registered population in UNRRA administered centres in the British zone were working. A Latvian man from Leeds worked for UNRRA in a DP camp in Germany as a motor mechanic, while a Latvian woman from Derby became an interpreter typist for UNRRA in an office in Schleswig DP camp.

An Estonian DP from Lübbecke DP camp wrote a letter to *The Manchester Guardian* on 27 June 1946 stressing the self-reliance and high employment levels of Estonian DPs. He stated that:

> '80 per cent of Estonians accommodated in DP camps in the British zone of Germany have voluntarily taken up employment – not excepting those disabled, enfeebled by age, and mothers with small children – and in the camps themselves, as far as the shortcomings of recent times permitted, everything conceivable is being done by self-initiative to improve our life, education, sanitary and welfare conditions.'

Some of the DPs who later came to Britain were only children or teen-agers when they first entered the camps, and they were able to resume their studies at schools set up within the camps themselves One Latvian DP was only twelve years old when he fled Latvia in the summer of 1944 with his parents. After making their way across Germany, they eventually entered a DP camp in Hannover and were subsequently transferred to a DP base in Greven. He attended school in the camp, learned English and later was able to travel to Britain as an EVW when he turned 18 in 1949.

Many of the children became ill during the difficult journeys across Europe and were able to receive treatment once they arrived in the camps. DP children were particularly susceptible to many of the common ill-nesses in the DP camps. For example, TB was common among DPs liv-ing in the confined, communal quarters of military barracks and similar dwellings. As with many other diseases, TB was exacerbated by the poor food rations. Two of the most common diseases caused by malnutrition were rickets and anaemia. Adults too suffered from a wide variety of complaints, again exacerbated by decreasing food rations. To offset the spread of diseases, UNRRA organised a fairly extensive medical pro-gramme among the DPs, with at least one medical officer and several nurses present in each camp. Infirmaries were also established within the camps and immunisation programmes were implemented. Those at risk were given vitamin supplements and a dental service was provided in a majority of camps. The result of effective organisation was to prevent a real crisis or epidemic developing among the DP population.

Despite the many negative traumatic experiences reported, life in the DP camps was described by some as a happy time. A Lithuanian woman interviewed in the Midlands, was only a small child when she came to the DP camps with her parents. Her family fled Lithuania on 9 October 1944 and during the next four years, stayed in a variety of dwellings and DP camps. From August 1945 to May 1948, the family were able to settle in Meerbeck DP camp, where they were given a private house in which to live. The camp accommodated mostly Lithuanian DPs and a variety of Lithuanian associations were set up. Comparing her experiences growing up in England after the war with the years in Meerbeck, she stated that:

> 'I recall the childhood being more pleasant after wartime Germany, where we lived in Meerbeck, those years. Now there … I have pleasant childhood memories.'

The diplomatic representatives of Estonia, Latvia and Lithuania wrote frequent letters to Ministers within the British Government stressing the plight of the DPs, both prior to and during the labour recruitment process. The Foreign Office files in the National Archives in London are full of letters and appeals from Latvian, Lithuanian and Estonian representatives in London, and from the various Baltic welfare committees. These appeals stressed the problems faced by the Baltic refugees and DPs in Europe and sought to pressure governments and international organisations to act to improve their situation.

The living conditions in the DP camps began to improve only after the end of 1946, when DP numbers began steadily to decrease due to the labour recruitment schemes organised by Western nations. The food situation in Germany also began to improve and some of the worst camps were closed. Nevertheless, remaining DPs were frequently moved from camp to camp as the DP Camp system was re-ordered, and their health suffered from the length of time spent in the camps.

One of the more positive aspects of the DP Camps is that after years of displacement and upheaval, the Baltic nationalities were able to come together, men, women and children, for the first time in months or even years. It was here that the Latvian, Lithuanian and Estonian diaspora began to form and when identities as refugees and exiles began to take shape. Camps became communities and national and exile identities were strengthened.

Particularly in the single nationality camps, the Estonian, Latvian and Lithuanian refugees began to create their own 'mini' Estonias, Latvias and Lithuanias. One Estonian DP stated that 'The DP camps were like little states in the middle of somebody's country'. Attempts to recreate the homeland in the confines of the camps was partly a way of remembering home, mainly because the refugees felt an increasing responsibility now that they had reached the safe haven of the camps, to act as the guardians of the homeland. They believed that because those in the homeland were now unable to maintain national cultures and identities as a result of Soviet repression, that they had a responsibility as exiles to maintain cultures and identities on behalf of the homeland. Andrejs Eglitis, a Latvian DP poet summed up the huge responsibility felt by the DPs in the poem 'God, Thy Earth is Aflame', which contains the line: 'We are the hope and blossom of our native land!'

Feelings of duty and responsibility to keep the Baltic cultures and identities alive on behalf of the homeland manifested themselves in a rich cultural scene and the reconstruction of national identities to fit the needs of DP life. The responsibilities of exile combined with boredom, nationalism and disorientation to fuel vibrant Latvian, Lithuanian and Estonian 'cultures in exile', both to restore the spirit of the homeland and its peoples and to pass the time. Participation in cultural events and organisations involved all DPs, many of whom had commemorated certain cultural traditions to only a minimal extent when they were living in the homeland prior to the war.

The celebration of homeland festivals and national holidays became important annual rituals in the DP camps, a new medium through which to express ethnic loyalties. Often, the celebration of these festivals, particularly those marking the hard-fought-for Latvian, Lithuanian and Estonian independence in 1918, were sad, sombre events. One Latvian DP stated that 'In the camps', the commemoration of Latvian Independence Day on 18 November, 'was a sorrowful day'. Lithuanians celebrated Independence Day on 16 February, while Estonian Independence Day was on 24 February. The commemoration of some of the other important national days, marked annually in exile, first began in the DP camps. The most significant of these was Deportation Day on 14 June. This day marking the night in 1941 when thousands of Baltic citizens were deported to Siberia became one of the most important commemorative events among Baltic refugees in exile, including those in Great Britain. It is still recalled among Baltic communities around the world today.

Choir groups, folk dance and singing groups, schools and sports groups were organised in the camps. A Baltic University was even set up to further the education of the homeland through its guardians abroad. Efforts were made to recreate as much as possible the life of the homeland. Although it was difficult to cook national dishes, except perhaps on special occasions like Christmas or St. John's Day, it was possible to replicate other traditions such as the building of traditional saunas in some of the camps. A Latvian man in Britain recalled the sauna built at Geesthacht DP Camp in Germany.

Dr. Kučius, President of the United Lithuanian Relief Fund of America, described how folk dances and other shows put on by the DPs in the camps helped to bring vibrancy to an otherwise dreary existence in the drab surrounds of the camps:

> *'The shows put on by the DPs, featuring their beautiful songs and national dances, with the performers, both men and girls,*

dressed in their picturesque and ancient national costumes, to
the accompaniment of native instruments, dispel somewhat the
dreary impression created by the ordinary run of camps.'

Theatre became a particularly important avenue through which to dra-
matise the plight of the DPs, and to recall a past, already remembered as
idyllic and happy. Folk plays were particularly common in Lithuanian DP
theatre productions. Theatre had been extremely popular in the interwar
period in all three Baltic States, as it remains today. It was thus inevitable
that the theatre re-established its popularity in the DP camps, particularly
given that it was a medium which could work with as few or as many props
and materials as were available. Many professional actors had fled from
the Baltic States along with other creative professionals, such as writers,
artists and musicians. The Estonian National Theatre was re-established at
Oldenburg and a Latvian theatre was set up at Meerbeck DP Camp.

In addition to theatre, opera and ballet were also performed. The entire
Latvian ballet had escaped to the west and had re-established at Lübeck.
At Oldenburg DP camp, a Latvian opera was launched. At Blomberg
a vibrant community of artists, musicians, theatre and film directors
was established. This included prominent Estonian musical artists and
Latvian artists and soloists. A Lithuanian Opera Artists' Centre of the
British zone was established at Blomberg, as were a Lithuanian Choir
Ensemble and the Lithuanian National Dance Group. Here, the Riga Film
Company began producing films and newsreels. At Meerbeck, a Latvian
choir was formed.

These groups put on a variety of performances in the camps. In 1947,
the Lithuanian Opera Artists' Centre at Blomberg succeeded in putting on
a performance of Rossini's Opera, *The Barber of Seville*, with self-made
costumes and decorations. This opera had previously been performed in
DP camps of the British and American zones fourteen times. Some of the
groups were able to tour the DP camps, despite the difficulties involved.
The 'Foreign Estonians' Male Choir': "Estonia" toured many of the DP
camps in the British zone, including Oldenburg on 10 July 1947.

UNNRA assisted with activities in the camps, including cultural,
sporting and recreational events. A wide variety of activities were set up
for DP children, including summer camps, and Scout and Guide organisations. In August 1948, the World's YMCA/YWCA Camp for Scouts
and Guides, 'Baden-Powell' was held at Havenoth, Timmendorfer Strand.

570 Lithuanian, 600 Estonian and 1,000 Latvian DP children between 10 and 16 years of age were sent to the camp, along with those of many other nationalities.

A Latvian interviewed in Nottingham described the cultural activities at Spakenburg Camp. She was then still of school age, and lived there with her parents:

> 'There were choirs, theatres and there was the church as well, of course. There were dancers and my father, he liked to do wood-work, so they had a workshop there, and there were about ten people who did all sorts of woodwork, and there were silversmiths and ... well, I went to school still, so I was busy, ... there were all sorts of people, teachers, professors, they were all there. Oh and in Germany we even had a Baltic University – Pinneburg.'

The subjects taught at the different schools in the camps were wide rang-ing, particularly in the larger camps, where there were a greater number of highly educated refugees resident. In Spakenburg, the school offered all the traditional school subjects taught in Latvia, including botany, physics, maths, Latvian and foreign languages. Some of the refugees who came to Britain were also taught English in the camps, although the standard of teaching was variable.

UNRRA was assisted by voluntary relief agencies in the establishment of educational facilities for DPs of all ages, from nursery school and kin-dergarten to professional training in universities and technical colleges. Many of the university lecturers and professors from Baltic universities had fled their homelands in 1944. The Foreign Office made lists of the locations of these academics and the Baltic nations' most eminent scien-tists in Germany. Many of them were in various DP camps in the British zone, including the DP Study Centre at Pinneburg, Hannover DP Camp, Göttingen DP camp, Blomberg DP camp and Geesthacht DP camp.

A list of opportunities for 'Occupational Training and Professional Re-education' circulated by the Control Commission in September 1946 showed the range of institutions offering educational and training opportunities for DPs in the British zone. The choices open to Baltic DPs included: the Hamburg D.P Study Centre (formerly Baltic DP University); the German Universities Scheme; the Latvian Agricultural Training School; the Estonian Agricultural Training School; farm work;

home making schools; the Art and Music school at Kabel; and the Baltic Technical School at Geestacht. The Flensburg Navigation School, sponsored by UNRRA, was opened on 1 September 1946, with 150 students attending the first course. A variety of maritime related subjects were taught at the school, which was run for the benefit of DPs only. All the students at the school were Baltic DPs.

The Baltic DPs in the British zone founded their own university, initially called the 'Baltic DP University', (later the 'DP University Study Centre') in Hamburg, which opened its doors on 14 March 1946. DP scholars from Latvia, Lithuania and Estonia founded eight faculties: Medicine, Chemistry, Construction Engineering, Agronomy, Mechanical Engineering, Natural Sciences, Mathematics, Philology and Law. The Nominal Roll of Professors of January 1946 listed 84 staff members, including distinguished Professors, PhDs and MAs from a wide range of DP camps. In December 1946, the enrolment numbered 1,100, of which two-thirds were Lithuanians and the remaining one-third was composed of Latvians, and Estonians in equal numbers. The same proportions applied to the teaching staff. However, the university faced difficulties and an unstable future right from the start. In early 1947, the British authorities moved the Study Centre to Pinneburg, twenty kilometres away, and while its facilities and conditions were improved, DP scholars requested the movement of the university to the American zone, where they felt education among the DPs was taken more seriously. The British authorities refused however and the university closed on 30 September 1949, though this was mainly because many of the students and teachers had accepted offers to resettle overseas.

Some Baltic DPs had the opportunity to study at German Universities. Occupation authorities demanded the reservation of ten per cent of the quota for German universities for DPs and these quotas were apparently filled. A Lithuanian publication advised college-age DPs to exploit these opportunities. In late 1945, applications for admission to the Marburg medical faculty were already being accepted and Lithuanian students would have dormitories at Erlangen. By May 1946, DP enrolment in German universities reached 600 in the British zone. The numbers were far lower than in the American zone, which had achieved 4,000 university enrolments by the same date.

In addition to the voluntary relief agencies working under agreement with UNRRA (e.g. the British Red Cross, the International Red Cross, the YMCA/YWCA), national and welfare committees were also established by the Baltic DPs. These organisations had both nationalist and welfare objectives, and aimed not only to restore independence, but also to ensure adequate care for DPs.

Newspapers were circulated among the DP camps to keep the refugees up-to-date on the situation in the homeland and the options regarding their future. Some DP centres produced their own newspapers or typed news-sheets. Throughout 1945 and 1946, the military authorities tolerated the circulation of a variety of newspapers among the DPs. Some were printed in Germany, others in Sweden. For example, in Lübbecke, the following newspapers were published: *Libekas Vestnesis*, a Latvian newspaper, *Laisvės Varpas*, a Lithuanian newspaper and *Sonumid*, an Estonian newspaper. The Foreign Office noted that the following Latvian papers published were in the British Zone in March 1946: *Latviešu Ziniu Dienesta Biletene*, published in Detmold, and *Latviu Sports* in Lübeck, Halle.

Some of the newspapers authorised by UNRRA contained English phrases to learn and articles about England and the English way of life. For example, a 1945 edition of the Latvian newspaper *Tēvzeme* contained an article about the English school system. A common section in the newspapers was a list of DP deaths. Newspapers also updated the DPs on international news such as the Nuremburg trials. Radio broadcasts and news films also provided news updates.

DPs also had the opportunity to read national literature in the camps. Latvian, Lithuanian and Estonian publishing houses were established in Germany and Sweden to cater for the emergent diaspora. Literature was also published in magazines and literary reviews. Between 1945 and 1950, 1,179 Latvian books were produced by DPs in Sweden, Denmark and Germany, including new exile literature and Latvian classics including works by Blaumanis, Poruks and Niedra. By 1950, there were sixteen Lithuanian publishing houses in Germany. These initial years of exile witnessed the birth of a vibrant exile literature, a genre that continued throughout the entire Soviet period.

Religion was also an important aspect of the homeland culture pinpointed for fervent maintenance, particularly among Lithuanians whose Catholicism was a significant component of their national identity. The large number of Lithuanian DP priests who had fled from the approaching atheist armies of Soviet Russia in 1944 contributed to the recreation of the religious life of the homeland. An estimated 227 Lithuanian priests were in DP camps in Germany, one quarter of the pre-war number of priests in Lithuania. Large numbers of seminarians were also accommodated in the camps, some of whom were able to continue their studies at Eichstatt. Estonians and Latvians had their religious requirements catered for by Lutheran ministers in the camps. Although religion among these nationalities was not, in most cases, inextricably linked to national identity in the way that Lithuanian-ness and Catholicism were, Lutheranism became increasingly important in exile. Religious ceremonies such as marriages and funerals were held in the camps, and became important events through which to express and perform ethnic customs and traditions.

Although the British Government was wary of nationalism fermenting in the DP Camps, it was initially fairly liberal regarding the cultural life of the refugees. At first, few restrictions were placed on the circulation of newspapers, and the cultural activities and welfare organisations of the Baltic DPs. Many of the Baltic refugees regarded the British zone as a model in this respect, and those in American and French DP camps were reported as wishing to transfer to camps under British control, since the cultural life there was deemed to be the most liberal.

Relations between the Baltic DPs and the British Military Authorities began to sour, however, as the months went on. During early 1946, the British military authorities began to implement changes in some of the camps in relation to circulation of newspapers, cultural activities and welfare organisations. The change in the name of the Baltic University to 'Study Centre' was symptomatic of the changes. In early 1946, the welfare and national committees, which had been organised by the DPs, were disbanded. All National Committees in the British zone were closed and their funds withdrawn, including the Red Cross, although the British authorities recommended that the Red Cross workers should continue their duties under British control. The British Government was concerned about the underlying nationalist objectives of some of these organisations. The military authorities were also worried about Soviet recriminations and the growth of Soviet propaganda suggesting that the British Government was aiding and abetting fascist elements within these organisations. In January 1946, the Northern Department reported the reasons for its decision to suppress the committees:

'We have not banned the Baltic Committees merely because we have refused to recognise the Ukrainian Red Cross. We are

against both for the same reason: viz., that welfare organisa-
tions of this nature would, and in the case of the Ukrainian Red
Cross did, provide cover for political organisation and activity.'[1]

In their place, the military authorities facilitated the establishment of
the 'Baltic Welfare, Education and Employment Organisation' in March
1946, which would enable close monitoring by both the military authorities and UNRRA. The military authorities outlined the functions of the
new organisation in July 1946:

'In order to advise Control Commission for Germany (BE)
and UNRRA on matters of Welfare, Education and employ-
ment among Balt Displaced Persons and other matters affect-
ing the well-being of Balt Displaced Persons, an organisation
to be called the Baltic Welfare, Education and Employment
Organisation has been established.'[2]

There was substantial opposition from some quarters of the Baltic DP
population regarding the suppression of national and welfare committees.
Many DPs felt that the individual committees carried out valuable work
and that the needs of each nationality might be overlooked as a result
of the establishment of the Baltic Welfare, Education and Employment
Committee. As a result of pressure from the Baltic DPs the government
made several concessions, including unblocking funds of the Latvian
Red Cross, with the money to be shared out through the Baltic Welfare
Committees to Estonians and Lithuanians.

Newspapers published by the DPs in their own language were also
closed and there was the threatened prohibition of Latvian, Lithuanian
and Estonian newspapers from abroad, purportedly 'due to the tendency
of such papers to contain anti-Soviet propaganda', although the publication of translations of British factual news reports was allowed.

Monsieur Torma, head of the Estonian Legation in London, wrote to
the Foreign Office in June 1946 stating his opposition to the fact that 'the
publication of *Sönumid,* the largest Estonian paper printed in the British
zone, has had to be discontinued by order of the military government'.
A. F. Lambert wrote to I. T. M. Pink at the Control Commission on 31
August 1948 stating that the Foreign Office had 'no objection to the publication in Latvian of factual news bulletins translated from the English'.

He noted in relation to Baltic newspapers from abroad that 'unless such newspapers from abroad are free from anti-Soviet propaganda, they should not be permitted.'[3]

During 1946, Charles Zarine from the Latvian Legation in London sent numerous letters to members of the British Government requesting greater cultural freedoms in the camps. In July he wrote to Mr Hankey at the Foreign Office about the effects of the restrictive measures on the DPs:

> '... the recent change in the attitude of the authorities has had
> a very bad effect. It is interpreted that they are considered to be
> a nuisance of whom the authorities want to get rid, and all the
> recent reverses ... are felt to be an indirect pressure to return
> home – to the Russians.'[4]

The restrictions on cultural life and associations in the camps served to intensify the national identities of the refugees, along with feelings of anger and disorientation. As a result of the pleas by the Baltic DPs and their representatives, however, some of the restrictions and implemented changes were rescinded, although particularly in regard to newspapers, the government policy tended to change frequently. In September 1946, a new order permitted the circulation of camp news-sheets in the language of the camp inhabitants and it was agreed that the publication of a Baltic weekly newspaper for the whole zone should be allowed. In 1948 it was reported that Latvians, Lithuanians and Estonians each had their own weekly newspaper in the camps, as well as camp news-sheets. The officially sponsored Latvian newspaper was called *Nedelas Apskats* (Weekly Review). However, the newspapers were withdrawn after 3 January 1948 due to worries about anti-Soviet content and lack of paper.

During their first months in the DP camps, the refugees' belief that they would soon be returning home and that the Allies would declare war on Russia and oust her from the Baltics furthered their identities as merely 'temporary' refugees. However, some of the younger refugees were already pessimistic about their future and reluctantly accepted that they would be absent from the homeland for a lengthy period. A Latvian woman in Leeds, asked if during the time that she was in the DP camp she had hoped continually that the war would end and that she would go back to Latvia, she replied, summing up the attitude of other young Latvians too:

> *'Yes, yes, at first yes we did, but we soon realised that that couldn't, that that wasn't going to happen because the Russians were still there. Yeah, so we came to the realisation that that would be it.'*

The DPs' desire to return to a free, unoccupied homeland was intense. As they recovered from their experiences from the war and as refugees wandering from place to place, the initial relief of finding refuge in the DP camps turned into a desperate wish to return to a free homeland, to see families once more and to restore their old lives. However, the Baltic refugees were unwilling to return to an occupied homeland under any circumstances. In the DP camps, the constant fear of repatriation heightened the ethnic solidarity of the refugees and increased resistance to Russian rule in the Baltics. Russian repatriation officers were initially able to enter the camps and attempted to lure the DPs back to the homeland. There were several incidents in the camps when Russian officers and Baltic DPs clashed. A few did accept repatriation offers, but the vast majority refused to return to a Soviet-occupied homeland. Rumours about the fate of repatriates spread like wildfire throughout the camps. DPs heard about cases where repatriates were sent to Siberia or suffered a horrific fate in their homeland. One Estonian DP explained:

> *'We have indisputable evidence that repatriates were destined for Siberia instead of for their native country or that they did not get farther than the prisons of the Soviet zone.'*

Soviet propaganda was distributed in the camps, attempting to refute these rumours, and outlining the positive experiences of Baltic repatriates. Although Soviet propaganda was banned during the Berlin blockade of 1948, for the rest of the time, the military authorities fell short of an official ban.

Soviet pamphlets and newsletters distributed in the camps drew attention to fascist elements within the DP camps, and stressed that emigration could only be advantageous to those States who regard refugees and DPs as cheap labour. Soviet propaganda aimed to increase repatriation among

Balts and to turn them against western nations. This effort, however, was largely unsuccessful. Only a tiny minority of Latvians, Lithuanians and Estonians from the British zone voluntarily repatriated to the Latvian, Lithuanian and Estonian Soviet Socialist Republics. It has been estimated that of an approximate total of 160,000 to 190,000 Latvians, Lithuanians and Estonians in Germany after the war, including those living outside the DP camps, only about two per cent applied for repatriation.

This description of life in the DP camps and the changes which occurred as the months went on, provides the context for the acceptance of recruitment offers by western nations. The worsening of the situation for the DPs and the growing uncertainty regarding their future prompted members of Latvian, Lithuanian and Estonian associations and the representatives in London, to propose radical solutions. In September 1946, Prof. Mykolas Krupavičius of the Supreme Lithuanian Committee of Liberation appealed to both the British Government and the United Nations Organisation about the present situation of the Lithuanian DPs and the possible solutions for their future.

'Under the present circumstances, the displaced Lithuanians will be able to stand only one more winter in the Allied zones of Austria and Germany, not only because they are an onerous charge to the local occupation authorities and are often treated with ill-will by the local German administration, which has too readily forgotten who bears the true responsibility for the presence of Baltic Displaced Persons in such numbers in Germany, but also because life in such crowded conditions, often with several families living in a single room, without regular work and employment, without prospects of a better future, has a demoralising effect on them. The time has come for the definite settlement of the European Displaced Persons problem.'[5]

CHAPTER 4

'A valuable addition to our manpower' – The recruitment of Latvians, Lithuanians and Estonians for labour in Britain

'I realised we won't be able to return to Latvia so we had to go somewhere else and more or less this was nearer. It was in Europe. It was a bit nearer Latvia and there was an opportunity to work in [a] hospital so I came like that...we knew there was no chance to go back to Latvia. There were Communists, Russians. We didn't want to go back there...and when you are young you are probably a bit more adventurous and why not do something about it, you know sort it out?'

Stranded in the DP camps with little hope of an imminent return to independent homelands, the refugees longed for a solution to their plight. In 1946, many months after arriving in the DP Camps, Great Britain was among the first countries to offer the refugees a possible way out, a potential hope for the future.

In Europe, a few months after the end of the Second World War, immense political and economic difficulties were created for the British Government by the hundreds of thousands of refugees stranded in DP camps in the British zones of Germany and Austria. Meanwhile, at home in Britain, severe shortages of manpower, one of the consequences of the economic conditions created by the Second World War, was causing critical problems in the health service, agriculture, and industries such as textiles and coal.

The numbers of DPs in the camps in Germany and Austria were enormous, with an estimated 650,000 DPs in the British zone of Germany alone at the end of the war with an estimated figure of 1.8 million DPs stranded in Europe as a whole, many of whom, like the Baltic refugees, had no homelands to return to, due to establishment of the Soviet Union and domination of much of Eastern Europe.

As the number of DPs grew and conditions deteriorated, humanitarian concerns also increased. The United Nations called on Western nations to shoulder a share of the responsibility for these refugees and increasing pressure was put on Great Britain and other western nations to find a solution.

A further problem was the growing financial burden of the DP camps. The British Government faced immense bills for post-war reconstruction at home and could ill afford the financial costs of running the DP camps. It was estimated that by 1947, the cost of the British zone of Germany to the British public was approximately 80 million pounds.

Faced with the DP problem abroad, back in Britain, the new Labour Government formed in July 1945, began the post-war reconstruction process. One problem which became immediately apparent was the shortage of manpower. There was also an uneven distribution of labour which had led to an undermanning of some essential industries, while others considered less 'essential' were able to recruit labour more successfully. Key industries, particularly coal, textiles and agriculture were facing the greatest difficulties, as their failure to attract labour became increasingly apparent.

There were also critical staff shortages in hospitals. The Economic Survey published in June 1946 noted that the additional manpower required to maintain the domestic coal fuel ration and exports at the current level, and to keep industry fully supplied with coal was 40,000, while an increasing rate of wastage and falling rate of recruitment was forecast to lead to a reduction in manpower of 40,000 over the year to March 1947. This put the numbers required in the coal industry alone at 80,000, while across all sectors the need was estimated at 230,000, rising to 630,000 by the end of 1946. Manpower shortages threatened not only to promote wage inflation, but also to destabilise the entire economy.

Manpower shortages were amplified by the fact that many of the women who had worked during the war, now stopped working to look after husbands returning from the battlefields. The country was in a precarious situation: the war had drained Britain's resources, gold and currency reserves had been exhausted and foreign debt was now well over three billion. Heavy shipping losses limited Britain's ability to export goods overseas, and manufacturing was at a critical low. The country was relying heavily on importing goods, just to supply the country with enough food and essential goods, while export levels were at severely low levels. The agriculture sector was not providing nearly enough food to feed the nation, and needed to be modernised to significantly increase production. Other industries such as textiles also needed massive investment and increases of manpower, to reduce reliance on imported goods and to increase exports. The Government needed to take urgent action and intervene decisively in the economy to prevent Britain from sinking further into debt and give a more optimistic time limit for ending rationing, which continued throughout 1945 and 1946.

The options for solving the problem of labour shortages had initially been discussed within the government in the autumn of 1945, at an inter-departmental meeting between the Ministries of Health and Labour to discuss the supply of nurses and domestics for hospitals. The shortage of hospital domestics had been acute during the war, and at the close of war, a near-crisis had developed, especially in TB Sanatoria. The idea of recruiting DPs for labour was dismissed initially, but deliberations continued during November 1945. Although the benefits to be gained were acknowledged by the Ministry of Labour, the associated difficulties had not yet been overcome. One of the potential problems foreseen by the Ministry of Labour was that once recruited, DPs would not stay in the jobs allotted to them and that there was no way that they could be forced to stay. In November 1945, P. Goldberg, an official at the Ministry of Labour, discussed the potential problems of the recruitment of DPs:

'Most of the available women were said to be Poles and Balts. Among the latter, the keenest applicants for the jobs would be well-educated women who at the time of the German occupation of their countries had been studying for the learned professions. Such women would no doubt delude themselves into thinking that they would be willing to do domestic work in hospitals in order to get the opportunity of leaving the DP camps, but:
'(1) they would prima facie not be the most suitable persons to bring over for rough domestic work.
'(2) After a few weeks at the hospitals they would no doubt find very good reasons for changing their minds, and in this

74

event there was no obvious way in which the Ministry could
compel them to remain in hospital employment.'[1]

Despite the potential problems associated with the recruitment of DPs, the Ministry of Labour faced pressure to reconsider the idea from various quarters and discussions continued apace throughout late 1945 and early 1946. Several small labour schemes were introduced in 1945 prior to the larger scale European Volunteer Workers schemes, in an attempt to solve the problem of the large numbers of POWs, by now in Britain in the scores of POW camps across the country, as well as the manpower shortage issue. Large groups of German and Italian POWs resident in Britain were recruited for various jobs in 1945 and 1946, and were legally regarded as 'aliens,' who did not have the same rights as British citizens. Various restrictions were imposed on their work and entitlement to live and work in Britain, including the requirement for regular registration with the local police. The newly formed Polish Resettlement Corps (former Polish Armed Forces who served with the British Army during the war and who did not want to return to a Communist Poland), were also used as sources of European foreign labour during this period. In July 1945, the MLNS also reached an agreement with the Belgian Government for the recruitment of Belgian women for domestic work in hospitals, on a six-month renewable contract basis. About 900 women were recruited on this scheme in 1945 and 1946. In March 1946, the 1920 Aliens Order was amended to restore to the Ministry of Labour and National Service (MLNS) powers to issue individual work permits. A number of work permits were issued to people from other countries who had found themselves in Britain (and Europe) at the end of the war, and who were able to fill vital positions in the British economy, such as dentists.

However, neither the work permit scheme nor the employment of POWs, Poles and Belgians were sufficient to meet the demand for labour. Therefore, meetings and plans continued apace regarding the introduction of a much larger scheme, specifically the idea to recruit DPs in Europe for labour in Britain. Meetings were held between the Foreign Office and the Ministry of Labour, and in April 1946, a proposed labour scheme was finally worked out and submitted to the Foreign Labour Committee. This scheme was called 'Balt Cygnet' and aimed to recruit Latvian, Lithuanian and Estonian women from DP Camps in the British zones of Germany and Austria, initially for hospitals and TB sanatoria, an area of employment particularly unattractive to British workers, and for which the earlier recruitment of Belgian women had been insufficient. A draft of a Memorandum on a DP scheme by the Ministry of Labour and National Service in May 1946 outlined the shortage of domestic staff in sanatoria:

> *'The need of the sanatoria for domestic workers is particularly acute for these institutions are often situated in remote country districts, and for this reason alone – i.e. apart from the widespread fear that inexperienced workers have of contracting TB if they are sent to work in institutions of this type – they have always been difficult to staff up with British women.'*[2]

Balt Cygnet was intended to be a small-scale trial scheme, which would be extended only if successful. The instructions for its introduction were outlined in the Control Commission for Germany's (British Element) Technical Instruction no. 8, 'Recruitment of Displaced Persons for employment in British Sanatoria: Operation 'BALT CYGNET', issued on 26 August 1946.'[3]

Initially, Balt Cygnet was designed to recruit 1,000 female DPs of Latvian, Lithuanian and Estonian nationality only for employment in British sanatoria. The conditions of service specified that: 'Women will be recruited in the first place for work in sanatoria as kitchen hands, general hands, ward maids, cleaners and laundry workers'. 'Women should be between the ages of 21 and 40, physically fit and willing to undertake domestic work of this character'. Women were not allowed to change their employment in the first twelve months without the consent of the Ministry of Labour and as aliens they were required to register with the police. No dependants were to be admitted, so the scheme was intended primarily for single women. Medical examinations screened out pregnant women and those with diseases such as TB.

The first party of 100 Baltic women departed from Lübbecke on 16 October 1946 and travelled by ferry from Cuxhaven to Tilbury. Thereafter, approximately 100 women travelled to Britain every week.

Even before the first group of women had sailed to England, however, discussions were underway to extend the scheme. On 17 September 1946, a memorandum by the Parliamentary Secretary to the MLNS on the 'Recruitment of Displaced Persons from Germany for work in British hospitals' had outlined the potential of an extension to the Balt Cygnet scheme and noted reasons for choosing Baltic women recruits:

'At its third meeting the [Foreign Labour] Committee approved the scheme put forward in FLC (46) 6, for the recruitment, on an experimental basis, of up to 1,000 women from DP camps in Germany for employment as domestic workers in our TB Sanatoria.

'One of our officers who recently visited a number of the Camps in the British Zone in connection with the scheme, reports that the women from the Baltic provinces, from whom volunteers are being sought, are of a very good type, and that it should be possible to recruit from among them suitable persons for employment in this country in numbers considerably in excess of the limit of 1,000 already agreed by the Committee. Indeed, out of a total of employable women of Baltic origin estimated by the Authorities in the British Zone at about 20,000, it is thought that there may be no difficulty in selecting as many as 5,000 very suitable volunteers for work in this country.

'They are generally of good appearance and habits and have been well looked after in the Camps. The general standard of education is good; most of them speak German as well as their own language, while many already speak English quite well, especially the younger ones.

'Careful selection, combined with strict medical examination of the type which is being undertaken under the supervision of the Medical Director of UNRRA, should produce a substantial number of women of useful qualifications and of good health who would form a valuable addition to our manpower and a not undesirable element in our population.'[4]

The prioritisation of Latvians, Lithuanians and Estonians at the start of the labour schemes has been analysed in some depth by Diana Kay and Robert Miles, who state that racialisation of labour played a major role in their prioritisation:

'The EVWs were not conceptualised as a single, homogenous category, but were minimally dichotomised. Nevertheless, they *were all racialised: the discourse of 'race' was implicit (as in references to 'blood' and 'stock') and explicit in the drawing of conclusions about the 'suitability' of EVWs, but in combination with evaluations of their social and cultural attributes. And where racialisation was accompanied by negative evaluations of the EVWs, or of the presumed consequences of their presence, one can speak of racism as being a component part of official discourse.*

'... the DPs became internally differentiated along a North-South divide. Those from the northern part of Eastern Europe (mainly the Baltic States) were regarded as eminently 'assimilable'. They were seen to be superior 'types', organised in strong and stable family groups, sharing in the Protestant work ethic and a more advanced industrial culture. By contrast, the going images of those from South Eastern Europe more closely approximated stereotypes of contemporary Third World Refugees. They were often depicted as 'simple peasant types', as being unversed in the ways of a complex industrial society and as being more 'racially' distinct, forming part of an ill-defined but alien 'Slav race'. As was the case with other countries recruiting from the DP camps, British officials exhibited an in-built, partially racialised bias towards the nationals from the Baltic States.'[5]

In Government documents relating to Balt Cygnet, the British Government frequently described Latvians, Lithuanians and Estonians collectively as 'Balts'. In this way, despite different cultures and histories, Latvians, Lithuanians and Estonians were homogenised by the British Government as one ethnic category. This partly reflected misunderstandings about the very different cultures of Latvians, Lithuanians and Estonians, but also suggested that the three nationalities were regarded equally in terms of their assimilation and recruitment potential. The correct use of the term Balts is as a description of the ancient tribe that only Latvians and Lithuanians (not Estonians) are descended from.

Government discourse highlighted the positive attributes of the 'Balts' throughout the planning of the Balt Cygnet scheme. The Baltic nationalities were regarded as excellent material for labour by both the Ministry of Labour and Foreign Office officials. Their views were influenced not only by pre-conceived racialised ideas, but also from reports of good behaviour in the DP camps, so to a degree, the Balts earned their good reputations. Ivor Pink informed Lambert in the Northern Department on 17 August 1946 that:

> *'Baltic DPs in the British Zone are, on the whole, better off than other DPs, not only because they have known how to organise themselves but also because their good behaviour has earned them the confidence and sympathy of the numerous authorities who look after them.'[6]*

Praise for the Baltic DPs was almost unanimous. In November 1946, N. C. D. Brownjohn, Major General of the Control Commission in Germany, too highlighted the assets of the Baltic DPs:

> *'The Baltic Displaced Persons are by far the best we have got containing a number of professional and better educated people. They give much less trouble and behave better than any of the other categories.'[7]*

Kanty Cooper, who worked among DPs in Germany, discussed the reasons for the prioritisation of Balts in her autobiographical work, *The Uprooted.* She stated:

> *'The Estonians, Latvians and Lithuanians were in a different category from the rest of the DPs. The majority had not come to Germany as forced labour like the Poles, Yugoslavs, Republican Spaniards and Greeks. They had come as refugees fleeing from the Russians who had occupied their lands between June and August 1940 while the German-Soviet Non-Aggression pact was still in force. They were enemies of our ally Russia and collaborators of our enemy Germany. Some of their men had joined the German army. But because they were cultivated, clean and reliable people they were usually the first asked for on emigration schemes. They belonged chiefly to the middle classes and many of them spoke excellent English. Most of the women would look more at home in the drawing room than in the kitchen, yet they were all prepared to work as scullery or ward maids for the first three months of their stay in England.'[8]*

Linda McDowell summarises the racialization of Baltic women under the Balt Cygnet Scheme:

> *'The imagery of a spotless, white femininity embodied in the term "cygnet" is indicative of the way in which these young Baltic women were constructed by British officialdom as "better quality" women and workers than other women refugees, especially Slavic women from rural areas'.* [9]

Another important reason for the prioritisation of the Balts was that as one of the largest non-repatriable groups in Europe, their existence in DP camps was causing increasing friction in Anglo-Soviet relations. The following statement by Political Division, CCG (BE) in December 1946 reflected the different status given to the Balts by Britain and the Soviet Union:

> *'The Soviet Government regards [the Balts] as Soviet Citizens while His Majesty's Government considers no person a Soviet citizen who was not a citizen of the Soviet Union and resident within its borders, as they were, on 1st September 1939.'* [10]

Thus, for Britain, repatriation of the Balts was not an option, which left only the options of resettlement or emigration. The main options discussed were absorption into the German economy or emigration overseas. The Baltic DPs themselves also regarded temporary resettlement in Europe prior to returning to the homeland once independence had been re-established as a fourth option. At this stage, Balt Cygnet was not regarded as a way of substantially reducing DP numbers, primarily due to its relatively small scale. However, as early as late 1946 and January/February of 1947, the Foreign Office and officials from the Control Commission in Germany became interested in the potential role of a larger scheme to reduce DP numbers. In October 1946, following the implementation of Phase 1 of Balt Cygnet, Brownjohn, wrote that:

> *'I consider ... the time has now come to invite plans for the two further schemes for employment of Balts in the UK. The first of these will involve the selection and movement of approximately 2,000 Balt women for employment as domestic servants; the*

second envisages the move of between 4,000 to 5,000 Balts for employment in Agriculture.'[11]

Although Balt Cygnet was initially primarily a project devised by the Ministry of Labour to address the urgent needs of British industry, the Foreign Office became increasingly involved with the plans for the labour scheme, as it became increasingly optimistic about the potential of labour recruitment schemes to ameliorate the DP problem in Europe. As early as September 1946, the potential of recruiting Baltic DPs for agriculture was discussed. In early September 1946, Mary Appleby at the Control Office in London informed Mr. Crawford at the Foreign Office that:

'Mr Goldberg was so impressed with the possibilities of the scheme and with the response which it is now meeting that he is asking the Minister of Labour to put a paper to the Cabinet suggesting that the scheme should be extended to allow 5000 instead of 1000 women to benefit. He also hopes to extend the categories of candidates from domestic servants in Sanatoria to domestic servants in General Hospitals and to nurses. He is very seriously considering advising the Minister of Labour that a further effort should be made to secure some of these DPs for General Domestic Service. He also told me that he was going to take up the possibility of bringing male DP labour to this country for agricultural and other purposes.'[12]

Agriculture was facing severe manpower shortages, and urgently required a significant increase in available labour to accompany the major investments that were being made to modernise farm machinery and increase food production at home. Again, low wages, poor accommodation and long hours put off many potential British recruits.

Meanwhile, coal shortages culminating in the coal crisis during the severe winter of 1946–47, which saw coal rationing due to an inadequate supply of coal, caused largely by a manpower shortage. The Atlee Government nationalised the coal industry in 1946 and set up the National Coal Board the same year to co-ordinate the newly nationalised industry, but it soon became clear that many collieries needed major investment. There was an international shortage of coal during this period; yet the coal shortage at home was so critical that for the first time, the government considered importing coal. Manpower shortages in this industry were critical; this was an era of effectively full employment, with so many working age men having been killed during the war, and remaining workers were able to pick and choose their employment to a greater degree than ever before. Working in the coal industry was not popular; it was badly paid, dirty and very dangerous.

Due to these manpower shortages, officials at both the Ministry of Labour and the Foreign Office were discussing expansion of both Balt Cygnet and the introduction of a much larger scheme, even before the first women had left for England on Balt Cygnet. The decision was taken however, to keep any potential future schemes quiet however, so as not to put off any potential recruits on phase one of Balt Cygnet, which was not proving quite as popular as officials had hoped. Many women were put off from participation in the scheme, as they believed they were going to be sent to do unpleasant jobs in what amounted to 'Plague Centres' in this country which no British woman would touch. Officials toured the DP Camps to answer questions and dispel the fears of potential recruits, which led to an upturn in recruitment and the eleventh and final party of Balt Cygnet women sailed to Britain on 5 January 1947, completing phase one. In total, approximately 1,200 women were recruited during the first phase of Balt Cygnet.

The formulation of Phase 2 of Balt Cygnet was consolidated in December 1946. This second phase 2 opened up recruitment for domestic work in General Hospitals as opposed to sanatoria, unless a woman specifically volunteered for this type of institution. Women had the option of being considered for nursing or midwifery training, if suitable, after the expiry of three months. Recruitment was still limited to women of Latvian, Estonian and Lithuanian origin. Women between 40 and 50 were to be considered for this scheme 'if they appear to be very suitable for this type of work and are physically fit'.

The first party of women on the extended scheme, the twelfth party on Balt Cygnet, left Cuxhaven on 11 January 1947. By the beginning of 1947, the scheme was proving such a success that the numbers recruited were substantially increased. From 25 January, the number rose to a target of 200 women each week. On 20 February 1947, Control Office informed Lemgo that 'Ministers have decided that stage now reached when substantial acceleration of Balt-Cygnet weekly arrivals absolutely essential'. On 21 February SUGRA 853 reported that 'the immediate target for Balt Cygnet is to be three to four hundred per week from 10 March, with expansion to five hundred as soon as possible thereafter.'[13]

From the Ministry of Labour's viewpoint, the sheer number of suitable Baltic DPs also played a role in their prioritisation. At the same time, the very number of Baltic DPs also posed a problem for the Foreign Office. Baltic DPs were among the largest of the DP nationality groups, along with Ukrainians and Poles. There were sizeable numbers of women and men aged between 18 and 50, and, importantly for the Balt Cygnet scheme, there was a huge number of suitable female DPs. In September 1946, there was a total of over 63,000 Baltic women DPs aged 18 or older. There were also over 77,000 Baltic men who were receiving UNRRA Assistance in Germany, the vast majority of whom were in DP camps. In total, there were over 180,000 'Balts' in Germany in September 1946. On 27 November 1946, it was reported that in the British Zone of Germany alone, there were a total of 13,309 Estonians, 45,413 Latvians and 23,882 Lithuanians both inside and outside Displaced Persons camps. Of these, 35 per cent were assumed to be women between the ages of 18 and 50.[14]

Towards the end of the Balt Cygnet scheme, the decision was taken to extend recruitment to Ukrainian women and to Baltic men, due to the growing shortage of suitable recruits. On 24 February, the Control Commission sent a telegram to the Control Office, reporting that 'Saturation point Balts will be reached end March unless consideration can be given to employment in England of males with dependants which would produce large response.'. On the same day, Control Office informed Lübbecke that 'We now have authority to recruit single women, not only from among the Balts but also from among the Ukrainians'. Lübbecke reported on 15 March that:

> 'Balt Cygnet has been going for some time and we have already shipped 1840 girls to the UK. It started off at the rate of 100 a week because the UK could not accept a greater number, this rate was stepped up to 200 a week last month. We have about 400 girls recruited and waiting to be shipped to the UK and the Ministry of Labour have increased their selection terms to cope with the wider nationality field, with the inclusion of Ukrainian girls, we hope this will result in increased recruitment. Shipping is at present a bottle neck as we have only been allotted 750 passages during the month of March and 900 during the month of April.'[15]

During March 1947, the recruitment of Baltic nationalities was also extended to the US zone.

With the recruitment of Ukrainian DPs, the exclusivity of Balt Cygnet came to an end. The Foreign Office was keen to recruit Ukrainians for many of the same reasons as the Balts: they were non-repatriable and therefore a potential source of conflict between Britain and Russia, and there were large numbers of suitable DPs for labour. However, the Ministry of Labour had its doubts towards their suitability for labour in Britain, describing them as uneducated 'peasant' types, who were not perceived to be as hard-working as the Balts, although the initial success of Ukrainian recruitment quelled these fears to some degree.

The last party of 52 women was dispatched on 2 May 1947, the 23rd party. In total, almost 2,500 women were received in the UK as part of the Balt Cygnet scheme.

Plans for a second much larger scheme, to be called Westward Ho!, were being formulated as early as January 1947, by which time the success of Balt Cygnet had become apparent. From the start, Westward Ho! was intended as a large-scale scheme, encompassing a wider range of DPs, who it was envisaged would fill a variety of jobs in areas of manpower shortage. Importantly, men would be included on this scheme. Although Balts were initially prioritised, recruitment quickly spread to other nationalities.

The proposal for a larger scheme was discussed at a meeting of the Cabinet on 30 January 1947. The Cabinet Minutes reported the discussion:

> 'The general view of the Cabinet was that there should be a much larger recruitment of suitable displaced persons, in order to meet the needs of undermanned industries, and that the present arrangement under which recruitment was virtually limited to female labour for domestic service in hospitals and similar institutions should be abandoned. Recruitment should not be limited to women, and skilled men who could undertake useful work in this country should also be admitted.'[16]

On 21 February, SUGRA 853 stated that:

> 'It was agreed at a meeting held today in the Control Office with representatives of the Ministry of Labour that they should

send representatives to Germany and Austria to arrange details
for opening up importation of DPs into this country on a large
scale as soon as possible.
   '... DPs will be moved to the United Kingdom from both zones
at a total rate of 15,000 per month commencing end of March.'[17]

On 26 February, W.B. Lyon from the Home Office wrote to Mrs Potter at
the MLNS, discussing the potential effects of the introduction of a large-
scale scheme on British immigration policy:

> *'In normal circumstances I doubt if the United Kingdom could*
> *properly be described as a country "concerned with migratory*
> *movements".*
>   *'However, it may well be that the position has been radically*
> *changed by present labour shortages.'...*

Miss Yates elaborated:

> *'Since the allocation to work here of the first thousand of these*
> *displaced persons was completed in 1946, Cabinet Policy has*
> *decreed that this Department should extend and accelerate*
> *the recruitment of many more displaced persons for the long*
> *term manpower shortages in British productive industry. The*
> *Department must therefore assume that in 1947 and thereafter*
> *this country will be recruiting permanent migratory groups for*
> *settlement.'[18]*

The details of the Westward Ho! scheme were outlined in the Control
Commission for Germany (British Element), Zonal Executive Instruction,
no.9 (Provisional): Employment of Displaced Persons in Great Britain –
Operation "Westward Ho" of 3 April 1947. Westward Ho! was open to
both men and women from the British Zones of Germany and Austria for
a wide range of occupations in Great Britain, including work in textiles,
coal mining, agriculture, brickworks and domestic work in hospitals.
Recruits were to be aged between 18 and 50, fit and healthy and required
to pass security screenings and medical checks. Recruits to Westward
Ho! had to remain in specified employment for one year and thereafter
could change their employment only with the approval of the Ministry

of Labour. They were to receive the same wages, draw the same rations, make the same unemployment and health insurance contributions and pay the same taxes as British working people. An estimated 60,000 to 100,000 DPs of different nationalities were to be recruited under this scheme.

Publicly, there was to be no distinction along the lines of nationality. The instruction stated that:

> 'There will be no distinction in recruitment on the grounds of nationality as this is primarily an industrial scheme, but it is the intention to give first priority to the stepping-up of recruitment of Baltic women for work in sanatoria and as domestic servants in Great Britain under the existing scheme known as "Balt Cygnet"; and thereafter that of Baltic and Ukrainian men. Initially Poles will have low recruitment priority until all those eligible for the Resettlement Corps in Great Britain have been "drawn off".'[19]

The Press Notice issued on 19 April 1947 by the Ministry of Labour and National Service outlined the Westward Ho! scheme:

> 'Volunteering will be made open to all persons in the British Zones of Occupation who fall within the Displaced Person's category. The scheme is primarily an industrial one to meet labour shortages and selection is made on the basis of suitability for work in the undermanned industries. Unlike the existing scheme for the recruitment of Balt women for employment as domestics in hospitals and sanatoria the new scheme covers both men and women, although some of the latter will continue to go into essential domestic employment.'

Under Westward Ho!, dependants were eligible to emigrate to Great Britain. However, it was emphasised that they would not be moved to Great Britain until the main flow of workers had gone.

The same reasons for prioritising Balts for Balt Cygnet underlay their initial prioritisation in the early stages of Westward Ho! The racialisation discourse among officials, apparent in discussions about the Balts' suitability for Balt Cygnet was extended in deliberations for Westward Ho! It required men and women for labour in a variety of employment spheres.

The minutes of the Third meeting of the Foreign Labour Committee, held on 14 May 1947 to discuss the scheme so far, suggested that the Balts were still deemed to be the best recruiting nationalities for all sectors of the economy. Not only were they regarded as the most suitable groups for domestic work and industry, they were also deemed to be the best agricultural workers. The meeting reported that:

> 'There was no reason to suppose that placing [EVWs in employ-ment] would be difficult, particularly in agriculture, where the Balts should prove excellent material.'[20]

In 1947, Boothby and Rouse, from the Refugee Department of the Foreign Office, had noted on a visit to an EVW holding camp in Britain that:

> 'The Balts have been found to be the most intelligent and the most suitable for skilled mechanical trades and the Ukrainians who are mostly of peasant or yeoman stock for agriculture.'[21]

In addition, the success of the Balt Cygnet scheme influenced the Ministry's continued prioritisation of Balts. The Latvian Minister wrote to M Hankey at the Foreign Office on 20 March 1947, that:

> 'The settling of Latvian women into work at British hospitals is going smoothly and there are already about 800 of them here. With very few exceptions the girls are extremely satisfied, and the Ministry of Labour and Welfare Officers are also praising them, so there is satisfaction to all concerned.'[22]

The first recruits under Westward Ho! arrived at the end of April 1947. In just one week, over 1,000 recruits were brought in via two ports – Tilbury, for women only, and Hull, for men and women. The third meeting of the Foreign Labour Committee reported that by 13 May, 4,200 workers had been brought to the UK under Westward Ho!, and a further 4,500 were due to arrive by the end of May. Of the total recruited by 13 May, about 42 per cent were women.

By April 1947, it had become clear that Westward Ho! would have to begin recruiting other nationalities, since the pool of suitable Balts was rapidly diminishing. While recruitment of Ukrainian women for

Balt Cygnet had been a success and therefore continued under Westward Ho!, policy towards some of the other nationalities was still unclear, particularly those, such as Byelorussian, who were regarded as Soviet citizens. Nevertheless, from mid-1947 onwards, Westward Ho! was gradually widened to cover many different nationalities as well as recruitment from American and French zones. The fourth progress report by the MLNS on the recruitment of EVWs for Westward Ho!, reported on 31 July that a 'wide nationality field [is] now open'. By November 1947, some 30,000 EVWs had come to Great Britain, including Balts, Ukrainians and Yugoslavs.[23]

The statistics for Westward Ho! revealed the gender imbalance in the first few months of the scheme. While there were 5,253 men shipped to the UK, there were only 1,485 women. In May 1947, the first full month of Westward Ho!, the nationalities of the women shipped from Cuxhaven to Hull were as follows: 205 Estonians, 466 Latvians, 235 Lithuanians and 579 Ukrainians. Ukrainians also accounted for the second largest number of men behind only the Latvians. By December 1947, over 14,000 Baltic men were shipped to the UK under Westward Ho!, compared to just over 3,500 women.

Practical difficulties influenced the gender of recruits. For example, in July 1947, accommodation difficulties in England led to a temporary suspension of all recruitment, except for single, unattached women.

Although the instructions for Westward Ho! contained provision for the admittance of dependants, the original zonal instruction stated that, 'It is HMG's policy that the bulk of accepted dependants should not be moved to Great Britain till the main flow of workers has gone'. However, officials began to voice the opinion that the postponement of the movement of dependants was acting to deter potential recruits, particularly those with families. The first movement of dependants thus began at the end of 1947. Priority was given to dependants of EVWs who were brought over in the initial stages of Westward Ho!, which in practice meant Balts or Ukrainians.[24]

During 1948, the field of recruitment was widened even further. The principal reason for the expansion was the need to increase the number of female recruits to cope with demand for female labour at home. The demand was so great and the need to clear the DP camps so pressing, that the government widened recruitment to those nationalities which it had previously rejected. Early in 1948, the recruitment of former enemy

88

nationals – Hungarians, Romanians and Bulgarians, began, and recruitment was later extended to include Volksdeutsche and Sudeten women.

The last recruits arrived during 1950. On 4 May, the '2000' scheme for the admission of refugees into the UK was announced. This was an extension of the Distressed Relatives Scheme, first introduced in 1948. The extension allowed for the admittance of 2,000 DPs 'for whom accommodation and maintenance would be provided by relatives, private persons or voluntary organisations, who were prepared to take continuing responsibility for them'.[25]

By December 1950, the number of Latvians, Lithuanians and Estonians recruited as part of the EVW schemes was as follows: 12,919 Latvians, with 1,322 dependants, 6,186 Lithuanians with 741 dependants, 5,154 Estonians, with 504 dependants.[26] In total, over 80,000 refugees from many different East European nationalities were brought to Britain under the EVW schemes, a significant addition to Britain's workforce during this period.

A Latvian woman who came to Britain in May 1947 described her motivations for accepting the offer to take up work in Britain:

> *'Well, Germany wasn't really a place for settling in, because after the war it was pretty devastated, and there wasn't really a chance to start again, so I thought I'd come.*
>
> *'It's fifty years ago this May, so one begins to forget, but I think it was a case of people between 18 and 50 and you had to be fit. They weren't taking invalids because it was meant to be mainly physical work. For men, it was mines and agricultural work and brick factories in Bedford and things like that, and women, they were mainly textiles, because there's some big textile companies around Bradford. Most of them are in Yorkshire.'*

A fear of repatriation also played a role in the DPs' desire to leave Germany. The refugees were keen to get as far away from the Soviet repatriation officers as possible. They continued their work in the British zone until 19 April 1950. Fears of being deported to Siberia were strong, and men who had served with the German army were especially fearful of their probable fate under the new Soviet regime. Although the screening processes for recruitment were stringent, Britain showed a greater willingness to accept DPs who had served in the German army than some of the other recruiting nations such as the United States. Among former army recruits therefore, the options of resettlement were limited.

Some DPs were attracted by the type of work offered by the British authorities. Agricultural labour was popular among men who had been brought up on farms, and hospital work appealed to some of the women. Most of the recruits, however, viewed the labour schemes simply as a short-term solution. Long term career aspirations were rarely considered when accepting labour and indeed, many of the DPs who accepted the recruitment offers cared little about the type of work available. They were simply eager to work, to earn money and to buy enough food to eat. An interviewer for the *News Chronicle* interviewed the first batch of eighty-seven women recruited for the Balt Cygnet scheme on 22 October 1946. The reporter stated that:

> *'Everyone I spoke to and they ranged from the eldest, over 40, to a 20- year old medical student, said that they had volunteered because they wanted to work and earn money.'*

Kanty Cooper was present in the DP camps during the implementation of the recruitment schemes. She recounted the statement of one woman who had been recruited:

> *'You have to be realistic ... I can't go back to my home. I can't live independently without money. I have no profession but I am strong, not afraid of work and, I hope, moderately intelligent. To clean a room or peel potatoes can't be hard to learn. I shall do whatever I am asked to do, however dirty.'[27]*

However, the type of jobs available did dissuade some DPs from coming to Britain, particularly those who were educated and eager to return to their professions. The stringent work restrictions were unappealing to DPs who wished to resume their studies or professions as quickly as possible, and they preferred to wait for offers from other countries which were reported to be coming soon. Some professional and educated DPs did come to Britain initially, but later emigrated as soon as they were able, to the United States, Australia or Canada, where they could pursue their careers with vigour.

For some DPs, the fact that Britain was the first country to offer a large-scale recruitment scheme was the most important factor. They were desperate to leave and simply took the first opportunity which arose. A Latvian DP stated quite plainly the reason why he and other Latvians came to Britain:

'Because that was first opportunity – to come to Britain, because we wanted to leave Germany and that was the first opportunity.'

Another Latvian agreed:

'Well, Britain was the first to offer. Ah no, first was actually Belgium, but [they] wanted coalminers only. They wanted somebody that had actually done coalmining first of all and Latvians didn't have any coalmining to speak of, so that ruled us out. Nobody really wanted to know what the coalmining was going to be like.'

Perhaps the most important reason cited for coming to Great Britain was that it was nearer to home than the USA or Canada and that return to the homelands once they had been freed from the Soviet yoke would therefore be easier.

An Estonian man interviewed for the Bradford Heritage Recording Unit accepted a recruitment offer for Westward Ho! and following screenings and medical tests came to England in November 1947 to work as an agricultural labourer. Clinging to a belief of return, he cited the main reason for coming specifically to England was that it was nearer to home than Canada, Australia and the US, where he also had been offered the opportunity to go. Another motivation was that since the English were Europeans like the Estonians, the two nations must be fairly similar.

A Latvian man explained why many Latvians chose Britain:

'Now I don't know if you've heard this before from somebody else, but that's been my idea and also, I suppose, a lot of other people's as well, that we always hoped, well, in an awful kind of way ... I don't know how to express it, that there would be another war and the Russians get kicked out, get kicked back where they belong. That's what we all hoped. Obviously, there would have been deaths and destruction. But that never happened. So that's why we came to England, a lot of us.'

A Latvian woman also stated her reasons:

I realised we won't be able to return to Latvia so we had to go somewhere else and, more or less, this was nearer. It was in Europe. It was a bit nearer Latvia and there was an opportunity to work in [a] hospital so I came like that...we knew there was no chance to go back to Latvia. There were communists, Russians. We didn't want to go back there ... and when you are young you are probably a bit more adventurous and why not do something about it, you know sort it out?'

Among most of the DPs, a variety of motivating factors influenced their decision, each based on a different individual set of circumstances. This is illustrated by the case of a first generation Latvian woman, now living in Nottingham, who was recruited for domestic work in hospitals as part of the Westward Ho! scheme in October 1947. She stated the main reason for accepting recruitment was a desire to leave the terrible material conditions that existed in the camps in Germany. She was single at the time, but lived with her parents in a DP camp in the British zone. She was then aged twenty and claims that her parents made most of the arrangements concerning her application for recruitment. The decision to come to Britain was made primarily by her parents. She stated:

'Oh, it was so bad. The conditions were so bad. We wanted to get away. The food ... it was so little and so, so bad, that you were thinking about food most of the time. And the conditions in Germany, well ... you realised that you weren't going back to Latvia ... not straight away, and so you had to go somewhere where you could find a job.'

Family considerations were also important for this woman. Her parents were allowed to enter Britain a year later as dependants and together they were able to recreate family life in Britain. Another motivation was the type of work offered. She had already been thinking about hospital work, so when the opportunity arose, she took it.

A Lithuanian woman who came to Britain also described the different reasons for her decision. The main reason was its proximity to home: 'because England is nearer Lithuania'. She also explained that she and other Lithuanians felt that they had to leave Germany because there was not enough food, and because so many of them were young, they were impatient to work.

Another factor behind the arrival of the Balts in Britain can be related to government policy. The government attempted to lure the DPs to participate in the schemes using a variety of methods. As well as posting notices on boards, the recruitment officers gave speeches and distributed leaflets outlining the attractions of the schemes. Leaflets advertising the schemes showed pictures of the recruits at work in British factories and were often printed in several languages, including Estonian, Latvian and Lithuanian. One leaflet aimed at different nationalities was entitled: 'She's Making Her Future in the British Rayon Industry'. It was printed in both English and German, and had photographs of happy recruits hard at work. Captions were printed under the photographs. For example:

> 'What work could be lighter and cleaner than this! Antonia is happily employed in the Coning Department of a modern rayon factory and enjoys handling the brightly coloured yarns.
>
> 'Zofita has been taught how to arrange the fine thread of yarn ready for weaving into the beautiful rayon fabrics which are world famous.'

Another photo showing a man read:

> 'This 26-year-old is employed on a manufacturing process called "spinning" which produces the rayon yarns. From here the yarns go through various finishing treatments and pass to the women's departments for processing.'[28]

The government's job was made easier as the recruitment schemes got into full swing and as positive reports from Baltic DPs already in Great Britain filtered back to the camps. Recruits were even invited to revisit the camps to tell their stories. It was reported in November 1947 that:

> 'One of the most successful means of inducing people to volunteer has been the visiting of DP camps by Baltic girls who came to U.K. to work under the original Balt Cygnet scheme some months ago and who have been able to give a first-hand account of their good treatment and happy lives in this country.'[29]

Extracts from letters from recruits already in Britain were displayed in Information Centres in DP camps to induce recruitment. For example, the following extract from a coalmining recruit:

> *'V.P. Age 23, Latvian, Arrived in England 14 November 1947 I am settled in England and in the Coalmining Industry. I am now on Grade I pay which is as much earned as by the fully skilled English coalface worker. In my leisure time, I play table tennis and billiards in the Hostel, also I like to watch football matches. I like to go out in the country and visit English Inns. I read and have my own English books. The Hostel food and accommodation is good and I would recommend other EVWs to England.'[30]*

As the new recruits began their journeys to Britain, many questions entered the excited, yet anxious, minds of the young recruits: What would Britain really be like? Would it be the land of lush, green pastures and thatched cottages as seen in books? Would they be welcomed and would they enjoy their new jobs? They were also mindful of those they were leaving behind in Germany and the homelands, and wondered when they would see their relatives and childhood homes again.

CHAPTER 5

'*I've never seen chimneys like it!*' – Initial Experiences in Britain

'We were the first strangers apart from the Poles, but we were strangers, and I think our culture was so different from the culture here, it was probably difficult to assimilate or to get close together. For starters, people did not speak the language anyway, speak English ...'

After being accepted as European Volunteer Workers (EVWs), the Latvian, Lithuanian and Estonian DPs began their journey westwards to start their new lives in Great Britain. Photographs from the period show well-dressed men and women leaving the camps in filthy army vans, with few belongings, usually just one suitcase and a warm coat for the long journey ahead. Tearful goodbyes were said to their friends, families and countrymen, the mix of excitement and apprehension tinged with sadness that they were journeying even further away from their beloved homelands to their new lives ahead.

The first stage in the EVWs' journey was their transfer to a Regional Collecting Centre. There were three Regional Collecting Centres (RCC), one in each of the three British zone regions of Germany (Schleswig-Holstein, North Rhine Westphalia, Land Niedersachsen). Each had a capacity of 1,000. In the RCCs, the DPs' personal details were recorded and they were screened for intelligence and TB. After checking that their passports were in order, they were issued with exit and entry visas. From the RCCs, the refugees were taken to the British Embarkation Transit Camp at Münster in North-west Germany (capacity 6,000) where they stayed for several days. A small reserve of clothing was held there and the refugees were issued with the necessary items and a couple of spares whenever possible. At the very least, each EVW was issued with a warm coat for the journey if they did not already have one.

After leaving the Collecting Centre at Münster, the EVWs boarded a train heading either for Cuxhaven in Germany, or the Hook of Holland. From Cuxhaven, the refugees boarded ships sailing either to Tilbury or Harwich (on England's south eastern coast) or from the Hook of Holland to Hull (in the north east) or Harwich. The boat trip was usually overnight and after disembarkation in the morning, the Latvian, Lithuanian and Estonian men and women were met by women from the Women's Royal Voluntary Service (WRVS), who welcomed them, gave them cups of tea and snacks and chatted to them about the next stage of the journey. Astrid Radze-Constable, a second generation Latvian in Britain, described how her Latvian father had felt sick after eating the fish and chips provided for the EVWs when they stepped off the boat in Hull, unused to the heavy, fatty food after years of scant rations in the DP camps.

John Tannahill noted his impressions of the arrival of the EVWs at the ports in his 1958 book, *European Volunteer Workers in Britain*:

> *'It was pitiful to see them arrive with their few belongings wrapped in a blanket. These were often a miscellaneous collection of rubbish, hoarded with the miserly care of the homeless, but sometimes included what was obviously loot, such as the two sewing machines brought by one girl.'*[1]

On arrival at the English ports, the refugees were given some pocket money to buy essentials needed for the first few days in Britain. One EVW recalled that she was given one pound (£1) on disembarkation at Harwich. A Latvian woman arriving two years later in 1948, noted that she was given 30 shillings on arrival (about £52 in today's money).

The WVS (Women's Voluntary Service) volunteers who met the EVWs off the ships, then accompanied them by bus and/or train to a hotel, hostel, holding camp or other temporary lodgings. Many of the participants in this study noted how friendly the WVS workers were. A leaflet issued by the WVS described some of its functions:

> *'WVS work in close contact with the Ministry of Labour Welfare Department through all the operations affecting the EVWs*

once they land here. We meet the boats at Harwich and act as
escorts and interpreters on the journey to the Reception Centre
in London. Next day our escorts accompany the party to one of
the Holding Hostels.'[2]

At the temporary lodgings which doubled up as reception centres, the
EVWs were issued with essentials and given information about the next
stage of their journey. EVWs who arrived in England via the port of
Harwich or Tilbury usually boarded a train to London, where they spent
a night in a hotel (Hans Place Hostel in W1), before continuing their
journey to the holding camps or hostels. One EVW woman recalls that in
the hotel, 'we were given cutlery, soap and towel, and were able to have a
bath again.' Doctors were also on hand when the recruits first arrived, to
check that the workers were fit and healthy.

A Latvian woman from Nottingham accepted work as a nursing orderly
on the Balt Cygnet scheme, which meant leaving her parents behind in
the DP Camp in Germany. She described the journey:

'I enjoyed the journey. I was with friends. There were lots
of young...ones from the school [in the DP Camp] as well.
First, we went to a transit camp, which wasn't very far away
from our camp, and then we were moved to Münster. That
was the big transit camp. And from there we were put on the
train, and we went to the Hook of Holland and during the
night we went on a ferry and came to Harwich, and I think
most of the night I stayed on the deck, and I was looking
at the stars, because I love sea, and I hadn't been near the
sea for a long time. It was very nice. By train we came from
Harwich to Liverpool Street Station – it was a dull day and
so it wasn't very impressive.'

Another Latvian girl, Kristine stated that when she travelled on the train
from Harwich to London:

'[It was] sometime in the morning, because we travelled during
the night and we stayed in a church building. I think it was Hans
Place in London, and apparently we were taken by double-decker
bus from the Liverpool Street Station to this building in Hans

Place, and my friend tells me that we went upstairs and I found a ten-shilling note on the bus but I can't remember about it. Well, if she said I must have done. I don't know what I did with it either. I just don't know. And after that after one night, we were sent to this transit camp. It's called Wigsley near Lincoln.'

Vida, a Lithuanian woman, arrived in Britain as a child of nine years old with her mother and brother, as dependants of her father, who had been recruited onto the Westward Ho! Scheme. She arrived in 1948 and spent a night in London, before travelling on to join her father in the house in the Midlands where he was living. She described the journey:

'We were driven to London. We came to London. We stayed over-night in London, don't ask me where … some sort of dark place to me, and then sat on a train. We were in a train and we travelled to Nottingham and my first recollection of England were chimneys! I'd never seen chimneys like it and I'd never seen houses so close together and dark. It was very different, very, very different. We arrived in May. I remember it was springtime in May. It was an overcast day and the WVS woman I recall was extremely pleasant and nice.

'I recall we were taken to this terraced house – I didn't know it was terraced at the time type of thing, up these narrow stairs and there was my father … and that's where we started our lives in Britain.'

In most cases, the refugees' first impressions of Britain as they passed through industrialised war-recovering cities were unforgettable, although hardly positive. The adjectives used in the descriptions of Britain on the journey from the ports to the holding camps are telling: they are of a dull, grey, drab, foggy, smoky and smoggy 1940s Britain. One Lithuanian woman noted that she had 'never seen chimneys like it'. The refugees' depiction of Britain reflected the huge contrast between this 'never seen before' landscape and the newly industrialising, green, rural and pictur-esque vista that was the homeland. It seemed that even experiences of war ravaged Germany had not prepared the refugees for the industrialised urban sprawl of many of Britain's towns and cities. Smoke billowed out of factories, wartime rubble lay strewn on street corners and rows of small terraced houses claustrophobically lined the flats and hillsides of northern and midland towns and cities. They were disappointed to find that Britain did not match up to the idyllic pictures in the books that they had read and that, like in Germany, the war had ravaged large parts of this oft-imagined land. Gone were the far-reaching lush green vistas of home, the pleasant sounds of birds and farmstead animals. Now there were sirens signalling the end of the factory shift, the clattering of engines and the noise of children playing on the streets, shouting to each other in unintelligible accents.

The book *Latvieši Lielbritanijā* described the first impressions of a group of Latvians arriving in England on 17 October 1947:

> *'Travelling by train, their first impressions were pleasant and reminded them of Latvia. On reaching the outskirts of London, the impact of poverty, dirt, huge factories and run-down urban housing areas was overwhelming. After the train, the experience of travelling by double-decker bus from the station to their hotel felt very strange. Registration, medical examination and an evening meal ended the first day in England. After a typical English breakfast, they were taken to work. On their journey through the centre of London they marvelled at the well-dressed people in the streets and the crowded shop windows. They felt happy to have escaped the ruins of Germany, but sad for their homeland so far away. Words from a newspaper reminded them: "England has been reached, but not yet Latvia".'*

Some of the reception centres also doubled up as holding camps, and in many cases, EVWs had no option but to remain there for weeks or months until work and onward accommodation could be found. Waiting times lengthened as the schemes were extended and numbers of EVWs arriving in Britain increased.

Baltic men and women were taken to hostels and camps dotted around various parts of Great Britain, including Devon, Yorkshire, Lancashire, Lincolnshire, the Midlands, North-East England, Wales and Scotland. Different holding camps and hostels were allocated to serve designated regions. For example, EVWs allocated to work in the East and West Ridings were allocated to Full Sutton Camp, Stamford Bridge, Nr. York or to Priory Road Camp, Priory Road, Hull. Many of the holding camps and hostels were housed in former prisoner-of-war camps or army barracks on the outskirts of cities and towns, or in the countryside. For example, Full Sutton holding camp near Hull, where many of the interviewees in this study recalled staying after arrival in Britain, was a former RAF camp about thirty-five miles from the Port of Hull. At Inskip holding camp near Preston in Lancashire, EVWs were housed in Nissen huts. Eden Camp in North Yorkshire was a former POW Camp and Harperley in County Durham, also a former POW Camp, housed 1500 EVWs after 1948. There were scores of holding camps and hostels around Britain, accommodating different nationalities. Most were a mix of Eastern European nationalities, although efforts were made to group nationalities together as far as was possible.

Local and national newspapers reported the arrival of the Baltic DPs all over Britain. *The Western Morning News* of Plymouth reported on 21 November 1946 that: 'DPs Arrive in Devon For Domestic Work: Six to be Employed in Sanatoria'. The article reported that:

> *'Six of the 54 displaced persons from the British Zone of Germany who landed at Tilbury on Monday, including Estonians, Latvians and Lithuanians arrived in Devon yesterday to take up domestic work at Hawksmoor (Bovey Tracy) and at Didsworthy (South Brent).*
>
> *'A welcome surprise for Ministry of Labour Officials and representatives of the Women's Voluntary Service who met the women was that several spoke sufficient English to make themselves understood, despite the fact that they commenced the study of the language only recently.'*

On 22 October 1946, the *News Chronicle* reported the arrival of eighty-seven EVW women, who were going to undertake domestic work in hospitals in Lancashire and Cheshire: 'Some carried all their belongings in a grey army blanket; others wore fur coats and smart hats'.

Once settled in the holding camps, the EVWs were issued with work, sometimes in as little time as two days. This would often mean another move to onward accommodation. Agricultural workers were moved to agricultural hostels in the countryside, while textiles workers were housed in boarding houses, often in the Victorian terraces, which had been built around the factories. Those who worked in hospitals or sanatoria were usually accommodated on site, for example, in nurses' quarters. Hostels and camps were run by different bodies including employers and charitable organisations such as the National Service Hostels Corporation, the County Agricultural Executive Committees, the YMCA and some private firms, including mill hostels.

The government viewed the holding camps and hostels as temporary accommodation and aimed to house the refugees in private billets as soon as possible. Hostels were perceived to hinder assimilation into the local community, yet in many areas they were the only option, since housing shortages in Britain after the war had put private accommodation at a premium. Women were prioritised in the accommodation sphere, with attempts made to house them as soon as suitable private accommodation became available.

The first batch of female refugees recruited for labour on the Balt Cygnet scheme were housed on-site in the hospitals or TB sanatoria, or in private billets with British families. As more and more women entered Great Britain under the Westward Ho! scheme, it became difficult to provide private accommodation for all of them. Many textile firms – major employers of EVW women – began providing mill hostels for their female recruits due to the shortage of suitable alternative housing.

In some cases, finding work for the EVWs took longer than anticipated and they spent weeks or months in the holding camps waiting for work. This was particularly the case for refugees in agricultural hostels during the winter months, although it also happened at other times of the year and was especially frustrating for the younger refugees who were keen to start work and earn money. One Latvian man who stayed in Full Sutton camp in Humberside (East Yorkshire) detailed in a diary the 'boredom and lack of purpose felt by those who were eager to work, but who were kept waiting for months'. Some of the men adopted an active approach to their problem and actually went out and found work for themselves when the employers failed to come to them. One Estonian man arrived in England on the 'Westward Ho!' scheme in May 1947, and was sent to Priory Road Camp near Hull. After being there for some time without being offered any employment, he and some of the other refugees in the camp decided to go around local farms and find work. He described the situation:

'We landed in Hull – Priory Road Camp that was the first one, but nothing moved so [a] few of us, I can't remember, six or

*seven of us, we went round farms in the summer and the farm-
ers took us on. We went hay-making and corn-stacking and did
some work.'*

Living in shared accommodation in hostels, camp or boarding houses
provided the refugees with a measure of emotional security when they
first arrived in Britain, and were a manageable stepping stone from the
DP camps in Europe. Older refugees were less enthusiastic than younger
recruits to enter the outside world and they enjoyed the companionship and
close-knit community of hostel life. However, it was also an existence of
communal eating and dormitory accommodation, housing between eight
to twelve men, 'an unnatural life', which many of the refugees had tired of
in the DP camps. Hostels were usually segregated, dividing men, women
and families and as they made use of former military barracks, were often
extremely isolated, sometimes miles from the nearest town or village.

One Latvian woman who initially stayed at Wigsley camp in
Lincolnshire, described the isolation of the camp. Asked what her first
impressions of Britain were, she replied:

> *'Well, in the first place we didn't see an awful lot of it, because
> living in the camp, you didn't see the life as such much at all,
> because the camp was on the site of a wartime airfield which
> was pretty much in the middle of nowhere, so the first impres-
> sions were ... you went to Lincoln shopping with what bit of
> money you had, which again was very little and the shops were
> pretty empty after the war as well. But no, we thought, it's quite
> nice, but ... the beginning was quite limited contact with local
> people because in the camp, the people who were in charge of
> various sections of the camp, they were British, and then from
> then downwards, it was all the DPs that had come in.'*

In some areas, the local WRVS helped the EVWs to settle in, for example helping them with their 'first shopping trip expedition, a visit to the
church, or the cinema, they start right away teaching English and collecting papers and magazines for them; they arrange hospitality and try to set
up concerts or social evenings in local clubs.'[3]

Conditions in the hostels and camps were extremely variable and initially, recreational facilities were frequently inadequate, although these

did improve. Again, recreational facilities varied widely from camp to camp. While one Latvian noted at Bearley camp, near Stratford-upon-Avon, there were 'diverse sports activities', another Latvian noted that in a different camp that although there were sports activities, 'socially it was rather quiet'. In another camp for agricultural workers in Hertfordshire, one Latvian reported that: 'Camp facilities were meagre', and 'gambling and drinking were the most popular pastimes at weekends.'

By 1949, it was reported that: 'Cinema shows, billiards, table tennis, football, volleyball and dances are provided in most hostels'. However, even the government conceded that light entertainment often did 'not satisfy the desire of many foreigners for creative activity, and there is considerable scope for hobbies and recreational pursuits of all kinds to be developed'.[4]

As they had done previously in the DP camps, the different nationalities organised their own cultural activities, both to fill their time and to provide a home from home for the refugees. Opportunities for learning English while living in the camps and hostels were limited, although English classes and lectures were held in some of the hostels. The difficulty of learning English in the hostel environment was furthered by the fact that inhabitants were generally not regarded as members of the local community, although this was not always the case. One Latvian remembered how EVWs from a camp near Leighton Buzzard, Bedfordshire, for those employed in the building materials industry were 'welcome guests at the local pubs, because they were good spenders.' In most cases, however, locals were somewhat aloof towards the EVWs, which increased the need for organising a full schedule of activities in the camps and hostels. One Latvian, quoted in *Latvieši Lielbritanijā,* described the situation in agricultural workers' camps in Sussex:

> *'There was virtually no socialising between locals and camp inhabitants, partly due to the inability to communicate in English and partly because the English farmers rarely invited anyone inside their homes, preferring to conduct business on their doorstep. Thus isolated, the Latvian EVWs organised their own churches and congregations, social activities, choirs and dance groups. There were also English classes, lectures and dances. Local branches of the Latvian organisations (e.g. the Society of Latvians in Britain, the Latvian Welfare Fund and the Latvian National Council) were established.'*

Even in camps where adequate facilities and activities were organised, it was common that as one Latvian noted, 'many still felt depressed by their uncertain future and the endless years of camp life'. Many of the hostel inhabitants, particularly the younger men and women, hankered for more freedom, privacy and better living conditions.

An additional problem with hostel accommodation was that relations between hostel inhabitants of different nationalities were reportedly far from amicable. Most of the hostels accommodated mixed nationalities, and Latvians, Lithuanians and Estonians often shared with Ukrainians, Poles, Yugoslavs or Byelorussians. Women who were housed in hostels were also frequently expected to share with other nationalities, although Balt Cygnet women initially shared only with their own or another of the Baltic nationalities. A government report undertaken in the spring of 1949 described the problem:

> 'Among the foreign workers there are nationals of all the coun-
> tries now under Soviet influence, a dozen or more nationalities.
> Between some of them there is a definite animosity, and it is only
> in hostels where there is a wise and friendly warden or manager
> (and often his wife) that the different races mix freely. As a rule,
> they prefer to remain within their own little national groups.'[5]

The participants in this study reported mixed experiences, with some stating that inter-ethnic relations in the camps were relatively harmonious. One Latvian woman stated that in Wigsley hostel, relations between the various nationality groups were:

> 'Quite reasonable. We used to play volleyball and things every night,
> so it was quite all right and the British officers were very nice.'

Accommodation facilities in both the hostels and private houses were extremely basic. Even women lucky enough to be housed by the authorities in boarding houses faced poor conditions. Many of the refugees who began their lives in hostels and camps were soon eager to move into private accommodation. This was especially difficult in the mining and rural areas where private accommodation was sparse as compared to that in the larger industrial towns. Private accommodation was often virtually uninhabitable, particularly in urban localities. In textile areas, many houses lacked sanitation and bathrooms. Large numbers of Baltic women left textile work quickly, primarily because the accommodation in these areas was so appalling. Most of the EVWs who lived in private accommodation had to share rooms and the conditions were cramped. It was not unusual for up to four single men or women to share one bedroom. One Estonian who had recently married and was working in textiles in Halifax found the living conditions for himself and his wife to be unbearable. He described the situation as follows:

'It were a house where we lived, like a room and a kitchen sort of thing. It weren't very old, but it was very small, two bedrooms and [the] bedroom was so small we couldn't get dressed together. We had to wait our turn. And well, we were fed up really, absolutely fed up because we got our dinners from factory ... We had recently got married and we tried to get somewhere of our own.'

With help from the factory management, they eventually found a flat of their own to rent:

'It was a pound a week. Two rooms, first and second floor and we had a small bathroom and like a kitchen and eventually my sister came to live with us. We came to work back end of September. That were in following March.'

Although initial accommodation was often poor, it did not differ markedly from that which many British people lived in, especially in urban areas, where many properties were unmodernised, lacked sanitation and were overcrowded by todays' standards. The war had destroyed hundreds of thousands of homes and brought major damage to many properties and streets. The rebuilding process was only just beginning and many areas were still effectively slums. In industrial towns, such as Leeds and Bradford, small back to back terraces lined the streets; they did not have indoor bathrooms or toilets, lacked central heating and there were no mod cons such as washing machines or electric cookers. In 'Austerity Britain' David Kynaston described the era:

'Britain in 1945 ... smoke, smog ... no automatic washing machines, wash day every Monday, clothes boiled in a tub,

scrubbed on the draining board, rinsed in a mangle, hung out to
dry ... Central heating rare, coke boilers ... the coal fire. Back-
to-backs, narrow cobbled streets, Victorian terraces, no high-
rises ... Meat rationed, butter rationed, lard rationed ... soap
rationed, clothes rationed. Make do and mend.[6]

A minority of Baltic refugees chose to remain in the hostels. A report
by the Ministry of Labour suggested that the hostel situation had
improved so much by 1949 that the EVWs 'have no wish to take advantage of the occasional opportunities of being housed in private billets'.[7]
However, this view is not supported by the evidence which suggests
that many were keen to move into private accommodation, particularly
those with arriving dependents and family groups. The hostel population in January 1949 was still high at 50,000 (all EVW nationalities).
This compared to an approximate total of 80,000 EVW nationalities
employed in Britain by the spring of 1949. Although a large number of
EVWs remained in hostels in January 1949, as the first to enter Britain,
Baltic refugees were also among the first nationalities to leave the hostels, and by 1949 a significant movement into private accommodation
had begun, albeit slowly, even while EVWs were still being admitted
into the country

The geographical distribution of the Baltic communities in the early
years reflected the areas where the EVWs labour placements were
located. The largest numbers were assigned to industrial areas of the
North of England (particularly the textile towns of West Yorkshire and
Lancashire) and the Midlands, although communities were also estab-
lished in Wales and Scotland and various regions in England. Among
Latvians the most sizeable communities developed in Bradford, Leeds,
Manchester, Nottingham, Mansfield, Chesterfield, Coventry, Leicester,
Birmingham, Wolverhampton, Corby, Bedford and Peterborough.
Smaller Latvian communities also developed in Scotland and Wales.
The geographical development of Lithuanian and Estonian communities followed a similar pattern, although due to their smaller numbers, particularly in the case of the Estonians, sizeable communities
were formed in fewer areas. Estonian, Latvian and Lithuanian women
arrived in Scotland primarily to take up positions in hospitals, joining
men already working in agriculture, coalmining and forestry. In Wales,
relatively small numbers of Latvian, Lithuanian and Estonian EVWs

worked primarily in TB hospitals, brickworks, coalmining and tin mines. Agricultural workers were distributed all over Britain. Forestry recruits were sent primarily to Scotland, while a popular destination for EVWs employed in the brickworks industry was Bedford. Steelworkers were sent to areas around Northampton, Corby and Bedford, as well as areas of Scotland and northeastern England. Recruits for nursing and domestic service were distributed in many different regions of Britain and coalminers were assigned mainly to Yorkshire, Wales, Lancashire and Scotland.

The refugees' early experiences of employment were variable. While some of the refugees enjoyed the work first assigned to them and remained in the same job even after a year, others were dissatisfied and tried to change their employment as soon as possible. There are instances of some Baltic refugees moving to half a dozen different camps or hostels and undertaking many different jobs by 1950. Some even transferred from the job to which they had first been assigned to another area of labour shortage almost as soon as they arrived. One Latvian who came to Britain to engage in agricultural work in 1947 aged 20 stated that he quickly changed his mind after seeing the dilapidated, cranky equipment, which was quite unlike the well-maintained machinery he had operated on the farmstead in Latvia. He described his experiences:

'After two months, a firm from Leeds came to see who wanted to work in [the] textile industry. And I had a look around. I didn't like the agriculture because I didn't like the rusty machinery all the farmers had left outside. It was so rusty and that was never my idea of farming ... I didn't want to go in coalmining. Some of them did but not myself, so I thought well we'll try textiles, see what it is like. So I joined the firm of W E Yates in Bramley and I spent there until 1964, working for them. First of all in the wool mixing department. It was very mucky, up to the eyes.'

Beginning life as an agricultural worker was very common among Baltic men. Heino, a young Estonian, was one of thousands of young Baltic men who undertook this kind of work initially. Like many of the Estonian refugees, he was familiar with agricultural work, although there were differences in practices and the scale of operations. According to Heino, some of the agricultural camps accommodating the EVWs had previously been used by the Land Army during the Second World War. He described his experiences:

> 'We were simply taking the place of wartime seasonal workers, living in the hostels and so that's what we did. We lived there and then the farmers, when they needed some hands, working hands, they informed the proper authorities and then we were put on the truck, and taken there and brought back in the evening. That was the first summer and then after, the second year I was taken on as a member of the staff of one of those camps and then the third, it was 1949 I think and they closed those camps and so they told us then, "Well, that's it. We're closing the camp and you have to find your own way round", and so we went on our own. We still had to register with the police, being aliens and we couldn't take any job that was not approved by the Ministry of Labour.'

After finishing agricultural work, he then carried out a succession of jobs, including working in the Navy, before gaining a permanent position in nursing, where he remained until he retired, describing it as a very 'satisfactory career'. He outlined his first experiences of work following the closure of the agricultural camp in 1949:

> 'First year, I went to Derby as a Christmas rush postman; quite a pleasant introduction. Played music while you worked and while we were sorting out the [mail]. Tended to get lost in Derby a little bit and then one of those textile factories just outside Derby, that was the first job and then that didn't last. It didn't suit me very well.'

Like Heino, most EVWs only undertook agricultural work for a short period before moving to other areas of employment, most popularly textile work. The range of jobs undertaken by EVWs within textiles was enormous and included various types of work in cotton spinning and doubling, woollens and worsteds, hosiery, rayon and silk manufacture, flax manufacture, textile bleaching, dyeing and finishing, and machine work in wholesale clothing. EVWs employed as textile workers had to work long hours and the tasks were usually very heavy, noisy and dirty. The hours of one Latvian woman who worked in a cotton mill in Rochdale from seven in the morning to five at night, with a 30 to 45-minute lunch break, were typical. Despite the long hours, another Latvian reported that she 'enjoyed' the work.

A young Latvian man, now living in Leeds, began working the night shift at Yates's Ltd. in Bramley, but could get little sleep in the hostel where he lived during the day and became exhausted. He quickly transferred to a daytime job in another mill. Frequent switching of jobs and firms was common among those working in the textile mills, since it was an area of severe labour shortage and there were always jobs available if the initial post was unsuitable.

A significant minority of Latvian, Lithuanian and Estonian men were engaged as coalminers during their first years including Scotland, Wales, the Midlands and the North of England. Coalmining recruits received intensive training and English language instruction for safety reasons. One Latvian woman noted that some of the courses lasted over three months. As with the other areas of employment, reported experiences of coalmining were variable. One Latvian felt that coalmining offered reasonable employment: work was in eight hour shifts and the food and living conditions were good. However, at Hardwick Camp near Chesterfield, Latvian mining recruits lived sixteen to each brick-built barrack, the food was poor and the accommodation was reportedly 'very cold'. Reports from Baltic refugees in other areas of work, such as forestry, brickworks, steelworks and domestic service were also variable. The refugees tended to describe both the positive and negative aspects of their work: for example, one Latvian woman noted that her work as a domestic was 'boring and humiliating, but not hard'. Another Latvian who worked in the building materials industry noted that the work 'was not easy, but the weekly wages of £4 10 shillings to £8 12 shillings, were considerably more than farm hands received, and less than six months after arrival everyone had acquired suits'.

Some of the refugees who had good English worked as interpreters or administrators in the holding camps and hostels. A Lithuanian man worked as an interpreter in an agricultural workers' camp in Penrith. He described his experiences:

> '[I] landed in Hull and [I] was in Transit Camp for about ...
> a couple of months, and then [I] came to Penrith in western
> Cumbria and it was [an] agricultural workers camp and ...

I became an interpreter. So I never worked on the farm. I just sorted, tried to sort everybody's else's problems. That's what I did in England when I first came.'

During the first few years of settlement, the patterns of employment shifts among EVWs brought about substantial migration from rural to urban areas. This was due mainly to the increasing unpopularity of agricultural work and the allure of the towns and cities. Frequently the move coincided with the transfer from hostel to private accommodation and the refugees' desire to improve their living and working conditions. Young male refugees who had spent a year or more in a men-only hostel, were keen to meet young women from their own nationality. One Estonian man who came to Britain aged 22 was first employed as a kitchen porter in an agricultural workers' hostel near Kinross in northern Scotland, before later moving to Bradford, a growing centre of the Baltic communities, where he settled permanently.

EVWs who wished to migrate from rural to urban areas exploited the opportunities offered by the completion of the initial labour contract, which stipulated that the refugees had to work in the specified post for one year and were thereafter able to change their employment so long as it was approved by the Ministry of Labour. Generally, this meant that the field of employment continued to be limited to areas of manpower shortage. There was a degree of misunderstanding among EVWs about the labour requirements, which had arisen due to language difficulties and lack of clarity in EVW recruitment literature. Some of the EVWs were under the impression that they were required to work in a Ministry of Labour-approved post for only one year and thereafter were free to choose their employment. Ministry of Labour controls were 'humanely exercised', and some of the EVWs were allowed to take up employment outside the approved field once they had completed the initial year of service. During 1949, almost 800 men and 300 women from the EVW population were placed in employment outside the 'approved field' of undermanned industries.'

A few were also released from their initial contracts early if there were special circumstances, particularly if they were moving to another approved field of employment. This was the case for a young Latvian woman, who had initially been employed as a caterer's clerk for the National Service Hostels Corporation Camps in Wigsley. She married her

...anian couple, Agota and Kazimieras's
...ing (See Prologue) in West Calder, Scotland,
(Karen Mitchell)

Agota and Kazimieras's first child, Stoneyburn,
Scotland, mid-1920s *(Karen Mitchell)*

Agota and three of her children,
Stoneyburn, Scotland, 1930s
(See Prologue)
(Karen Mitchell)

DP Girl Scouts in Germany,1940s *(Alexandra Māzers)*

Balt Cygnet women leaving Lübbecke DP Camp 1946/47 *(Alexandra Māzers)*

...p of nurses recruited from DP camps for labour in Manchester, England *(Susanna Brazauskas)*

Group of EVW nurse recruits from the Baltic States in Britain *(Alexandra Māzers)*

Scenes of Lithuanians in a DP hostel in Britain *(courtesy of Susanna Brazauskas)*

Lithuanian man Ksaveras Adickas at work in a Rochdale textile mill spinning cotton reels *(Irene Adickas)*

up of EVW nurse recruits in Britain
xandra Māzers)

Estonian Mining representative Kalju Ranik
with other EVW Mining reps in Worksop,
Nottinghamshire *(Angela Wall)*

ian Farm Workers relaxing after work at Windlestone Hall Camp in North East England, 1948
line Szelewski)

Latvians at Hamsterley Hall DP hostel/camp, late 1940s, County Durham *(Glynis Harrison)*

Latvian EVWs from Hamsterley Hall, socialising at a pub in Rowlands Gill, County Durham, late 1940s *(Glynis Harrison)*

European Volunteer Workers doing paperwork at a DP hostel in England, late 1940s *(Sarah Dauksta)*

Windlestone Hall DP hostel in County Durham, 1940s *(Sarah Dauksta)*

Latvian man with his English girlfriend at the DP camp at Boughton, Northants., England, late 1940s *(Sarah Dauksta)*

Latvian volleyball team, England, late 1940s *(Sarah Dauksta)*

Pauline Szelewski's Latvia[n] father with wandering minstrels in a DP hostel in England *(Pauline Szelewsk[i]*

Latvian men working on the land in County Durham England, late 1940s. *(Sara[h] Dauksta)*

Baltic EVW men celebrating in a hostel in England, late 1940s *(Pauline Szelewski)*

' men carrying out age works in the tryside, late 1940s, nd *(Pauline Szelewski)*

an men at Scarborough h, late 1940s *(Sarah sta)*

Latvian men at Hamsterley Hall DP Hostel in County Durham keeping the camp clean and tidy, late 1940s *(Glynis Harrison)*

Latvian man working in the English countryside, late 1940s *(Sarah Dauksta)*

Lithuanian dance group in Manchester, late 1940s *(Irene Adickas)*

Joint Baltic Deportations Day Commemoration in London in early 1950s
(Reet Järvik)

Latvian DVF (Daugavas Vanagi) badge. The DVF was set up in 1948 to cater for the needs of Latvian ex-servicemen who had been displaced from their homelands. *(Alexandra Māzers)*

na Brazauskas's Lithuanian parents shortly after re-emigrating to a in the early 1950s *(Susanna Brazauskas)*

Latvian Midsummers at Newport (Nieuport) House, Almeley, Herefordshire, 1996 *(Sarah Daukst*

Latvian Jānis Day celebrations at Newport House in 1996 *(Sarah Dauksta)*

an dancers at Mūsmājas, Wolston, near Coventry. The Latvian countryside property closed in (Sarah Dauksta)

an dancers at Mūsmājas (Sarah Dauksta)

Midsummers Festival at Latvia
countryside house Catthorpe M
(Straumēni), 2016 *(Sarah Dau*

Latvian dancers at
Midsummer's Festival at
Straumēni, 2016 *(Sarah
Dauksta)*

Estonian dancers at their
annual Estonian Children's
Camp held at Catthorpe
Manor each summer 2012
(Reet Järvik)

Estonian Dancers at the annual Estonian
Children's Camp held at Catthorpe Manor,
2012 *(Reet Järvik)*

Imants Māzers at Lübbecke
DP camp Germany
(Alexandra Māzers)

Latvian boy, Imants
Māzers in 1950s England
(he came to England as an
EVW dependant age 4)
(Alexandra Māzers)

Imants Māzers returning to
Latvia for a visit in 2014,
with his daughter Alexandra
Māzers, the first time since
he left Latvia in 1944
(Alexandra Māzers)

husband in Wigsley camp, and when he secured a post working in offices in a large textile firm, she was also offered a position. Both she and her husband spoke good English. Her husband had been an interpreter for the Ministry of Labour, during which time he had become acquainted with the personnel manager of one of the large textile firms, who invited them to work in offices at the firm. According to her, the Ministry of Labour:

> ... 'released me because ... they knew my husband, but the Hostels Corporation didn't want me to go. They said, "You can't go. I mean you came over on that engagement and you have to stay", but I went to [the] Ministry of Labour in Lincoln, they said, "Yes. Yes. We'll give you a paper ..." So it proves it's who you know'.

Most of the refugees reported that they adjusted to different working practices successfully and those who had never been employed previously quickly became proficient in their jobs. Adjustment was usually easier for the younger refugees who had not yet embarked upon their careers. They were generally more open-minded about the work available and in a sense, had fewer expectations, having no benchmark against which to base their aspirations. If the refugees found their initial job unsuitable, they were usually able to find a satisfactory alternative within the Ministry of Labour's designated manpower shortage areas.

The opportunities to restart careers or education were limited during the first years in Britain. A few of the Baltic refugees were able to continue their education, although this was certainly not the experience of the overwhelming majority. In December 1949, the British Government decided that EVWs who had been awarded open scholarships to universities and who had worked well for eighteen months could be released from employment to undertake a full-time course lasting two years or longer. The course had to be approved by the Ministry of Labour and the applicant was required prove that they could be self-supporting while studying, which was extremely difficult and only achievable by a few. By 1950, the numbers of EVWs able to enter universities was minimal. In the eighteen months following this ruling, forty-four applications from among all EVW nationalities were received and the majority accepted. There are no specific figures on how many of these were Latvians, Lithuanians or Estonians, but the numbers are likely to be small.

A few professionals were also able to continue their careers, although this was rare. Linda McDowell describes how some of the women who were sent to work as domestics in hospitals under Balt Cygnet, made such a good impression that Matrons put them forward for nursing training:

> 'The "superior" quality of Baltic domestic workers many of whom had completed some form of higher education before or in the early years of the War was recognised by individual matrons and by the National Advisory Council on Nurses and Midwives, who agreed to proposals that suitable candidates should be trained as nurses'.[8]

Some Latvian dentists were allowed to practise in Britain from the start due to shortages of dentists at the time, and there were also rare cases of professors and other highly qualified individuals being permitted to come to Britain to work on the individual work permits discussed earlier, without engaging in the EVW schemes. However, the majority of Baltic refugees who remained in Britain had to settle for fewer educational and professional opportunities than they would have liked.

On the completion of the initial labour contract, small numbers of Baltic EVWs returned to Germany, some as early as in 1948. A few had taken up labour in Britain on the assumption that it was only a temporary contract and therefore returned to Germany after a year. Others proved to be unfit for work in England, while a third group went back to Germany to re-emigrate to Canada with their families. In addition, the evidence suggests that a few of the Baltic refugees returned to their homeland, although the numbers are impossible to quantify.

The speed at which the refugees restored some semblance of a family life in Britain varied enormously. Some of the Baltic EVWs were lucky and re-established solid family structures within a few years. This was achieved in three ways – through dependants being admitted into Britain, through spouses or other family members also participating in the EVV schemes and finally, through marriage in Britain.

The rapidity with which some Baltic refugees recreated family life through marriage in Britain is illustrated in the following two cases. A Latvian woman was married to a Latvian man less than a year after arriving in Britain aged 26. She was married at Keighley Parish Church in West Yorkshire and recreated many of the characteristics of a traditional

Latvian wedding. The service was performed in Latvian by a Lutheran minister and the bride wore a white dress with a myrtle head-dress. This woman gave birth to her first child in 1950. Another Latvian woman was married in 1949 at the age of 23 to a Latvian man. She became pregnant and stopped working at the textile mill in Lancashire where she had been employed. She gave birth to a son in 1950. Shortly afterwards, she and her husband moved to Bradford, which was by then the centre of a vibrant Latvian community.

Marriage offered a way for the young refugees who had no family in Britain to create stability in their lives. It was hardly surprising that long-term relationships were formed quickly, due to the large numbers of single men and women employed as EVWs in Britain. Some of the young couples who married in Britain had met in the DP camps, while others met in the hostels and community centres in Britain. Many of the young women who married during this period were in their mid-twenties and eager to settle down and start families.

Some refugees recreated a kind of surrogate family by sharing houses with other members of their own community. Although the conditions were often cramped, these arrangements provided security and support for the refugees during the difficult first years.

The need to recreate something resembling family life during the early years in Britain was furthered by the continuing lack of contact with family in the homeland. Until Stalin's death in 1953, many of the Baltic refugees in Great Britain were too frightened to attempt to contact their relatives in the homeland, concerned both for their own safety and that of their friends and relatives. The Stalinist regime in the Baltic States disseminated propaganda deriding the exiles as 'deserters'. The exiles felt that if family members were exposed as relations of 'deserters', the Soviet regime would take its revenge. On the other hand, the exiles were keen to let their relatives know their whereabouts and that they were safe. Complicated methods of communication were therefore devised, including the use of third parties to communicate information and the development of sophisticated coding techniques.

If a majority of the Baltic refugees can be said to have adjusted to new working practices relatively quickly, how were they received by British workforce – by fellow British employees, employers and trade unions?

Perhaps the most important point to make is that for the most part, Ministry of Labour policies had been carefully formulated to facilitate the entry of the EVWs into the British labour market and to mitigate neg-ative responses from the British labour force. Agreements between the Ministry of Labour and the Trade Unions were negotiated at a national level and were aimed avoiding any problems when deploying the new workforce. Most of the agreements stipulated 'full union rates of pay, union membership and a clause which stated that foreigners would only be employed in the absence of suitable British labour'.[9] The employment of the EVWs in undermanned sectors reduced hostile responses. Workers had little grounds for accusing the EVWs of stealing jobs from British men, although a few such accusations inevitably surfaced. Ensuring that wage levels of EVWs were kept at the same rate as British employees also reduced charges of cheap or slave labour. The involvement of EVWs in trade unions also helped the process of successful integration into the British labour market.

However, hostile responses did occur in some areas and varied widely from one locality to another. Negative attitudes arose from several fac-tors, including the perceived threat to jobs and accommodation, as well as from cultural and political clashes, particularly the alleged fascist ten-dencies of the newcomers and their hostility to Britain's wartime ally, Russia. Positive images came primarily from everyday contact with the EVWs and from an awareness that the refugees were helping in the post-war reconstruction of Britain. Differences in responses towards the EVWs also arose as agreements negotiated by the Ministry of Labour and the trade unions at a national level sometimes ran into difficulties at a local level. The specific factory or workplace, the branch of industry, the characteristics of the local economy, local and EVW attitudes, as well as the national economy and political climate all contributed to the range and diversity of responses and experiences.

There are few reported instances of discrimination or hostility from either fellow workers or employers. Most of the refugees described ami-cable relations with their British workmates during the first few years of settlement. The fact that in many work places, especially in towns, there were usually very few workers from their own nationality employed in the same factory or institution, necessitated getting to know British work-ers. Even in large textile companies, it was common for only a handful of any one nationality to be working in a particular factory.

There were some difficulties with communication, which led occa-sionally to misunderstandings and hindered the formation of friendships between the locals and the refugees. A good English language ability being an important factor which eased relations with the locals was noted in the 'Report of an Enquiry by one of HM Inspectors of Schools during January, February and April, 1949 into the teaching of English to foreign workers':

> 'Industrial tensions become exaggerated when the foreigner and our own workers cannot talk things over, and the foreigner's impression that he is "slave labour", or is being victimised in some way, is deepened, while some of our own people are inclined to forget that a man who cannot speak English has the same flesh, blood, nerves and affections as himself, and is inclined sometimes to dismiss him as "one of those foreigners".'[10]

Many of the respondents in the study stated that they worked harder than many of the local employees and were thus viewed as excellent workers by employers. However, this characteristic also occasionally made them unpopular with fellow workers. The same report from the HM Inspector of Schools in 1949 noted that:

> 'Nearly all the foreigner workers are industrious and thrifty. Employers of all kinds are in general very satisfied with them, and, as a result, some of the workers have become unpopular with our own people working beside them because they do not fully understand restrictive practices.'[11]

Tannahill noted that:

> 'The anxiety of the EVWs to earn money quickly was sometimes criticised, but they soon learnt that to arrive early in the morning and start their machines or to work through the lunch break was unpopular with their workmates and was forbidden on safety grounds by the management.'[12]

A Latvian woman described the differences between English and Latvian approaches to work in the following terms:

> 'I think the Latvians used to work a different way than the locals because we were told, "Take it easy. Slow down." I

remember that because ... in Latvia, if there was a job you get it done, and then you have a rest, but apparently here you couldn't. You had to spread the job out. You were supposed to be doing something all the time. You couldn't, just finish the job and then stand on one side. No that wasn't the thing at that time anyway.'

She recalled that because she and another Latvian employee were such hard workers:

'I think there might have been a bit of jealousy at times, I don't know, but I think we were a happy crowd.'

During these initial years, she socialised with both new English friends and other Latvians.

[The English girls] 'used to ask us to their homes for tea. No, it was a happy time. Oh and there was a Latvian men's camp, an agricultural camp too, and we used to meet the boys there as well'.

One Latvian woman claimed that there was discrimination from employers in one of the factories where she worked, although she had a more positive experience when she changed factory.

Suspicion and opposition to the EVWs from English workers certainly existed and promoted discord and friction, as evidenced by newspapers and journal articles from the period. The *Cowdenbeath Advertiser* reported in November and December 1947 that there was anger at the eviction of Scottish industrial workers from an NCB hostel to make room for DPs.[13] Nevertheless, as conflicts are more newsworthy than lack of conflict, for every reported incident, it is likely that there were many more trouble-free and amicable working relationships. Occasionally, newspapers did print news stories reporting positive relations between the EVWs and the local population. For example, on 6 April 1947, the *Dunfermline and West Fife Journal* reported that at the Townhill Miners' Hostel in Dunfermline, British, French, Africans, Poles and British Hondurans lived together with 'no hint of any antagonism'. Although cases of racism and discrimination existed, they were relatively isolated, and in general, relations both between the Baltic workers and fellow British workers and employers were harmonious.

John Tannahill summed up the initial reactions of local British populations towards the EVW community as 'tolerance, tinged with some suspicion, which is mainly economic but is partly ... political'. The British public received the refugees 'with their customary lack of effusion. Sometimes there was opposition; sometimes (and this too could be hurtful) there was indifference. But many of the EVWs speak with gratitude of widespread tolerance, helpfulness and patience.' Indeed, the variety of local responses mirrored that of the British workforce and was based the specific locality, the individual EVW, local and national attitudes, political viewpoints and availability of accommodation in the area.

Availability of accommodation in the local area was indeed an important factor, as in some areas, locals charged the EVWs with taking much needed accommodation, which in many areas was at a premium during the early post-war years. In some areas, signs were even put up in boarding houses stating that East Europeans were not welcome. If the EVWs were seen to be enjoying a higher standard of living than locals, this also caused acrimony.

In most cases, the British population was unable to distinguish between the different East European nationalities. Latvians, Lithuanians and Estonians were frequently called 'Poles', due to the large numbers of Polish ex-servicemen who had been based in Britain during the war and who were demobilised in 1946 and subsequently transferred into the Polish Resettlement Corps (PRC). A Lithuanian woman explained the mistaken identities of Baltic refugees in Britain, as a result of the Polish resettlement:

> 'When we coming in England, here well, they only know Polish,
> Polish – "Are you a Pole?", you know. First thing they ask you,
> as soon as you open your mouth, "Are you Polish?" ... because
> they must know Polish people here, there's so many people. "Are
> you Polish?" "No, I'm not – Lithuanian". "Where is that?"'

Some EVWs reported examples of abuse and a hostile reaction among locals. One woman reported that:

> 'By the locals you were to put it bluntly a bloody foreigner ...
> We were Displaced Persons, foreigners even. There were no two

ways about it. We were foreigners. We were very much told so, quite often'.

A Latvian EVW who came to Britain to work in a brickyard, where they made 18–20,000 bricks a day: 'I worked my guts out.' Yet, he noted that local people still called him 'an idle and bloody foreigner'.

The degree of animosity felt by the refugees from the local community sometimes depended on different interpretations of a certain situation. For example, while one Latvian man reacted badly to being called a Pole, his wife did not feel that this was abusive.

An Estonian man pointed out that British people were suspicious of the Baltic refugees, because initially, prior to the start of the Cold War, the British and the Baltic refugees had very different attitudes towards Russia, Britain's wartime ally:

> ... *'Russia and England were Allies and most of Estonians, they were sort of, well we didn't like Russians and [the] English couldn't understand why we didn't like Russia because Russia was their ally.'*

Referring to local attitudes towards the EVWs, Kenneth Lunn raised a related point:

> *'In political terms, there were tensions based on the alleged "fascist" tendencies of the newcomers. There had been well-publicised incidents of anti-Semitism among the Polish forces in Scotland during the war years and sometimes vehement anti-Soviet views expressed by Poles and other East Europeans were taken as indicators of fascist sympathies.'*

One Lithuanian woman who entered Britain as a child dependant felt that the refugees were accepted only because they were 'orphans of the war'. She described how the differences in culture and language made it difficult to become friendly with British people:

> *'We were the first strangers apart from the Poles, but we were strangers, and I think our culture was so different from the culture here, it was probably difficult to assimilate or to get close*

together. For starters, people did not speak the language any-
way, speak English.'

The British government aimed to assimilate, to 'merge' the Baltic and other East European EVW populations into the British community as rapidly as possible. In the late 1940s, assimilation was regarded as a straight-line process, where one culture (generally the minority culture) merged into another culture (the dominant culture, that of the majority) until ultimately no traces of the former were visible. The aim therefore was that Latvian, Lithuanian and Estonian cultures and identities would eventually merge into the British culture and identity and that at the end of this process, no remnants of the original homeland culture and identity would be discernible.

Although the British Government was clear on its long term aims, the means by which to achieve these goals were not adequately thought out in advance of the refugees' arrival. Many of the policies were only formulated after the implementation of the Balt Cygnet and Westward Ho! schemes, when it quickly became apparent that assimilation would be a long-term process, possibly taking place over more than one generation. Several policies were enacted alongside these schemes, including the dispersal of the communities nationally, locally and in the workplace. Others were implemented after the arrival of the EVWs, such as providing English language lessons, educating the EVWs about British society and establishing mixed Baltic/British social groups and activities. Many policies were only a limited success, for example, the attempt to move the communities into private accommodation as quickly as possible. Allied to these approaches was a lack of support for Baltic cultures and identities. Apart from a handful of local authorities providing space for weekend schools for children, national and local authorities provided few facilities for the maintenance of Baltic cultures and communities. One Lithuanian woman described the situation as follows:

'Once we were here there were no concessions given to us what-
soever about anything. Neither the language ... the whole idea
was immediately that we would assimilate as quickly as possible
... there was no assistance whatsoever.
'You were given no assistance to retain your identity at the
beginning, whatsoever, simply because that was the Iron Curtain
[and] there would be no return.'

119

Government reports and recommendations in the years during the implementation of the EVW schemes reveal government thinking in relation
to policies which it believed would hasten the assimilation process. The
British government regarded the fact that by 1949, significant numbers of
Baltic EVWs, particularly men, were still living in hostels as one of the
most serious obstacles to achieving assimilation and believed that much of
the reluctance to move out of the hostels and settle elsewhere was due to
the tenacity of the return myth. J.G. Stewart at the Ministry of Labour and
National Service informed H.H. Sellar in May 1949 that 'particularly in
the more isolated areas, it seems that they are continuing to exist in somewhat isolated communities and are not taking any real roots in this country'.
Stewart advised Sellar that:

> ... 'what is most needed is to get the EVWs into clubs and soci-
> eties of all kinds which will enable them to meet British people
> in an informal way, encourage them to learn more English than
> they need simply for the purpose of their job and for simple
> types of shopping, and enable them to form individual friend-
> ships with British people.'[14]

Regional Welfare Officers were employed by the National Service
Hostels' Corporation to take charge of the welfare of EVWs in each
region and to implement strategies to encourage assimilation. Stewart
wrote to the Regional Controller of All Regions on 16 August 1949,
recommending a series of measures to facilitate the assimilation of
EVWs into British life. These included teaching EVWs English,
securing accommodation in private lodgings and the organisation of
social events, where EVWs mixed with the British population. He
concluded that:

> 'It is generally agreed that EVWs living in private lodgings have
> a greater opportunity and incentive to become assimilated into
> the community than those living in hostels. [Every effort should
> therefore be made to] encourage and assist EVWs to find pri-
> vate lodging accommodation.'

He also noted that social clubs which attempted to mix EVWs with the
local population were very successful. He stated that:

'In a number of regions, the Women's Voluntary Services and other voluntary organisations and groups of interested people have started clubs to which both British persons and foreign workers are encouraged to belong, so that the assimilation of the latter may be encouraged through joint social activities.

'It is impossible to over-estimate the importance of activities of this kind: informal social activities leading to individual friendships between EVWs and British people provide the most effective means of assimilation.'

Stewart also emphasised the importance of learning English:

'An individual worker with an elementary knowledge of the language stands a much greater chance of successfully fitting himself into the life of the community and of participating fully in its activities.'[15]

In addition to language classes and the organisation of social events where EVWs mixed with local British people, other measures were implemented to aid assimilation. A booklet was prepared for EVWs by the Central Office of Information called *To Help You Settle in Britain*. Another booklet entitled *Contemporary Life in Britain* aimed to familiarise the refugees with the British way of life.

One of the major obstacles to assimilation as the government saw it, was that the refugees only regarded their stay in Britain as temporary, and therefore they had little motivation to integrate. One government report described the EVW as a 'bird of passage', to describe how the refugees saw themselves. This term had similarities with the Lithuanian interpretation of DP – *Dièvo Paukšteliai*, which translated means 'God's Little Birds'. This meaning of the abbreviation DP is revealing of the refugees' belief that someday they would return. Exile writers and poets also used the metaphor of birds to describe the refugees' situation, as demonstrated in the story by Latvian writer, Knuts Lesiņš: *The Dove*. The comparison suggested that Britain was but a temporary resting place and that when the metaphoric seasons turned, the refugees, like migrating birds would return to their homelands.

The timescale of the envisaged return shifted considerably during the early years in Britain. During the first months or years, the refugees believed that they would be able to go back to the homeland shortly, but as time passed, the possibility of being able to return seemed an increasingly distant prospect. Individuals held their own beliefs about when the communities would be able to return. One Latvian interviewee, now living in Leeds stated that:

> ... 'we realised straight away we wouldn't go back, as long as there was a communist government. We wouldn't go back. No way...'

Her comments (which have almost certainly been influenced by hindsight) contrast with the testimonies of other individuals, who talked about how they believed in an imminent return throughout their early years in Britain.

The tenacity of the return myth transcended developments in the homeland from 1946 to 1950, which even during these early years of incorporation into the USSR, pointed towards lengthy Soviet rule over the Baltic republics. News reaching the Baltic communities was fragmentary and often misleading due to the difficulties of receiving accurate information throughout the Stalin era. Nevertheless, Baltic exile communities across the world linked up and exchanged information via newsletters, radio programmes, reports and newspapers. Community newspapers in Great Britain printed information received from these sources, from the western media and any information coming out of the homeland, for example from relatives.

During the early years in Britain, the three communities heard about disturbing events in the homelands. Intensive Sovietisation of the Baltic republics included a second wave of deportations in 1948 and 1949 when tens of thousands of ethnic Latvians, Lithuanians and Estonians, deemed to be 'enemies of the state' (including women and children) were forcibly deported, many of them resettled in Siberia and the Asian republics to work on collective and state farms. In Latvia alone, an estimated 70,000 Latvians were deported from 24 to 27 March 1949. Deportations continued until 1952 and precipitated the total collectivisation of agriculture in all three Baltic republics. Repression of religion had begun in earnest and the Sovietisation of industry was already leading to the influx of Russian migrants into the Baltic States as manpower.

In the early years of settlement, homeland developments had two main effects on the Baltic communities in Britain. Firstly, they did little to weaken the return myth, which the communities continued to propagate. The communities clung to the hope that guerrilla activities in the home-lands and efforts to establish governments-in-exile would be successful. The diaspora joined together in the political campaigns for indepen-dence. Secondly, events in the homeland heightened the exiles' sense of duty towards the homeland and contributed to the development of exile identities and cultures. Not only were the Baltic States now subjugated nations, but their whole way of life, culture and national identities were perceived to be in jeopardy.

There is no doubt that a belief in return hindered the resettlement pro-cess during the first few years. In his 1955 UNESCO symposium notes, *Flight and Resettlement*, H B M Murphy defined resettlement as follows:

> *'Resettlement begins when the refugee ceases to regard his state of life as a purely temporary one and begins to plan for a future based on his present environment. The planning need not have been very conscious – some individuals never consciously make plans – and ideas of a change of life later, by repatriation for instance, under a new regime need not have been abandoned; but some mental gesture of acceptance of current conditions must have been made. Where this is not done, as happens with those people whose minds remain wholly in the past, or with those who live an asocial life from day to day, then resettlement cannot be said ever to have taken place.'[16]*

He believed that the resettlement process 'implies a pushing out of new roots, and an acceptance and nourishing of these roots by the new envi-ronment'. Clearly, while some of the younger refugees did enter the resettlement phase before 1950, possibly an overwhelming majority did not begin to glimpse a future in Great Britain until the early 1950s. For many, this process took much longer.

Some older DPs turned inwards towards their own community and this reaction to life in Britain occurred among refugees of all ages and from all walks of life, but was more common among the older refugees, for whom displacement had disrupted a settled family life and halted careers. For refugees in their thirties and older, starting afresh would prove to be more difficult than for younger refugees. For the former group, migration to Britain was accompanied by disorientation, disillusionment and despair, all of which deepened as the return myth weakened. The realisation that they may never see family and friends in the homeland again and would probably be unable to restart their careers and education, began to sink in.

The disorientation and disillusionment of many of the refugees combined with the effects of experiences of war and displacement to produce a relatively high incidence of mental illness among Baltic refugees. According to Murphy's 1952 study, the incidence of mental illness and suicide among the three Baltic nationalities was far higher than among the resident population. This was also the case among other East European EVWs who came to Britain. The most common diagnoses among European refugees in 1949 included schizophrenia and depression. Other diagnoses recorded were paranoia, schizoid, manic depression, psychosis, mania, anxiety state, anxiety neurosis, psychoneurosis, primary dementia and delusional state. Suicide statistics among the Latvian population were considered 'remarkably high'; fourteen suicides (12 men, 2 women) among the Latvian community between October 1949 and September 1951, equalling 6.09 males and 2.56 females per ten thousand of the population. 'merit the mournful claim to be the highest for any published data on a representative community'.[17]

In seeking to understand the higher rate of suicides and mental illness among the EVW populations, Murphy's study pointed to the characteristics of the DP population, which differentiated it even from other immigrant groups:

> '*The chief factor in refugee status which is responsible for an increased susceptibility to mental disorder cannot yet be said to have been defined, but there seem strong theoretical grounds for inculpating four interlocking factors, namely: (a) loss of homeland, where a feeling of homeland had previously existed; (b) experience of persecution, including physical injury and starvation; (c) cultural difficulty in adjusting to new conditions; (d) general social isolation.*'[18]

He found that the loss of family in resettlement for many EVWs was one of the most important factors in promoting mental health problems. Bülbring stated that it was not surprising that mental illness and especially, neurotic complaints, were more common among the refugees than in the English population, 'considering the hardships many of them have undergone, as a result of war, deportation, forced labour, P.O.W camps D.P. camps, separation from home, families and friends, uncertainty about their fate and long periods of more or less severe malnutrition. In addition, the insecurity of not having really settled, their homesickness and hope for return to their homeland, their anxiety about the future all aggravate mental strain'.[19]

Physical ailments were also common during the early years among many of the refugees, their health having been weakened by the long years of war and displacement, with a high incidence of tuberculosis commonly reported among the EVW population. A Latvian man interviewed for this project reported suffering from 'Galloping' TB, the local name for a severe form of tuberculosis, in 1949 and was obliged to spend a prolonged period in hospital. Commentators of the period and interviewees also reported an inclination to heavy drinking, particularly among older, single male EVWs.

While many of the refugees suffered mental and physical problems during the first years of settlement, others had more positive experiences. Often this was due to an optimistic approach to settlement. This characteristic marked out the second group of Latvians, distinguished by John Brown in his 1970 study of Bedford, published as *The Un-Melting Pot: An English Town and its Immigrants*:

> *'Others looked outwards, impatient of the hostels and their ways, eager to explore the possibilities of the new country, to make their own way. These stronger spirits turned their minds to learning English, to seeking lodgings in town. Here, their task was long and painful, as it had been for the Poles.'[20]*

Younger refugees were more likely to adopt a positive approach to life in Britain. Most of them had still been in school or had just embarked on higher education or a career, and did not yet have families of their own. They had lost some of the most important years of their adult lives during the years of war and displacement and were keen to make up for lost time. Despite difficulties such as ignorance of the English language and the shortage of accommodation, they were pleased at last to have found somewhere to settle, if only temporarily, so that they could begin to carve out new lives for themselves. Those who were able to send for dependants to join them, also felt positive about the migration to Britain.

For this group, arrival in Britain represented an 'opportunity to resume something resembling a normal life'.

Maria, a Latvian woman, was recruited onto Balt Cygnet aged twenty, to work in a hospital in Newark, Nottinghamshire. She arrived in Britain in October 1947, having left her parents behind in the DP camp in Germany. The hospital was a former workhouse with four geriatric wards, and as a nursing orderly, Maria was '*cleaning, lifting patients, feeding [them]*'. The job was a new experience for Maria who had only recently finished her schooling in the DP camps: '*I had never worked before!*'. She did the job for two and half years before her parents joined her in England under the dependents scheme in 1949, which enabled some close family members to join the workers in Britain. After labour restrictions were lifted in 1951, Maria started working in a hosiery firm, then in a lace firm in Nottingham, when she 'started going to evening classes…I had to pass English at that time GCE ['A'] Level'. Maria then went on to study for a degree in Pharmacy at University in the late 1950s, which later led to a job and lifelong career as a pharmacist in Boots. She worked there for thirty-seven years, during which time she also married and had children.

However, even among young refugees who felt positive about resettlement, difficulties settling in were reported. Despite being pleased to come to Britain, one young Latvian reported feeling 'sick' during the early days of settlement, while a young Estonian man noted that Estonian refugees were 'disorientated for quite a long time…':

> … '*we felt rather traumatised. Most people felt you could write what three, four, five years off their lives. In fact, they were so cross with losing all your families and background.*'

One of the factors which was of the utmost importance in shaping attitudes towards settlement was the relationship with the local population. The experiences of one young Lithuanian dependant, who was eight years old when she arrived in Britain as an EVW child dependent in 1948, shows how local attitudes, which she described as both unfriendly and ignorant, increased feelings of being a foreigner, and thereby heightened a sense of alienation. She also explained the pressures to assimilate in the early years:

> '*By the locals you were to put it bluntly a bloody foreigner so you tried to make yourselves as English as possible, as quickly*

as possible. You were given no assistance to retain your iden-
tity at the beginning, whatsoever, simply because that was the
Iron Curtain [and] there would be no return. Nobody knew any
more about Lithuania as time went on... Nobody. Even [in] the
schools the maps were Soviet Union full stop and that was it.
    'You grew up [with] almost a kind of, almost a deep down
hate inside you for ... being alienated at the beginning.'

For this woman, feeling like a foreigner motivated her to make herself more English. For other refugees the opposite was true. Alienation made them feel ever more isolated and promoted withdrawal into the refugee community. For these refugees, feelings of alienation promoted resistance to integration, and heightened national identities and the desire to maintain ethnic cultures.

Although a large percentage of the refugees felt like foreigners and outsiders at the beginning, among many of the younger refugees, this feeling quickly dissipated as they settled in at work and within the local community. One Latvian woman was asked if she has ever felt like an outsider in Britain. She replied, 'Maybe at the beginning, but not really.' Others, like the Lithuanian woman described above, did feel like 'foreigners', throughout their early years in Britain.

The requirement that EVWs had to register with the police whenever they moved to a different locality certainly reinforced the fact that their formal status identified them as aliens. For some, this heightened their sense of being outsiders, often for many years, long after they had begun to feel at home in Great Britain. Registration also induced fear among some of the refugees that the information given may be used for repatriation purposes.

During the first years in Britain, the new communities began to assess the spiritual, practical, financial and cultural needs of the new DPs. Latvian, Lithuanian and Estonian community structures developed rapidly, despite the continuing belief in return. Initially they were intended mainly as support structures for the refugees during their 'temporary' stay in Britain, to campaign for the restoration of independence and to provide support for DP populations in Germany who were unable to re-emigrate. As the years passed and return seemed an ever more elusive goal, more solid structures with long-term aims and objectives emerged.

127

On 21 December 1947, Latvian refugees in Britain renewed the work of *Daugavas Vanagi* (*DVF*), the Latvian Welfare organisation which had been established in a Belgium prisoner-of-war camp in 1945, calling it in English, the Latvian Welfare Fund. In 1950, the DVF purchased a property in London, 72, Queensborough Terrace, which became the British branch headquarters and the social centre for Latvians in the London area. *Latvians in Great Britain*, a publication produced by the Latvian National Council in Great Britain described the initial functions of the DVF:

> '*In the early years, a particular concern of the DVF was the plight of those of their countrymen in Germany and Austria who because of physical disability or old age or having large families were unable to emigrate. Support in the form of food, clothing and money was provided. Those with tuberculosis were sent medical supplies.*'

In November 1949, the Latvian National Council in Great Britain (*Latviešu Nacionālā Padome Lielbritanijā*), was established at the Latvian Legation in London as a representative body for Latvians in Great Britain. Twenty-five elected members were to form the Council, and the first elections were held in 1950 with the participation of some 7,000 voters. The statutes of the Council accepted in November 1949 laid down the aims of the organisation: to represent the Latvians living in Great Britain; to care for their cultural and material well-being; and to work for the re-establishment of an independent state of Latvia.

The Association of Estonians in Great Britain (*Inglismaa Eeestlaste Ühing*) was founded in 1947 'to serve the interests in this country, both those resident from before the Second World War and those displaced by the war'.

The Lithuanian Association in Great Britain (DBLS – *Didžiosios Britanijos Lietuvių Sajunga*) was also founded in 1947, on 2 July. The first DBLS AGM took place on 22/23 November at Great Cumberland Hall, near Marble Arch in London. During this meeting, the DBLS statutes 'accepted the World Lithuanian Charter and proclaimed this to be the Great Britain Lithuanians' declaration.' At the second DBLS AGM in 1948, it was agreed that shares would be issued in order to buy necessary central premises in London, to act as a base for the Lithuanian community in Great Britain. It was envisaged that central premises would house an office, library, club, newspaper editing and flats for employees and visitors to London. Lithuanian House Limited was formed in July 1950 by the central committee of DBLS to handle the community's financial affairs and central premises were bought in October 1950 in Holland Park, London.

Local branches of the Latvian, Lithuanian and Estonian organisations were quickly established in areas of Latvian, Lithuanian and Estonian communities. The publication *Lithuanians in Bradford* noted that the Bradford branch of the 'Lithuanian Association in Great Britain' was founded in 1947. Other branches were quickly established in areas of Lithuanian community. The DVF and the Association of Estonians in Britain also set up local groups in diverse areas of Britain during the early years. In addition to clubs in many areas of England, branches of the DVF were set up in Armadale, Edinburgh and Swansea. In the early years, local branches of Latvian, Lithuanian and Estonian organisations were established not only in towns and cities, but also in hostels and camps, for example in agricultural or mining areas. Occupational groups and organisations were also set up. For example, in 1950, the Group of Latvian Foresters in Great Britain was founded as was the Doncaster Latvians' Coalminers Group on 18 September 1948.

However, due to the wide geographical dispersion of Latvians, Lithuanians and Estonians in Great Britain, groups and clubs could not be established in all areas and some Baltic refugees had to get by without the support of community structures or cultural and social activities. For example, writing about Latvian community life in Scotland in 1948, one Latvian noted that only Latvians 'who lived and worked in Edinburgh and the surrounding area participated in the Latvian community life'.[21] Nevertheless, until the re-emigration of thousands of Latvians, Lithuanians and Estonians to the New World in the 1950s, large numbers of Baltic refugees were still housed in hostels and camps where there were other members from their own nationality. In most cases, this prevented isolation in the absence of formal community structures.

The post-war Baltic refugees established community structures largely separate from pre-war Baltic communities in Britain, even in Scotland, where there were still significant groups of Lithuanians who had migrated at the end of the nineteenth and the beginning of the twentieth century. The pre and post-war communities were starkly different in many ways, and in some areas, conflicts arose. For example, the bulk of the members of pre-war communities had emigrated from the Russian Empire, not from the independent Baltic States, and apart from intellectuals and political émigrés, a majority had underdeveloped national identities. Many spoke Russian. Writing in the Lithuanian Youth Newsletter LYNES in February 1985, one Lithuanian discussed the relations between the post-war Lithuanian community and the pre-war Lithuanian communities during this period:

> *'The end of the Second World War brought yet another wave of Lithuanians into the wider world, displaced persons (DPs) who were welcomed as labour. But when this group met with the established locals, there were many conflicts. Language for one, outlook for another and money too; they were all from the same nation but different. In some places, there was acceptance and they lived happily. In other the conflict was too strong and divergence increased. Eventually, as the older earlier generation died, the DPs took over and ran everything.'*

The diplomatic representations of the three Baltic nations in London, which had been set up during the inter-war period of independence, continued to play a large role in supporting the Baltic exile communities in Britain and in Europe. Even after the arrival of the first Baltic refugees in Britain, they continued to wield pressure on Allied governments, requesting greater support for Baltic DPs in Germany. The diplomatic representations campaigned vigorously in the first years after the war for the restoration of homeland independence, and letters were written to the Ministry of Labour requesting improvements in various aspects of the refugees' living and working conditions in Britain. The aims of the refugees vis-à-vis the homelands were also fostered by the Baltic Council, established in 1947, to undertake campaigning work and promote political, social, economic and cultural ties between the Baltic countries and Britain.

Community newspapers informed the diaspora not only of developments within the communities in Britain, but also of changes within the worldwide diaspora and perhaps most importantly of all, of events in the homelands. For example, among the Latvian community, *Londonas Avīze* (London News) was set up in 1942 to inform Latvians in Britain about developments in Latvia and among the worldwide and British Latvian diaspora. Another newspaper, *Latvija,* which had been published in a DP Camp in West Germany since 1946, was also circulated.

The establishment of solid community structures and organisations provided stability and security for the refugees. A Latvian woman from Leeds described the importance of the Latvian community in the early years:

'It was a very strong community and at first it was really good for us because it was somewhere to go, somewhere to meet people. I missed Latvia very much when I first came here, very much for quite a long time and just to meet somebody Latvian, it was like meeting a close relative really, right at first, the first years and so it was nice to go, to meet to do something and to take part in something, various activities. That was quite important to start with.

'It was sort of a little home from home. Yes, there were people with similar feelings, we were together ... various activities, it helped a lot in those early years really. It was really good for me anyway...'

To a degree, solid community structures and organisations also partially fulfilled the gap left by loss of family, providing support and close friendship. One Latvian described the Latvian organisations as a 'big family', helping keep the Latvians together.

During the first few years, the cultural and social life of the Baltic communities was particularly rich. Although some of the refugees were keen to save as much money as possible and therefore restricted their social activities, many of the refugees had a full social life in the early years, despite working long hours. One Estonian reported that he went out every night, whereas others socialised at weekends. Solid community structures and vibrant cultural and social activities also meant that, according to one Lithuanian interviewee who came to Britain as a child in 1948, the communities were able to operate in a kind of 'cell' outside work, precluding the need for socialising within the British community.

The communities organised most of the cultural and social events by themselves and felt that they were given no help or support at the beginning by the authorities in relation to cultural maintenance. One Lithuanian living in Nottingham reported that:

'Once we were here there was no assistance whatsoever. At the beginning, I only recall we were allowed to use school halls

*for our concerts for a number of years and then the Saturday
school for a while, and then I don't recall that any more, probably because people did emigrate and numbers decreased.'*

From a very early stage, among all three Baltic communities, song and
dance formed an important part of cultures in exile, as they had earlier
in the DP camps. According to the publication *Latvians in Great Britain*:

> ... *'in exile, song along with dance proves [proved] to be the
> strongest means of maintaining language and tradition and of
> instilling in both performer and listener alike an acute aware-
> ness of national identity.*
>
> *'After arrival in Britain, Latvians immediately established
> choirs. Men far outnumbered women, and those living in agri-
> cultural hostels and other close communities soon formed male
> voice ensembles. A programme of a major Latvian event in 1949
> shows the participation of five mixed choirs and seventeen male
> voice choirs and ensembles.'*

The organisation of sports activities was also popular. Activities had both
social and cultural functions. For example, Lithuanian scouting, which
was begun in Britain in 1947, combined a mixture of social and cultural activities for Lithuanian children. Other cultural activities included
a thriving book trade among the Latvian community and weekend language schools for children, to teach the Latvian, Lithuanian and Estonian
language to the younger generation. The maintenance of language among
the first generation and its transmission to younger generations, was
regarded as a vital defence against Russification in the homeland and
assimilation in Britain.

Annual national days and festivals were celebrated and commemorated, including new days created in exile, such as Deportation Day.
In exile in Great Britain, the anniversaries of Latvian, Lithuanian and
Estonian independence became particularly important, a trend which had
begun in the DP camps of Germany. While the commemoration of this
day had been purely a celebratory event in the independent homelands,
in exile, however, these occasions were tinged with anger and sadness.
Speeches were given in hostels, camps and centres of Baltic community
up and down Britain. For example, thirty years after the establishment

of Latvia's independence in 1918, on 18 November 1948, a speech was given by Adolfs Pērkons at an agricultural camp in Wainhouse Corner in Devon. The speech stressed the significance of 18 November when thoughts turned 'to the years spent working and building their home country', but in 1948, 'only God' knew when they would be able to return. Pērkons then gave a short overview of the history of Latvia and its people and the maintenance of Latvian culture – their folk songs, folklore and applied arts – despite aggression by neighbouring powers. He concluded by stating that Latvians in Great Britain were lucky to be able to celebrate this thirtieth anniversary in a free country, and that the Latvian nation trusted that stand of the Western Powers, who did 'not recognise the annexation of the Baltic States'.[22] Speeches in camps, hostels and clubs all over Britain mirrored these themes, as did commemorations of Lithuanian and Estonian independence.

As in the DP camps, religion also played an important role among the exile communities. In a rare example of the British government supporting the EVWs' cultural needs, the EVW schemes contained provisions for the spiritual welfare of the refugees. The zonal instruction for Westward Ho! specified that arrangements would be made 'with the National Hostels Corporation to safeguard the spiritual welfare of DPs in Great Britain by sending DP pastors and priests to British camps'.[23] With this arrangement, priests and pastors representing the different religious denominations of the three nationalities were able to come from the DP camps to Great Britain, to care for the spiritual needs of the refugees. For example, on 28 April 1948, the IRO reported that a Latvian Archbishop who was a DP left the British Zone of Germany to come to Great Britain in order 'to care for the spiritual welfare of the EVWs employed in Great Britain'.[24]

Due to the dispersion of the EVWs in Britain, church representatives usually served a large area covering different parishes and camps. Even before the implementation of these arrangements, Lutheran clergyman Roberts Slokenbergs, had been one of the very first post-war Latvian refugees to enter Britain, and became pastor of the London Latvian Evangelical Lutheran Church congregation, founded in October 1945. In 1949, Latvian Lutherans held their first annual synod and Latvian services started to take place all over Britain. For example, in Edinburgh, the Latvian Evangelical Lutheran Church held services from July 1948 onwards. Catholic leaders also travelled to Britain to care for Lithuanian and Latvian Catholics, and Estonian Lutheran communities were also provided for. The Lithuanian community in Great Britain was granted permission to hold Lithuanian church services in Catholic churches in many parts of Britain. In 1948, the Lithuanian community in Bradford appealed to the Bishop of Leeds, John Poskitt, to allow Masses to be celebrated in Lithuanian. Permission was granted and the first Lithuanian Roman Catholic Mass in St. Ann's Church, Bradford, was conducted on 14 March 1948 by a Lithuanian priest Jonas Kuzmickis.

During the early years of exile, religion served many functions. Church representatives and services provided the refugees not only with spiritual guidance, but also with practical support. Latvian, Lithuanian and Estonian church services recreated an element of life in the homeland and enabled members of the communities to offer mutual support to one another during difficult times. Church services provided another place, in addition to the clubs and associations, where the communities could meet and socialise. For Lithuanian communities, Roman Catholicism had been an important element of Lithuanian national identity throughout the national independence period and before. The significance of Catholicism in relation to national identity grew stronger during the Soviet period, not only in the homeland where it was undergoing severe repression by the Soviet State, but also among exiles. Although the religio-national link had never been particularly strong in Latvia and Estonia, Lutheranism also grew significantly in importance among exiled Estonian and Latvian communities, and among homeland populations during the Soviet period. Church services provided a platform for the commemoration of the loss of independence and for the expressions of hope for the restoration of independence. Prayers were spoken for loved ones exiled in Germany, and for those who remained in the homelands, for liberation, and for the safe return home of all the refugees.

By 1951, adaptation to life in Britain remained sluggish for several reasons, including the large hostel population (even by 1949) and the continued uncertainty of a long-term stay in Britain. Adaptation only began to take place at a steady pace once the refugees had secured private accommodation and began to fend for themselves by, for example, shopping, using public transport and generally looking after themselves, all of which necessitated learning English and conversing with the locals. Not surprisingly, adjustment was quickest among those refugees who were keen to leave the hostels and camps and make their own way in

Britain. These were usually the refugees who adopted a positive outlook and wanted to make the most of the opportunities offered to them. This approach was most prevalent among the younger, single refugees.

One of the most important factors cited by the government as respon-sible for retarding adjustment, was the slow rate at which the refugees learnt English. When they first came to Britain, most of the Baltic refu-gees did not know the English language, and by 1950, progress remained sluggish. 'Not a word' was the reported knowledge of English of one Lithuanian woman when she first arrived in Britain and although some of the refugees had undertaken lessons in the DP camps and knew some basic words and phrases, they formed a minority. Opportunities for developing the language were limited among those living in hostels or in Baltic households. Even at work, learning English was not always easy. One woman who worked in a textile factory stated that, despite the fact that there were only a few other Lithuanians working there, there were few possibilities to learn English with the 'machines going', making it almost impossible to communicate above the noise. Regional accents also presented difficulties for EVWs struggling to learn English. One Estonian reported that he 'couldn't understand a word they were saying in Yorkshire'. During the first few years, the Baltic refugees continued to use their homeland language in most spheres of life. The maintenance of a large hostel population even by 1949 meant that few needed to learn English. Even at the workplace, many found they could get by with only basic English skills.

As recommended by the Ministry of Labour, local authorities and var-ious voluntary bodies had begun providing English classes for the new arrivals but they were neither very successful, nor well attended. There were various reasons for this response by the refugees. The first was that after a hard day's work at the factory or in the fields, most of the work-ers were simply too tired to attend a language class. Secondly, many of the teachers were not particularly skilled, and taught rather dull classes, often directly from a textbook. This was hardly a suitable approach for exhausted workers. Thirdly, and perhaps most importantly, the continu-ing belief in a temporary stay in Britain did not provide motivation to learn English.

The 'Regional Reports on Progress of the Assimilation of the European Volunteer Workers' revealed the authorities' assessment of the state of the East European EVW communities by February 1950, and the degree

135

of assimilation already achieved. The North-Western Region stated the following:

> *'Assimilation of EVWs proceeding slowly but surely. Many EVWs however regard their present stay as a temporary expedient until they can return home or emigrate. The peasant class tend to keep to themselves and display no eagerness to learn English.'*

The report from the Northern Region also highlighted how the myth of return was perceived to be hindering 'absorption': 'Some EVWs are uncertain as to their future and this has a detrimental effect on their absorption into the British community'. According to the report from the East and West Riding: 'Assimilation will clearly be a long-term process', while the Southern Region noted that:

> *'Foreign Workers in private lodgings settle down most satisfactorily. Those in hostels where EVWs predominate tend to cling to their own national groups. A large proportion do not want to become assimilated as they look on their stay here as being temporary.*
>
> *'Areas where EVWs have been given entertainment or exhibitions on nationalistic lines and where there have been British audiences show the best results in assimilation. Success depends on local British residents who will take an interest and assist in a practical way and on EVWs who will co-operate.'*

The report from Scotland also suggested that 'the settling down process is speediest where workers are dispersed as individuals'. The view that dispersal into private lodgings promoted quicker integration was echoed by the report from Wales:

> *'Gradual but steady drift from hostels to private lodgings where there is a much greater opportunity and incentive to become assimilated, but provision of houses in which foreign workers can live with their own families will be a factor even more conducive to their integration.'*

Finally, the Midlands region stressed the link between age and the potential for integration:

'Younger workers are much more likely to become integrated into the British community than older people who tend to remain aloof.'[25]

CHAPTER 6

'We got disorientated for quite a long time' – The 1950s

'The lifting of labour controls on 1 January 1951 marked a watershed for the Latvian community. The EVWs now had more choice in finding work and the small communities in hostels and camps began to break up. Furthermore, many thousands who were dissatisfied with their prospects in Britain and realised that there could be no early return home to Latvia, further emigrated in the early 1950s, principally to Canada. Of the 14,000 or so Latvian EVWs and their dependants who had arrived in Britain after the war, perhaps about 9,000 remained.'
Jānis Andrups, A History of Latvians in Great Britain

During the 1950s, homeland developments were also pivotal to the evolution of the communities. Not only was the increasing intractability of Soviet rule over the homelands a stimulus for mass re-emigration to the New World, it also gave rise to the settling in of the communities in Britain.

Although Stalin's death in 1953 and the accession of Khrushchev to power brought some hope that the Soviet Union's grip on the Baltic nations would ease, events soon conspired to quash any optimism. Among Lithuanians, the end of the Forest Brothers' campaign to free Lithuania in 1954 was a turning point, while for all East European nationalities in Britain, the brutal crushing of the Hungarian Revolution in 1956 emphasised the brutality and tenacity of the Soviet regime.

Developments in the homelands not only threatened the Latvian, Lithuanian and Estonian nations, identities and cultures, they also transformed the economy and environment of the three Soviet republics. The influx of Russian immigrant labour to fulfil the manpower requirements of rapid industrial development led to decreases in the indigenous share of the population, most severely in Latvia and Estonia. In Latvia for example, the combination of Russian immigrant labour and the decrease in population, as a result of war, displacement and deportations, brought the ethnic Latvian share of the population down from 75.5 per cent in 1935, to 60 per cent in 1953.

The impact of Soviet industrial expansion on the environment was enormous. Huge Soviet style industrial complexes and towering apartment blocks housing immigrant newcomers were constructed, shadowing clapboard cottages and largely European-designed architecture, built on a human scale. These large-scale imposing structures were metaphors for the Soviet Union's hegemony over the Baltic nations, and formed part of the homogenisation of the Soviet Republics.

News and rumours about developments in the homeland had far-reaching consequences for the diaspora. John Brown, for example, noted the effects of Soviet consolidation in Eastern Europe on the Latvian exiles of Bedford:

> *'As EVWs, Latvians had to work three years as indentured labourers before they were 'freed'. By this time, the early fifties, political relationships between East and West had deteriorated to a seemingly implacable condition of cold war. Soviet control of Eastern Europe had tightened and for the people of the Baltic States, integral parts of the Soviet Union, hopes for freedom and independence had become hopelessly remote. It was time for the Latvians of Bedford to take stock, to face the bitter realisation that there was no way back, at least not for a very long time. They would have to dig in where they were, carry on as best they could, or seek opportunities elsewhere, perhaps even further away from their own country.'[1]*

For some of the EVWs in Britain, particularly the older refugees, the realisation that they would not be returning to their home countries anytime soon was too much. Feelings of disorientation and disillusionment manifested themselves in a variety of physical and mental health problems, which in some cases led to breakdowns and even suicide. John Brown noted that among the older Latvians in Bedford, 'Several committed suicide. Others were broken in mind or retreated permanently from reality.' 'Some became alcoholics.'[2]

Feelings of being in limbo and uncertainty about the future also continued among some of the younger generations well into the early fifties. As one Estonian noted, the refugees were 'disorientated for quite a long time', until the economic struggle and the building of family life took over from the mid-fifties onwards. Employment restrictions were lifted in the early 1950s, enabling Latvians, Lithuanians and Estonians in Britain to seek employment of their own choice. Many of the refugees had already changed jobs from their original placement to another area approved by the Ministry of Labour. For example, many men had already moved from agricultural labour to work in textiles. A large number continued within these areas for several years and some even remained in textiles throughout their whole lives. Others chose new career paths.

John Tannahill's survey of the EVW communities in the mid-1950s reported the types of employment which Latvians, Lithuanians and Estonians left in particularly large numbers following the lifting of labour controls, and those original 'undermanned industries' which remained popular at least until the date of his study in 1956. He observed that the most striking fact was the extent of the flight from agriculture, the beginnings of which had already begun to take place before 1950 but large numbers also left coalmining, forestry, brickmaking and allied industries, hospitals and private domestic service. However, although coalmining experienced heavy wastage in the first two years until 1949, this trend did not continue, with 3,806 EVWs still in the sector on 30 June 1956. High wages and the availability of colliery houses were obviously important. The only original undermanned industry which had experienced a rise in EVW employment by 1950, the textile industry, also encountered a drop during the 1950s, but this was relatively small compared with any of the other original undermanned industries. There seemed to be little change in the iron and steel industries.

The drop in numbers can be accounted for partly by emigration, but also by a desire among the remaining EVWs to take up employment of their choice, usually positions with better prospects or higher wages. A small number, particularly the younger refugees, began to take college and university courses to improve their employment opportunities during the 1950s. One Latvian woman studied for a pharmacy degree at university with the help of her parents who had come to Britain as dependents. After first working as a nursing orderly, then in a hosiery firm and a lace firm, she was subsequently able to gain employment in a Boots pharmacy in Nottingham, as a result of her new qualifications. This gave her career stability and good prospects. She worked in Boots for thirty-seven years until she retired.

The scope of jobs taken up by Latvians, Lithuanians and Estonians in Britain during the 1950s was wide-ranging. Positions undertaken outside the original fields of employment included bus driver, postman, a position within the Merchant Navy, porter for a furniture shop, pharmacist, shop manager, hospital porter, salesman, kiln operator, cabinet maker, and glassworks worker.

A few of the refugees became self-employed as a route towards social or economic betterment. John Tannahill mentions one or two cases of EVWs in partnership buying a small farm. In towns, some EVWs opened small foodstuffs shops to supply the needs of their fellow nationals. One young Latvian in Manchester opened a bookshop which he combined with a selling agency for leather or wood 'objets d'art' made by other Latvians. One of the Latvians interviewed in the 1990s earned a living by buying and renovating houses and selling them on, or letting them out.[3]

The choice of employment was often influenced by changes in individual circumstances during the 1950s, such as getting married, moving to a new locality, buying a house, starting a family or having to care for elderly relatives. The decision to return to education, to take up a new career, or resume an old line of work from the days of the homeland, reflected the new sense of greater permanency among the post-emigration Baltic communities in Britain.

What is striking about the Baltic exiles in Britain is that, unlike those who emigrated to the USA or Canada, relatively few became professionals, such as lawyers, doctors, dentists, teachers or accountants. Some of the refugees did enter professional careers, including several Latvians who became university academics and there are other examples of Baltic refugees entering high-status white-collar jobs. However, in comparison to the Baltic exiles in the countries of the New World, the numbers were small.

After the lifting of the labour controls in 1951, many of the more highly educated or more ambitious EVWs in Britain, took the decision to re-emigrate to countries of the New World, including Canada, the USA and Australia (and far smaller numbers to Venezuela, Uruguay and Argentina), when the opportunity arose. A higher proportion of Lithuanians re-emigrated to the USA or Canada, since many had connections with the earlier wave of immigrants who had left the homeland in the late nineteenth and early twentieth centuries.

Some former refugees were also keen to join family who had emigrated straight to these countries from the DP camps after the Second World War. This was the case for Susanna Brazauskas's Lithuanian parents, who had initially come to Britain on the EVW schemes in 1946 and 1947. Susanna's mother had been recruited to nursing and her father initially worked in agriculture after being recruited onto the Westward Ho! scheme in 1947, but later making a switch to psychiatric nursing. They had met in the DP camps and married in England in late 1947, where they later had their first daughter Ruth. However, about five years after migrating to Britain, they decided to re-emigrate to Canada to join family, and it was there that Susanna, their second child, was born. Other motivations were also at play. Susanna explains:

> *'I think they were motivated to join family. As well, I recall my dad mentioning that he had to wait five years to get a council house [in England], but in Canada he could buy a home right away. He had completed psychiatric nursing training at Shelton Mental Hospital in Shrewsbury. My Aunt Albina (dad's sister) was living in Winnipeg at the time and my Aunt Ella (mom's sister) was in Vancouver and both Portage la Prairie (an hour outside of Winnipeg) and Vancouver had mental hospitals back then. I am unclear as to why they chose Manitoba to settle. I have a hunch that it may be because my dad was quite a nature lover and Portage la Prairie had a population of about 13,000. My dad was hired at the Manitoba School (later renamed the Manitoba Developmental Centre) but was required to retake the psychiatric nursing training. My mom worked as a seamstress in a sewing factory until I was born.'*

Just like Susanna's parents, many Latvians, Lithuanians and Estonians were frustrated with the lack of opportunities to further their careers and by the quality of life in Britain. According to one Latvian, large-scale migration to Canada took place among Latvians 'because Britain wasn't interested in the intellectual, just the muscle power', and 'because the laws were different' in the New World countries, enabling young Latvians to pursue educational and career opportunities of their choice.

A Lithuanian woman in Manchester noted that the post-war Lithuanian community in Manchester was halved by re-emigration: 'Again it's the standard of living. People used to say that there were more opportunities over there'. Australia became an increasingly popular destination because at that time 'it was Assisted Passages even. You could go for ten pounds'.

The precise numbers re-emigrating are not known, although it is estimated that a quarter of the total number of EVWs recruited left Britain during the 1950s. The publication *Latvians in Great Britain* states that 'several thousand Latvians re-emigrated' during the early fifties, and the book *Latvia and Latvians* by Juris Sinka notes that 'a large number went on to other countries, mainly Canada and Australia'. In John Tannahill's small sample, 48 per cent of Lithuanians emigrated, 44 per cent of Estonians and 23 per cent of Latvians.[4]

Another reason for emigration to the New World was that in the early days it was perceived that unlike in Britain, in the New World 'various substantial communities could continue to exist within the State, enjoying facilities such as the provision of books in their own language in the public libraries, and the immigrant could soon forget that he was a "foreigner"'[5] The EVWs' experiences during their first years in Britain had made them very aware of their status as aliens and as foreigners.

Re-emigration left many centres of Latvian, Lithuanian and Estonian community depleted and consequently affected cultural and social organisations. For example, the publication *Latvians in Great Britain* noted that re-emigration forced many of the smaller Latvian choirs and ensembles out of existence. A Latvian echoed this, stating that Latvian 'society would have been much richer, if we hadn't lost that many'. Whereas larger areas of Latvian, Lithuanian and Estonian communities, such as in Bradford, Leeds or Manchester survived re-emigration and retained vitality, smaller areas of Baltic population were weakened. The smaller communities in Scotland and Wales were hit particularly severely by re-emigration, although community structures in and around the cities of Edinburgh and Swansea survived. Re-emigration coincided with the closure of many hostels, and left some of the Baltic refugees isolated.

Among those who decided not to re-emigrate, a gradual adjustment to life in Britain took place among a majority of the refugees during the 1950s. This period saw the refugees gradually taking on aspects of British culture and traditions while at the same time continuing to try to maintain their homeland cultures and identities as vigorously as was possible.

Vida, a Lithuanian child dependant, described adaptation to British culture within her family. She had come to Britain with her mother and brother to join her father, an EVW, in 1948. The family was thus an all Lithuanian family unit:

> 'I would say it has taken us near enough to gradually adopt English customs, near enough to about, after about five years...
>
> 'I recall various foods that we used to have as a child and the strange thing is, I remember those foods very well, because we stopped after a five-year gap, you sort of take in the foods of the country you live in. We had some Lithuanian youngsters at our [scout] camp last year and they were still eating the same sort of soups that I recall we used to eat years and years ago, when we first came to England, white carrot soups, milky carrot soups and also things made with flour, just simply little dump-lings things and so on that we used to have a lot of. I recall all that type of food which we gradually now keep on just special occasions, maybe festive occasions.'

The example of food reveals the difficulty of maintaining the homeland culture in the different circumstances of life in Britain, especially during the rationing years immediately after the end of the war.

Although it was considerably easier to maintain the homeland cuisine in Britain than it had been in the DP camps (which provided barely enough calories for the refugees, let alone the opportunity to cook traditional recipes, except on the rarest occasion), nevertheless, in the post-war conditions of Britain, many of the ingredients required to cook tradi-tional cuisine were difficult to obtain in many areas, many items were rationed, and otherwise expensive. However, because a large percentage of the Latvian, Lithuanian and Estonian diets in the homeland were based on staple foodstuffs such as potatoes, grains and dairy products, many of the refugees were able to cook modified versions of daily homeland recipes, once they had moved into private accommodation. As with some of the other aspects of Baltic homeland cultures, food attained a signifi-cance in exile in Britain, previously absent in the homeland. The signif-icance of cuisine as an element of national identity and culture became most marked when consumed at a religious or national celebration. For example, among Lithuanians, the twelve-course meal eaten on Christmas Eve, called *Kučios*, was hugely symbolic. On occasions such as this, food became an integral part of expressions of national and ethnic identity among the exiled communities.

After working for several years, some Baltic refugees were able to save enough money to buy houses, an acknowledgement and acceptance of their long-term futures in Britain. Saving up for a house was one of the primary goals of the young refugees and they lived frugally for years in order to be able to purchase their own properties. One Lithuanian woman joked that another reason the Lithuanian families had to buy houses was because due to living two or three families together in rented accommodation, they were 'falling out'. Overtime and part-time jobs, combined with thrift, enabled Baltic refugees to save money for house purchase. Few were able to buy their own houses individually by this stage, however. During the 1950s, couples or groups of young men bought houses together. Many couples were keen to work hard to buy a house before planning for a family. The comparatively low prices and plentiful supply of houses in the textile towns of the north proved to be particularly popular with Baltic refugees. Tannahill wrote that:

> *'The buying started in the North where the houses were cheaper. Sometimes a group bought one of the large old-fashioned houses; more often, a married couple selected a small terraced house, which might even be scheduled for demolition in a few years. But before long houses were being bought in the Midlands and in London too.'[6]*

By the mid-1950s, some EVWs began to qualify for council houses or N.C.B. (National Coal Board) houses. Some of the EVWs moved to New Towns, particularly Corby, where Development Corporation houses were relatively easy to acquire and employment was plentiful. Different local authorities had varying rules regarding the allocation of council housing. Whereas some required at least an application for naturalisation, others such as Bradford City Council did not. By 1956, the majority of the married and many of the single EVWs owned their own houses.

Some of the EVWs chose to stay in the remaining hostels, although many had closed their doors by the mid-1950s. By mid-1956 the EVW

hostel population of 50,000 in January 1949 (includes all EVW nationalities) had been reduced to about 3,000. Most of the remaining EVW
hostel residents were over 40 and were either single or had left behind
families in the homeland. Some EVWs left the hostels for life in the
towns but later returned.

The creation and consolidation of family life was another way that the
Baltic refugees began to settle in Britain. By 1960, a sizeable second generation of Latvians, Lithuanians and Estonians had formed. According to
available statistics, in the Bradford area from 1951–55, British women
headed the table of brides for Lithuanian men and took second place to
the 'home nationality' for Latvians and Estonians.[7] A Lithuanian woman
reported that in Manchester, the most popular nationalities of brides
among Lithuanian men were Italians, British and Germans. The popularity of Italian women among Lithuanian men may be partly due to a
shared Catholic religion. Few Latvian and Estonian men married Italian
women. There were numerous cases of Latvian, Lithuanian or Estonian
men marrying outside their nationality, but few Baltic *women* marrying
outside their nationality. Due to the disparity in numbers of men and
women who came to Britain, most Baltic women were able to marry
within their nationality.

Marriage within the same nationality offered refugees the opportunity to recreate family/household traditions from the homeland, as
far as the conditions of Britain allowed. These traditions included
national cuisine, birth, wedding and funeral customs, the transmission of values through the generations and gender relations within
the family.

Maintenance of culture within intermarriages was more difficult.
John Tannahill cited clashing cultures as one reason for the failure of
marriages between Baltic men and British women. He noted that cultural and class differences were often to blame, particularly differing
gender roles among British and Baltic women. A Latvian he interviewed
placed the blame for failure on the British side on two grounds. First,
'British girls were too independent to accept the husband as master of
the house'. Second, the 'British girls met by EVWs at dances and elsewhere were sometimes of rather poor upbringing who had little sympathy with the different backgrounds of their husbands'. A Lithuanian
apportioned the blame equally, citing three pitfalls of mixed marriages:
a tendency for the British wife to pay insufficient attention to cooking;

146

a tendency for the EVW man to drink excessively; and finally, the difficulties of different religions.[8]

Large numbers of Baltic men did not marry at all, the failure of some
unions with British girls tending to make some of the remaining single men wary of contracting such a union hastily. Other men may have
felt too old to marry and start families. Some men had left wives in the
homeland or had lost them during the years of war, occupation and displacement. While carrying out this study, there were several incidental
remarks about men and women who had married more than once, having
left behind a spouse in the homeland. Unable to contact them, and often
not even knowing if they were alive, some of the refugees decided to
remarry once in Britain.

During the 1950s, communication with relatives in the homeland
improved slightly. After Stalin's death, some refugees began writing to
relatives and friends for the first time, although they were still cautious.
One Latvian woman stated that the refugees began sending letters in
1953. They also received letters from family in the homeland, although
sometimes letters were sent via Germany to avoid identification of relatives in Britain. Letters received and sent were reportedly opened by the
Soviet authorities and often doctored, with black lines concealing sections of the letters.

Furthermore, the Krushchev 'Thaw' which began in 1956–7, led to
some concessions regarding the granting of exit visas enabling relatives to join family members abroad. As a result of talks with the British
Foreign Secretary, Khrushchev agreed that a number of relatives from
the Baltic States and other Eastern European countries would be able to
join families in Britain. Foreign Office files contain lists of all those who
submitted the necessary applications 'to the appropriate Soviet authorities for permission to leave the Soviet Union for temporary or permanent
residence with relatives in the UK, Australia, New Zealand and South
Africa'. Records show 133 applications submitted to join relatives in the
UK, of which 64 were residents of the Baltic States. On 13 May 1959,
Soviet exit visas were granted to a number of Baltic residents, mainly
the elderly to join their relatives in the UK. From the documentation in
the National Archives, it is impossible to state accurately how many exit
visas were granted to Latvians, Lithuanians and Estonians to join relatives in Britain as records are incomplete. According to Foreign Office
records, thirty-five exit visas were granted on 13th May 1959, mainly to

the elderly. This number included fourteen (of whom only one was male) who wished to join relatives in the UK. Nineteen were Latvians, eleven were Estonians and two were Lithuanians.[9]

During the 1950s, Baltic community structures and organisations continued to develop, despite the severe depletion of numbers by emigration. The communities were now financially more prosperous and able to start buying properties for Latvian, Lithuanian and Estonian clubs and headquarters. Clubs and properties were purchased in the centres of Baltic community.

In 1955, the Lithuanian Association in Great Britain purchased Headley Park, known as *Sodyba*, as a holiday/retirement home for the Lithuanian community, near Bordon in Hampshire. Headley Park was first named *Prieglauda –Vasarvietė*, a fairly literal translation of its functions, broadly meaning retirement home and summer residence, but in 1956, its name was changed to *Sodyba*, translated as 'Homestead'. The new metaphoric name reflected the intended character of Headley Park, which aimed to recreate aspects of the Lithuanian homestead, in effect to reconstruct home both for retired Lithuanians and Lithuanian holiday-makers. *Sodyba* quickly earned its name, growing typical farmstead produce and running fishing and rifle clubs. It not only provided a home for elderly Lithuanian refugees, but was also a centre where various annual youth and cultural events took place.

New premises were also bought for Lithuanian House Limited. In 1953, the Latvian National Council began to lease Nieuport House in Almeley, Herefordshire 'for use as an old people's home and as a venue for children's summer camps'. During the same year, the London Latvian Evangelical Lutheran Church started to lease Rowfant House near Crawley in Sussex for similar reasons. Both properties were later purchased by the lessees.

During the 1950s, political activities continued to focus upon attempts to restore Latvian, Lithuanian and Estonian independence, especially after Stalin's death when hopes were briefly revitalised. Links between the diaspora of different nations were strengthened in an attempt to increase pressure on western nations to restore independence. Links between the three Baltic communities and with other East European diaspora both within Britain and across the world were also forged. One result of this was the establishment of the Assembly of Captive European Nations (ACEN), in New York on 20 September 1954 by representatives of nine 'captive' countries – Albania, Bulgaria, Czechoslovakia, Estonia, Hungary, Latvia, Lithuania, Poland and Romania. This organisation sought to heighten pressure on western governments by joining forces with one another. The communities supported the attempts made by Baltic diasporas across the world to bring about the re-establishment of independence, for example through the formation of governments in exile. BBC Monitor reported on 23th January 1953 that the Estonian Exile Government had been formed in Oslo.

The communities in Britain kept up-to-date with homeland related news primarily through community newspapers published in Britain, but also via various newsletters, newspapers and reports published abroad and by the diaspora and various organisations across the world. For example, the *Newsletter from Behind the Iron Curtain*, published in Stockholm by the Estonian Information Centre, provided reports on communist activities in Eastern Europe. This contained a variety of information relating to communist activities in the Baltic States and other East European countries. For example, copies from 1952 and 1953 contained information relating to religious suppression in Lithuania.

The libraries and clubs of the Latvian, Lithuanian and Estonian associations in Britain usually held copies of newspapers, newsletters and reports for the communities to read. Few publications came directly from the homeland and these were primarily propaganda, sometimes subtly disguised, although more often, quite blatant. The three Baltic communities used all the channels at their disposal to urge the British government to take up their cause. In addition to pressure from diplomatic channels, the communities organised street protests and demonstrations and gave speeches within each community. Representatives from the Latvian, Lithuanian and Estonian Associations in Great Britain also wrote letters to government officials. The Chairman of the Lithuanian Association in Great Britain, M. Bajorinas, wrote to Winston Churchill on 4th November 1953. His letter contained the following message:

'It is the fervent hope of all Lithuanians that this great nation, following its centuries old traditions of freedom and defence against aggression, will in no circumstances recognise the annexation of Lithuania and other Baltic States by Soviet Russia, and will not leave these unfortunate peoples in the clutches of the eternal enemy of humanity – Soviet Communism.'[10]

Diplomatic pressure also continued. In 1954, the Latvian, Lithuanian and Estonian Ministers in England made appeals to the British Government to bring up the question of the Baltic States in the forthcoming conference of Foreign Ministers of Great Britain, France, the USA and the USSR in Berlin, taking place on 25 January. Charles Zarine of the Latvian Legation wrote to Anthony Eden, Secretary of State, stressing that, 'all Latvians, wherever now living, are looking for the day when their country shall again be independent and free ...'[11]

Appeals were sent by the diplomatic representatives of all three Baltic nations based in Britain (A. Torma – Estonian Legation, C. Zarine – Latvian Legation, B. K. Balutis – Lithuanian Legation), prior to the visit of Marshal Bulganin, Chairman of the USSR Council of Ministers and Nikita Khrushchev to the United Kingdom in 1956, to pressurise the British government to raise the issue of the Baltic States during their visit.

Although when the EVWs entered Great Britain in the late 1940s they were the largest organised group of labour migrants in Britain's history, trends in the 1950s served to conceal their prominence within Britain. One important factor leading to a growing acceptance of EVWs as members of British society was the changing immigration trends during the 1950s. Beginning with the docking of the *Empire Windrush* at Tilbury Docks in June 1948, thousands of immigrants from the Caribbean and Indian Sub-Continent began arriving in Britain over the next decade. A majority of colonial immigrants during the 1950s were from the British West Indies and they settled in many of the industrial cities where Baltic and other East European populations resided, such as Bradford and Leeds. The numbers of colonial immigrants rose year on year, reaching a peak in the 1950s of 46,000 in 1956. Numbers only significantly dropped temporarily in 1958 and 1959.

As these new immigrants tried to find employment and accommodation, the focus of British society's attention shifted away from the East European groups, who were becoming increasingly invisible, towards the more numerous and visible colonial migrants. Greater public toleration of the Baltic refugees also increased due to the deepening of the Cold War, which tended to heighten sympathy for their plight.

By the end of the 1950s, therefore, much can be said to have improved for Latvians, Lithuanians and Estonians in Britain, now no longer 'refugees' as such, but 'exiles', living outside of their homelands, but with, in many cases, positive futures to look forward to and present circumstances that were significantly more satisfactory and prosperous than they had been a decade earlier.

The communities of 1960 contrasted markedly with those in 1950, not only in terms of physical volume and composition, but also in relation to attitudes towards settlement and the sense of permanency felt among the refugees. The diminution of hopes for independence brought about by the failure of Khrushchev's rule to bring any significant change to the political status of the Baltic States within the Soviet Union was vital in producing acceptance of a long-term stay.

One Estonian summed up the process of change among the Estonian community in Great Britain during the 1950s – trends which were also experienced by the Latvian and Lithuanian communities:

> '*Initially in the fifties, early fifties, I think we tended to regard this as a very short term thing being in exile. In fact, [we] got disorientated for quite a long time, but then gradually the economic struggle took over. You had to create your homes and support families but initially political activity in the fifties, early fifties was quite active. Demonstrations and petitions ... But then from the mid-fifties onwards then there was mostly this rebuilding of the life abroad that took over.*'

CHAPTER 7

'I've got used to being here' – 1960–1985

'Since the war I do not hear anything of my family. Now I feel like English. But when I go to social evenings with Latvians, I feel like Latvian again. My wife is Irish. My children are English. They all like it here. I would be very happy to go back to Latvia, just for holiday...but you would not get visa. You frightened to go. And sometimes I see people begin to think of home, they do not know where they are. I try to put it out of my mind.

'Sometimes I think of myself, with big beard, walking in my own country. And no one recognises me, not even my own brother. Stranger in my own country ... You don't hear of many people going back.'

These are the words of a Latvian man interviewed in Bedford in 1969 by John Brown. They reveal the huge changes undergone among many of the refugees in just two decades.

Fifteen years later in 1984, a Latvian refugee interviewed by Bradford Heritage Recording Unit stated that she felt 'quite English' and that if Latvia became independent she would not return because she felt too old to start again. She felt that maintenance of the Latvian language was only for sentimental reasons and that the Latvian community in Great Britain would 'die out'. An Estonian man interviewed in the same year stated that although he was 'Estonian', his loyalties were with England. These comments contrast sharply with notions surrounding the myth of return in the 1950s and the responsibilities of exile.[1]

Between 1960 and 1985, growing families rooted the Latvian, Lithuanian and Estonian communities in Britain. In the 1960s, the youngest of the married refugees were now in their thirties and for-ties and busy bringing up children. Family life was facilitated by the growing financial prosperity of the exiles and the fact that almost all had bought their own houses. Some had even purchased their own cars. A few, primarily younger men, married for the first time during the 1960s and began to have families, although a sizeable minority remained single, possibly about half in some areas, particularly older refugees.

Although there are few available statistics on the demography or marital patterns of Baltic refugees in Britain during this period, John Brown noted the family and age structure of Latvian refugees in Bedford, as of 1 June 1969. The population of 176 native-born Latvians (151 men and 25 women) in Bedford were all over the age of forty. Eighty-nine of them were single, four of them women. Twenty-one were married to Latvians (amounting to 84 per cent of Latvian women but only 14 per cent of Latvian men in Bedford) and the others to spouses of other nationalities. Of the wives, twenty-seven were English. Brown also noted the number of second generation Latvians in Bedford. Of the eighty children of the first generation, twenty-three were of Latvian parentage, the rest of mixed marriages. All the children were under twenty. Twenty-three of the families were childless, including nine Latvian couples.

Some aspects of the situation in Bedford were representative of the general Latvian community in Britain, most obviously, the age of the first and second generation and the large number of mixed marriages and single men. However, the Latvian community in Bedford was slightly different from that in some of the other areas however, primarily in the disproportionately high percentage of men to women. Latvian men outnumbered Latvian women in the original EVW population to come to Britain, with men composing approximately three-quarters of the original population. However, the percentages were even higher in Bedford due to the male dominated brick industry, the principal employer of EVWs. John Brown noted that in 1948, 98 per cent of the 300 Latvian EVWs in Bedford were employed in the brick industry.

Among those who were able to recreate family life in Britain, the nationality of one's spouse influenced the extent of adaptation and integration into British society. Among Latvians in Bedford, homeland cultures and identities were most successfully maintained among same-nationality couples and in most cases, intermarriage had a weakening effect on homeland cultural maintenance. Same nationality couples spoke the homeland language at home, cooked homeland cuisine regularly and

153

were more likely to maintain some of the norms, values and traditions of the homeland.

In contrast, those who had married outside their nationality usually spoke English in the home, and rapidly embraced English culture, although this effect was dissipated if the man had married a woman of non-British background.

This dichotomy, is, however, overly simplistic. One inter-married Latvian, now living in Leeds, noted that being married to an English woman 'didn't really affect' his Latvian culture and identity, which he described as strong. He noted that his wife's encouragement was an important factor in this maintenance, stating that: 'My wife is very supportive'.

While families were growing in Britain, contact with family in the homeland remained minimal. Continued censorship meant that even among those who were not too scared to write, relatives on both sides had very little sense of the realities of the lives of loved ones. A Latvian man discussed the correspondence he had with his brother in Latvia:

> *'... he was very cautious what he wrote. I were writing fairly, fairly openly, but then again I knew that if I wrote far too openly or gave any information away then ... my brother would suffer ...'*

Although a few refugees met relatives during homeland visits with *Intourist*, the Soviet travel agency, these tightly structured package tours only allowed visits to the capitals and one or two 'tourist' destinations, such as Sigulda or Jūrmala in Latvia. Visitors were not allowed to diverge from the schedule and were forbidden to travel independently outside the capital. They were therefore unable to return to their pre-war homes and villages. Meetings with relatives were short and reportedly monitored. There were rumours about hotel rooms being bugged and tourists being followed when they left their hotel.

Indeed, many refugees in Britain lived through the entire exile period not daring to attempt to contact lost relatives and not knowing whether they were dead or alive. To some extent, refugees with families of their own in Britain were able to turn their attention and thoughts to their own family, but single refugees had to find other ways of coping, perhaps by focusing on friends, hobbies, work or the organised community.

By the 1960s, most of the refugees had become settled in their employment, having found a line of work that suited them. Many refugees climbed the ladder of their chosen career, and were satisfied with their jobs. A sizeable minority remained in the original undermanned areas of employment, such as textiles, but many had moved on. Of the 176 Latvians who remained in Bedford in 1969, 62 still worked in the brickyards, five were self-employed, five were working in the same trades that they had before the war, but many had learned new skills in 'several spheres of life'.[2]

Work was a major factor facilitating the integration of the refugees during the 1960s and 1970s. Not only did these employment experiences promote fluency in English and broaden the refugees' social sphere, British labour became increasingly accepting of them, particularly as the numbers of colonial immigrants increased during the 1960s. Levels of integration at work were such that many of the refugees reported 'feeling British' at work and some even blamed their employment for weakening homeland language skills.

Retirement, a process beginning in the 1970s for the older refugees, had mixed consequences for the integration process. On the one hand, it provided the opportunity to re-engage with the community and with one's past. Retired members of the communities reported an increase in their participation in community activities. An Estonian who retired in 1984 after working as a psychiatric nurse explained the difference retirement made. He had moved to Chesterfield in the early 1960s, mainly for work purposes, where there were very few other Estonians. He described becoming 'immersed' in his working and family life, and, as a result, he 'practically lost touch with the majority of Estonian communities.' 'I have [had] one or two [Estonian] friends, continuously but I practically lost the use of the Estonian language.' However, during his retirement, he re-engaged with the community and became actively involved in the Estonian Association in Great Britain, where he was elevated to the position of Club Secretary. He described the process:

'While you're nursing, it's a lot of training. It's four and a half years training. I was at Open University for five years, so while those things were going on, you couldn't think of sitting and being Estonian. You just had to get on with whatever you're at. You could not have been doing all this clerical work. I couldn't have done that, anything like that ... Estonian language, well I almost forgot it. Yes, I think it's since retirement [that] I've again got a bit gradually more interested in things Estonian and I don't know whether I feel more Estonian because of that.'

155

As well as promoting community participation, some interviewees also talked about reminiscing about the homeland and their childhood years more frequently as they got older. An Estonian interviewee noted that:

> '*I think it is to do with age. It's nothing to do with politics or being abroad, I don't think, or being in a foreign country. It's just that I think that's what old people do.*'

He described how he remembered his childhood in an idyllic, 'story-book' way and that 'You forget the nasty bits', 'this is part of the ageing process'.

Not all the refugees reported an increase in reminiscence, however. In the 1990s, one Latvian woman was asked if she reminisced more about Latvia as she got older. She replied: 'No, no. Not really. Not really. I've forgotten most of it now'.

The decline in organised community participation due to family and work commitments was summed up by an Estonian man, who noted that: 'notwithstanding the continuation of cultural, social and political activities', 'for all that, signs of decline in…interest in the Estonian national-cultural activity were unmistakable perhaps from [the] mid-seventies onwards…' The 'rebuilding of the life' took over from the middle of the 1950s onwards:

> '*In fact, I know this from my own experience. I tried to fit myself in, in various ways including [the] Merchant Navy for a while but then I came back and went into nursing in 1956. And there . were quite a few in this hospital, quite a few Estonians, but gradually I got absorbed in my career and my family here, and then early sixties [I] came to live in Chesterfield and practically lost touch with the majority of Estonian communities.*'

Another Estonian man interviewed in 1984 described how he let his participation in the nearby Estonian community 'lapse' after marrying an Irish girl and starting a family. He stated that he was not currently 'very deeply' involved. His job as a cook at Leeds Road Hospital in Bradford had left him little time for connecting with the community and he noted that although he felt sad that he had drifted away, he also felt a little indifferent. He claimed that he had become 'carried away' with his wife and family. Another reason for declining participation was the increasing geographical distance of many refugees from centres of Baltic community. From 1960 onwards, a continued trend of geographical dispersal both within cities and within Britain as a whole, also impacted on community structures. Within cities and towns, as members of the communities became more financially prosperous, they began to move away from the original areas of Latvian, Lithuanian or Estonian community towards more affluent suburban areas of towns and cities, thus following the general trend throughout the British society at the time.

However, many were still able to maintain links with the organised community as they now owned cars and could drive to clubs. Improvements in public transport also facilitated continuing community engagement. Not all moved away however; one man living just yards from the Latvian club in Leeds, and a significant number stayed within 15 or 20 minutes travelling distance of a Latvian, Lithuanian or Estonian community centre.

The decline in community participation brought about a need to increase revenues from other sources in order to keep club buildings open. Many clubs opened their doors to the wider local community as a way of increasing income. For example, *Sodyba*, the Lithuanian retirement and holiday home, established a Rifle Club in the 1960s which drew members from both the Lithuanian and local communities. Rowfant House opened its licensed social club to locals from the surrounding districts and several clubs welcomed the local populations to drink at the bar. For example, Bradford's Lithuanian Club and Leeds Latvian Club both welcomed the locals in, which in addition to helping to keep the clubs open, also aided the integration process.

In some areas, Latvian, Lithuanian and Estonian communities also continued to share facilities with each other and other East European nationalities as a way of mitigating poor or non-existent facilities. For example, in Bradford, where the Latvian and Estonian clubs were in the same road, members regularly drank at each other's bars. The Lithuanian Youth Newsletter, *LYNES* reported in June 1980, that Lithuanians danced at the Polish Catholic Club in Wolverhampton and that Lithuanians held get-togethers at the Ukrainian club in Nottingham.

Of the three communities, the Latvian community was arguably the most successful at maintaining community participation during this period. It benefited from being the largest of the three communities, and had a very strong organisation base and structure. This gave it financial clout, and the ability to partially address local weaknesses and problems with centralised funds and support if necessary. In 1978, *Latvians in Great Britain* noted that the DVF retained 32 local branches with 2,100 members. The Latvian National Council in Great Britain was also a solid organisation, serving the interests of Latvians in Great Britain and extending the work done by the DVF in social, cultural and political fields.

The main Lithuanian organisation, the DBLS, had significantly lower membership levels, but was nonetheless able to survive and even flourish despite falling membership levels. Despite some differences of opinion within the organisation about its future direction, the focus on bringing younger second generation Lithuanians on board from the 1970s onwards was a key factor in ensuring the survival of many clubs and branches. A few branches did close during this period, but in 1981, the Lithuanian Association of Great Britain's AGM noted there were still twenty local branches of the Lithuanian Association.

Not all clubs survived through the 1980s; for example, LYNES noted that the Leicester branch, which was reportedly one of the most progressive, drawing Lithuanians from a wide area, and organising a full schedule of activities including social and cultural events, sports groups and a Saturday school, suffered irreversible decline. In January 1999, LYNES noted that: 'Regrettably as numbers declined so did the activity'. Attempts were made at revival with little success, and despite continued cultural activity, the DBLS Leicester branch was officially closed in 1982.

However, decline in some areas was partially offset by more positive developments in other areas. For example, Lithuanians in Scotland acquired a new club in Mossend, Lanarkshire, one of the few examples where 'old' and 'new' Lithuanian refugees pooled resources to buy a club building for joint use. Lithuanian DPs and the 'old' Lithuanian refugees from the late nineteenth and early twentieth century got together to raise funds from voluntary contributions to buy St Margaret's Episcopal Church, to use as their meeting hall in 1950. The club moved to new premises in 1979, due to redevelopment plans by Monklands District Council, who agreed to erect new premises. During the early 1980s an extension was built.

In contrast to the DVF and the DBLS, the Estonian community structure – the 'Association of Estonians in Great Britain' (*Inglismaa Eestlaste Ühing*) was a fairly loose society, which did not have individual

158

membership, but 'acted as a co-ordinating body' and as a collector and disseminator of information. Various organisations were affiliated to I.E.U, including the clubs in London, Leicester and Bradford, societies in other areas and those representing ex-servicemen and the younger generations. Due to the small size of the Estonian community, only a few clubhouses and societies were maintained. In comparison to the DVF, which was able to purchase over twelve large properties during the period of exile, Estonians bought only three. Remarkably however, all three of the clubs have remained open and active until the present day.

Decline in community participation not only affected clubs and branches, it also contributed to the extinction of some community publications, which suffered growing financial difficulties. Examples were the London Lithuanian paper, which became integrated into *Europos Lietuvis*, a weekly paper, and the London Latvian paper – *Londonas Avīze*, formed in 1942 which became integrated in 1971 into a European-wide paper for Latvians printed in Germany – *Brīvā Latvija*.

The decline in community participation must not be exaggerated however and throughout this period, active involvement and participation in social, cultural, political and religious activities continued among Latvians, Lithuanians and Estonians in many areas. Clubs provided an important outlet for socialising and enabled the exiles to discuss and share information about aspects of their lives in Britain and developments in the homelands. Clubs would usually be open at least several nights a week and Latvians, Lithuanians and Estonians would chat over beer or whisky, gin and tonic, or brandy, and enjoy meals prepared by the women (or in the case of Lithuanian House in London, a very talented man, Kazys) of the club. They would also gather regularly during the daytimes and prepare food together and organise film viewings or invite guest speakers. Important festivals and national days continued to be celebrated with vigour and often included performances by dance or singing groups. There were also regular meetings with other community groups in different parts of the UK, as well as internationally. The groups organised cultural shows and events for the wider general public with the aim of raising awareness about Latvian, Lithuanian and Estonian culture. For example, in 1975, a large exhibition of Lithuanian art was held in Bradford Central Library.

In addition to the social and cultural activities, political campaigning also continued, with the aim of releasing the homelands from the tight grip of the USSR and bringing attention to their plight to the British Government and public. An important aspect of political campaigning was to highlight the issue of political prisoners in the homeland and to campaign on their behalf. This role increased significantly from the 1960s onwards as Brezhnev's oppressive regime placed huge numbers of dissenting individuals into prisons, labour camps and psychiatric prison hospitals and as links with the dissident movements grew. Community members were urged to take an active part in these campaigns. For example, in January 1983, *LYNES* called upon its readers to send birthday cards to Lithuanian prisoners of conscience.

The growing international dissident movement from the 1960s onwards unified exiles in different countries and brought together political resistance in the homelands with a growing international protest movement. Community publications encouraged the diaspora to support dissident activity. For example, in August 1980, *LYNES* called on second generation Lithuanians to participate in Lithuania's Underground Press and to help Lithuanian's persecuted believers. It asked young Lithuanians to acquaint themselves with the *Chronicle of the Catholic Church in Lithuania*, a *samizdat* journal aimed at highlighting the plight of the suppressed Lithuanian Catholic Church.

Joint political campaigning in co-operation either with the global diaspora, the dissident movement, or other Baltic and East European communities was regarded as the most effective method of protest during this period, given the small size of the communities in Britain. Particularly significant during this period was the Captive Nations' Committee, an association of so-called captive nations including Latvia, Lithuania and Estonia, together with other Eastern European countries suffering under Soviet rule. This organisation was established to highlight the plight of these nations to western governments and the General Public and to carry out political campaigning on behalf of the homelands.

The soaring publication and circulation of books and periodicals was one of the most obvious vehicles for spreading the dissidents' campaigns across the world. In Britain, this stimulated exile publication and increased access to exile and dissident literature from all over the world. Clandestine sites for the distribution of dissident literature were established within Britain and publishing houses such as the Lithuanian Nida Press flourished. Nida Press produced Lithuanian 'literary books, memoirs and annual almanacs of *belles lettres* "*Pradalgės*" (The Swathes)' and published *LYNES* initially. Nida Press also published works from the other Baltic communities, including the well-known *Latvia and Latvians* by Juris Sinka.

The dissident movement was particularly significant among the Lithuanian exile community which linked the repression of Catholicism in the homeland to the suppression of the Lithuanian ethnic nation. Religion quickly became a key focal point of the growing opposition movement in the homeland and consequently, the religio-national link among the diaspora also strengthened. Lithuanians in Britain played an active role in supporting the religious dissident movement. In fact, there was even an underground publishing and distribution centre in Britain.

Throughout this period, Lithuanians in Britain attended church services held in the Lithuanian language. St Casimir's Lithuanian Catholic Church at The Oval in Hackney had been built in 1912 to serve London's growing Lithuanian community and it remained a vibrant centre during this period. In Nottingham, the Lithuanian Marian Fathers' *Židinys*, was also an important centre for Catholics in the East Midlands and further afield. Lithuanian priests travelled around Britain to celebrate mass in their language in Catholic Churches and to attend community events and commemorations and to provide spiritual guidance and support to community members. The Carfin Grotto in the West of Scotland, which had become a destination for Catholic pilgrimage in the early twentieth century and was dedicated to the 'Our Lady of Lourdes' shrine in France, continued to attract Lithuanian Catholics who attended on annual pilgrimages. Masses were also held regularly for Lithuanian Catholics residing in Scotland.

Amongst Latvians and Estonians, the significance of freedom of religion as a national-cultural trait was also strengthened during exile, with church services acting as an important vehicle for expressions of culture among the diaspora. As with the Lithuanian community, church services were well attended by Latvians and Estonians for whom Lutheranism was the main religion. It could be argued, however, that the link between religion and nationalism was not as strong as within the Lithuanian community.

In many cases, attendance at Lutheran church services became a casualty of the increased focus on work and family life during this period. A Latvian man from Leeds, noted that his participation in church services had dwindled as his work life took over, in the same way that it had affected his participation in the local Latvian club.

Other Latvians and Estonians did attend services regularly, however. The 'Latvian Evangelical Lutheran Church in Great Britain' had been established shortly after the Second World War and organised services in Latvian across Britain. In 1966, the Lutheran Church of St Agnes and St Anne in London was rededicated for use by Estonian and Latvian Lutherans, with the help of the worldwide Lutheran community.

During this period, the communities also organised group donations to homeland residents. Most clubs and societies held a variety of collections, some intended for individuals, others to support schools or other institutions. Vieda Skultans noted how her mother, a Latvian who had come to Britain as an EVW, worked for a Polish company in London who sent gift parcels to Latvians in the homeland. Sending parcels via a company such as this one eased the process as there was a good deal of red tape involved. Vieda noted that at one point her mother was sending up to 200 parcels a week on behalf of Latvians in London.[3]

From the 1970s onwards, there was a growing need to address those requirements of an ageing population which were not met by the British social services system. Social services placed members of smaller minority groups such as the three Baltic populations within old people's homes which did not cater for different nationality groups. Many refugees wanted to spend their last years within the homeland community. The largest of the three communities, the Latvians, faced the most acute problem numerically and the community felt that significant provision was needed. The solution was to acquire properties which could serve multiple functions. In 1988, a report written by the British Refugee Council *Age in Exile: A report on elderly exiles in the United Kingdom* noted that there were 'four residential (homes) for retired people run by various Latvian organisations'. According to the report, they 'provide residential care mixed with holiday accommodation and also are used for conferences, meetings, concerts, seminars, and children's holiday camps'.[4]

The first property, Rowfant House in West Sussex, was leased in 1953 and purchased entirely by voluntary contributions. In 1961 it was bought by the London Latvian Evangelical Lutheran Church. Voluntary workers restored the neglected property and gardens within the twenty acres of park land. In 1988 it had thirty residents. Accommodation for weekend guests was also available and it also housed a licensed social club. Residents took part in the wide range of activities held at Rowfant House, including concerts, lectures, church services and the traditional Jānis Day celebrations. Although there was no nursing care, a local doctor visited regularly.

Mūsmājas, at Wolston, near Coventry, owned by *Daugavas Vanagi's* Coventry Branch, began as a licensed social club and was used for week-end schools, meetings and various cultural activities. Standing in fifteen acres of parkland, *Mūsmājas* was adjusted to house up to fourteen perma-nent residents and had spare rooms for weekend guests. The 1988 report noted that it also had residential nursing staff.[5]

Nieuport House in Almeley, Herefordshire, was run by the Latvian National Council and had been rented from the Hereford Local Authority since 1953. The property could house up to fifty residents and also accom-modate weekend guests. Nieuport House hosted annual summer camps for children, youth conferences, seminars, fancy dress parties and Jānis Day celebrations. It housed a library and social club for residents only.

Finally, the increasing need for further retirement accommodation led to the purchase in 1975 of Catthorpe Manor in Leicestershire, called *Straumēni*, to cater primarily for retired members of the community, but also to be used as a meeting and cultural centre for Latvians of all ages. In 1988 *Straumēni* housed fifty-eight residents. *Straumēni* was bought by *Daugavas Vanagi*, entirely from voluntary contributions. The manor provided and continues to offer retirement accommodation and medi-cal facilities whilst simultaneously operating as a general centre for the holding of community events. It has the air of a Latvian village tucked away deep in the Leicestershire countryside. Catthorpe Manor stands in acres of grounds, with bluebell woods, pagan structures and a small lake. The complex houses Latvian newspaper publishing facilities, a bar/café, event halls, independent retirement accommodation within the Manor, catering facilities, guest rooms, a sick bay, a library and information cen-tre, retirement bungalows, landscaped gardens and a chapel. *Straumēni* has been one of the main locations for St. John's Day celebrations as well as the location for *Daugavas Vanagi* AGMs.

The 1988 report on elderly exiles in the United Kingdom also noted that Latvians had access to the British Refugee Council residential home, Agnew House. Neither the Lithuanian nor the Estonian community had such extensive facilities. In terms of provision from central and local gov-ernment, or from voluntary agencies, Estonians and Lithuanians received no specific residential provision other than housing assistance from the British Refugee Council. In comparison to the Latvian community's four retirement properties, the Lithuanian community only had one – *Sodyba,* in Hampshire, also known as Headley Park. As with the Latvian properties, *Sodyba* also doubled up as a centre for Lithuanian cultural activities and Scout and youth camps. LYNES noted that in August 1980, *Sodyba* had thirteen retired residents.

The Estonian community had no separate provision for the elderly and no comparable residences. This meant that older refugees who were unable to look after themselves were obliged to use local authority provisions, as did some Latvians and Lithuanians. There were not enough places for all Latvians and Lithuanians in the retirement homes like *Sodyba* and some people wished to remain near their families. Some received local authority help within their own homes and the local Latvian, Lithuanian and Estonian communities also helped by providing hot lunches, social events and other provisions such as a 'Talking Book' scheme organised by the Latvian Welfare Fund, for older Latvians with poor vision. In some areas, the communities also organised visiting schemes to the elderly.

The way in which first generation refugees decided to bring up their children (as Latvians, Lithuanians, Estonians, as British, or as both), reflected their varying beliefs in the permanency of exile and the importance of their role as guardians of the homeland.

Language was regarded by many exiles as the cornerstone of Latvian, Lithuanian and Estonian identities and as the most important element in the transmission of culture through the generations. The Lithuanian Charter, a set of guiding principles for the Lithuanian exile communities, adopted by DBLS and DBLJS, stressed its importance:

> *'The strongest bond of any national community is language. To a Lithuanian the Lithuanian language is his national pride. The family is the lifeblood of a nation … A Lithuanian passes on to future generations the existence of the Lithuanian Nation that his parents preserved, so that we may live for ever-more.'*

Many refugees were torn between their sense of duty as exiles and a firm belief that Britain was to be theirs and their children's permanent home. The dilemma about how to bring up one's children had emerged in the 1950s, but became particularly pressing as the children reached school age. Many parents felt that it was more of a priority that their children learned and understood English, so that they were not at a disadvantage at school, could make friends easily and felt a sense of belonging in Britain. Some refugees did not even teach their children the homeland language because they feared it might prove a handicap to learning or getting on. Names were changed for the same reason. A Latvian woman, now living in Leeds, explained her dilemma about whether or not to bring up her children as Latvians. When asked how she and her Latvian husband raised their two sons, and whether she taught them Latvian, she replied:

> *'When they were babies I did speak Latvian. That came naturally, that's how I felt, I could talk to them in Latvian. Then when they came to school age I knew they had to learn English. Besides they were mixing with English children and somehow they picked up the [English] language.'*

When her children showed no interest in attending the Latvian weekend school, she did not force them to attend:

> *'I tried to take them to [the] Latvian [school]. There was Latvian Sunday school, Saturday school, they didn't like it and I thought, well why should I force them to do it if they don't like it? No they didn't really like it. I don't think it [Latvia] interests them.'*

She explained her motivation for not imposing the Latvian language on her children and encouraging them to learn English:

> *'They're living here and they should feel at home. They shouldn't be sort of half and half which is really I don't think that's very good really, if you feel like that.'*

Her decision not to force the Latvian culture upon her children was based partly on a recognition that they would not be returning 'as long as there was a communist government', and reflected her belief that settlement in Britain would be permanent:

> *'I wanted them to feel at home here since we weren't going back I was going to help them to feel them to belong here, to belong somewhere. They have to have a home somewhere. And of course that did change my attitude as well.'*

165

Some parents were keen for their children to learn the homeland language, however, and went to great lengths to achieve this. Nevertheless, even within this group of parents, there was an acknowledgement that their children had to learn English and they were aware of the difficult task of bringing their children up as Latvians, Lithuanians or Estonians within British society.

Children from single nationality households were more likely than those from intermarried households to be raised as Latvians, Lithuanians or Estonians. That single nationality households usually spoke the homeland language at home aided this process. However, as the above comments show, external influences were great, and hindered many parents' wishes that their children maintain the Latvian, Lithuanian or Estonian cultures and identities. Even though most pre-school children of single nationality parentage learned the homeland language as their first language, when they reached school age, they became fluent in English rapidly and homeland language skills weakened. By the time the second generation left school, many had poor homeland language ability. The sons of the Latvian woman first mentioned in this section had lost most of their Latvian by their twenties and thirties. One had 'sort of forgotten nearly completely', although the other still 'understands Latvian quite well'. Both had married English wives, spoke English within the home and rarely spoke Latvian. Interestingly, the development of the second generation was an enormous influence on the integration of the first generation. For all-Latvian, Lithuanian or Estonian families, children introduced British influences into the household and their fluency in English aided English language skills among the first generation.

The weakening of homeland language and cultural maintenance among the second generation had a significant impact on the organised communities. Until the 1960s, Latvian, Lithuanian or Estonian was the only language used in community publications, speeches, events and AGMs, but it became increasingly apparent that if this were to continue, many members of the second generation would in effect be excluded.

Nevertheless, it was not until the 1970s, when the second generation and some of those who had come to Britain as child dependants took matters in hand and that positive steps towards meeting the needs of the youth were taken. According to the January 1997 edition of the Lithuanian youth newsletter *LYNES*, the first generation agreed eventually that 'Lithuanian youth should organise its own activities, rather than being led by the older generation'.

Beginning in the early 1970s, Latvian, Lithuanian and Estonian youth (often in their twenties and thirties, but regarded by the older generation as 'youth'), began to develop youth groups, activities and publications which aimed to lure second generation members back into community participation and were designed to enable those with poor language skills to participate. Lithuanian youth were the most innovative and organised, inspired by the success of youth programmes and organisations in the USA and Canada. In January 1978, a newsletter for Lithuanian youth was published, first as the 'Lithuanian Youth News-Sheet' (later as *Saulė* and then *LYNES*), as a supplement to *Europos Lietuvis*, the newspaper of the British Lithuanian community. The first news-sheet was a small two-page edition. The newsletter was written both in English and Lithuanian and was intended to unify Lithuanian youth, to provide information about the community, stimulate interest and participation and to reach all members of the community, including isolated youth who did not live in an area of Lithuanian community.

As early as 1979, *LYNES* began to call for the establishment of a Lithuanian Youth Association in Great Britain and in 1981, the DBLJS (*Didžiosios Britanijos Lietuvių Jaunimo Sajunga* (The Lithuanian Youth Association in Great Britain) was established. The Constitution of the Lithuanian Youth Association in Great Britain accepted at the DBLJS General Meeting in January 1981 specified that 'The languages of the DBLJS are Lithuanian and English', and that 'The members of the DBLJS are young Lithuanian descendants, people of other nationalities who have married Lithuanian descendants, and those who closely involve themselves with Lithuanians'.

Among the Latvian and Estonian communities, youth organisations and activities were also established. In 1973, an Estonian youth organisation – *Tulevik* (meaning 'The Future') was founded 'with the aim of promoting Estonian youth's involvement in the Estonian social-cultural activities in this country and abroad'. In addition to organising choirs and ensembles, the main event in the *Tulevik* calendar was the organisation of an annual summer camp. Within the Latvian community, there was a branch of 'The Association of Latvian Youth in Europe', and 'The Latvian National Council in Great Britain' also had a youth section, both of which organised a variety of social, cultural and educational activities.

167

The new youth organisations co-ordinated a range of activities in Britain involving the second and third generations, complementing those arranged by the first generation. For example, summer camps, language classes and social events were organised. Among younger Lithuanians, *Vakaronės*, traditional social gatherings of Lithuanians, described by *LYNES* as 'a sit-in, a talk-in, and a drink-in', usually at a volunteer's house, often with a special cultural theme, such as Lithuanian folk customs and mythology, became especially popular among second generation Lithuanians in London and Nottingham. *LYNES* noted in 1986 that *Vakaronės* were held every six weeks or so in London and that the Nottingham-based Lithuanians were planning their own *Vakaronės* season in 1987. The December 1986 edition of *LYNES* noted that the theme of the next *Vakaronė* in January 1987 was 'the traditional Lithuanian folk wedding, its customs and traditions'.

LYNES outlined the activities of Lithuanian youth in London in 1985. There was a football team called 'Lithuania Victoria FC', composed of about twenty members all from the Lithuanian Sports and Social Club in Victoria Park Road, London, E9. The team played in Lithuanian national colours. The dance group *'Lietuva,'* originally formed in 1969 was still going strong, performing in Britain and in Lithuanian Folk Dance Festivals abroad.

Events and activities were also organised with other East European youth. For example, at a special Baltic Evening in Swansea in 1983, dance groups of the Latvian, Lithuanian, Estonian and Ukrainian youth in Britain performed. The June edition of *LYNES* reported that 'strong links have now been formed with the youth of Estonia and Latvia in England. None of our communities is large and perhaps survival and the way forward for us lies in unity and support for each other'.

The second generation linked up with youth in other parts of the world for the purposes of Youth Congresses, Rallies and Festivals. At these events, the younger generations were able to learn or improve their knowledge of the homeland language, learn about its history and culture and participate in various cultural activities. The international organisation of Lithuanian youth (PLJB) organised a World Youth Congress every 4–5 years to 'bring together youth from all over the West'. For example, in 1983, the fifth Lithuanian World Youth Congress was held in Chicago. In the winter of 1987/88, the *VI Kongresas* was held in Australia.

Scouting was also particularly popular among Lithuanians, with both girls and boys joining up, and participating in a wide variety of events and activities both in Britain and further afield, in Europe and America. International scout camps gave young Lithuanians the opportunity to meet up with other members of the Lithuanian diaspora across the globe. These events were facilitated by the expansion of low cost air travel.

The effects of growing up within British society manifested itself in the ethnic identities of the second generation, of whom a majority regarded themselves as British or half-and-half, with only a handful describing themselves as Latvians, Lithuanians or Estonians. In June 1981, *LYNES* discussed the identities of second generation Lithuanians, and explained why the vast majority thought of themselves as British, even those born of all-Lithuanian parentage:

> *'Second generation Lithuanians are either born or have spent a large part of their childhood here in Britain and have been subject to the influences of this country in their most formative years. While the home maintains Lithuanian influences to a large degree, for children educated and articulate in English, these are often moderated by the English way of life. Also the range of activities offered by the British social scene is vast, and the second generation often has to decide between British and Lithuanian attitudes on certain issues.'*

The author then contrasted the maintenance of the 'Lithuanian connection' for first and second generation Lithuanians. For the first generation the link is maintained 'because it fulfils a need for them, whereas their descendants can actually choose whether or not they maintain these links'.

Not all those among the second and third generations who chose to maintain links with the communities came from same nationality parentage. A young Lithuanian explained his motivations for maintaining the 'Lithuanian connection' in the June 1983 edition of LYNES:

> *'Being of mixed parentage I have not grown up a Lithuanian speaker and my interest in Lithuanian affairs were non-existent until 1982. Since then, I have gone from strength to strength in terms of community involvement: participating in most DBLJS activities and joining the 'Lietuva 'dance group. In this time, I have endeavoured to learn Lithuanian and can now hold,*

albeit basic conversations in Lithuanian. My basic motives are political and I would like to see greater involvement by young Lithuanians in this sphere.'

The acquisition of British citizenship, a process that had begun in the 1950s and continued through the 1960s and beyond, provides a good illustration of the variations in the integration process among members of the first generation Latvian, Lithuanian and Estonian communities in Britain.

Gaining British citizenship provided the refugees, formerly legally designated as aliens, the same privileges as British citizens, including the right to a British passport and the entitlement to vote in elections. In a sense, this represented the a more formal aspect of integration into British society, enabling the refugees not only to take part in the political process of the country in which they lived, but also to gain access to certain social and economic institutions previously denied to them.

British citizenship could be acquired through naturalisation by two methods. Baltic women who married British subjects could apply for British nationality. Secondly, as aliens, the refugees were eligible to apply for naturalisation under the Second Schedule of the British Nationality Act of 1948. Under the provisions of the Act, the refugees were eligible after living in Great Britain for a period of eight years. Thus, the process of acquiring citizenship began from the mid-1950s onwards. The numbers acquiring citizenship are difficult to quantify but it seems that a majority of the younger refugees did acquire British citizenship, with some, more commonly older members of the communities, resisting acquisition.

John Tannahill reported that by 1958, the extent of naturalisation among non-emigrating refugees was 'still very small'. Excluding the women who married British subjects the proportion of those naturalised probably did not exceed 5 per cent. However, he estimated that the proportion would rise over subsequent years since it was only three or four years since most EVWs qualified to apply for citizenship. Within the groups of 128 EVWs interviewed by Tannahill in 1958, nearly one third said they 'had it in mind'.[6]

Bruno Rullis, a Latvian, was one of a small number of refugees who took up citizenship in the 1950s. He had applied for citizenship in 1955 as soon as he was eligible, primarily in order to apply for his mother to come and live in England. Bruno described this early period of Khrushchev's rule as a 'slack' time, when a number of exit visas were granted to enable relatives to join EVWs in Great Britain and Australia.

Aside from financial considerations (naturalisation cost £20 in 1958, a large amount in those days), there was division among the communities and individuals over the question of British citizenship. Many were initially undecided and waited several years before taking the final plunge. In the 1960s, some regarded British citizenship as a betrayal of one's identity and homeland and felt that it might prejudice their chances of returning. Others viewed naturalisation as a practical measure, to gain the same rights and privileges as the native British. It would also enable them to travel to the homeland without fear. There may also have been a fear among a few refugees that they still might be forcibly repatriated. Some refugees applied for citizenship for the sake of their children or if they took up certain jobs which required British nationality, for example, one refugee took up British citizenship so he could join the Royal Navy.

One of the reasons cited for not taking up citizenship was a feeling among many of the refugees that naturalisation would not make a great deal of difference to their lives and some felt that even with citizenship, they would still be regarded as foreigners. This was the feeling of one Latvian man who never applied for citizenship. He stated as his reason, 'Well among English, we're still foreigners whether we have citizenship or not.' Finally, inertia also played its part in failing to apply for citizenship. Some always meant to get around to it, but never quite managed to apply. Often when they did eventually try to secure citizenship, the cost or length of the application dissuaded them.

A Latvian woman from Leeds who married another Latvian took up British citizenship during the early 1960s at a cost of £25. She felt that it was important to take up British citizenship because 'it made you belong more. You could go to the library and borrow a book, otherwise you had to guarantee that you live here …'

A Latvian woman in Derby who also took up citizenship in the early 1960s described her reasons for doing so:

> 'Some people objected to doing it. They were Latvians. They would stay Latvian. My dad said you can change a citizenship. You can't change what you're born, you know the nationality you're born with is yours. But if you live in a country and you

work there and you're a citizen of that country then it's right and then again you've got a voice. See if you're British citizen, then you've got an MP who you can appeal [to] on your behalf. If you're not, you're a non-entity. You're nothing. And if you travel abroad, you've got nothing behind you if you're not anybody's citizen, you see. There is a travel document people could get for travelling, but they needed visas and things, more than you did with a British Passport. So we thought it over and decided that it was the right thing to do, because if you live in a country, and you work for it, you're sort of loyal to that country.'

This woman then, distinguished nationality from citizenship. For her, British citizenship was not a betrayal of one's ethnic identity. As she stated:

... 'if you're a Scot you're a Scot. You're British, but you're a Scot, like if you're a Welshman, you don't really lose that, because what you have is British. You can't become English or can't become Scotch. It's really what you're born, you know by blood you belong to something, but you can be British and have a voice in the life of the country in which you live.'

Another Latvian man who married a Latvian woman and maintained a very strong Latvian identity and active participation in the local Latvian community still felt that it was important to take up citizenship. He explained the main reason as being too fearful to visit his homeland without a British passport:

'Oh yes, first you see, you are not very safe. Very, very afraid of what may happen. You see when [those] Bolsheviks [were] in the country you are never sure what may happen. And so I visited my country with British passport – that is safer.'

In the 1970s and 1980s, the main reason for taking up citizenship was to enable the refugees to travel to the homeland, which became easier and more popular during this period. As time passed, considerations related to the changed perception of where home was, also became important.

By the 1970s and 1980s, many refugees felt that Britain was now their home and since they were unlikely to be returning to the Baltic States, citizenship could provide them with a greater sense of belonging. Generally, however, practical motivations were the main impetus, particularly as the cost of citizenship continued to rise. While the homeland remained part of the Soviet Union, they did not feel that it was home, but for many (although certainly not all), Britain was *becoming home*.

CHAPTER 8

'We were living in the past' – The impact of homeland independence on the Latvian, Lithuanian and Estonian communities in Britain

'When I [went] to Latvia it [was] all different. We don't fit in you know. We are foreigners over there. Same as we're foreigners here. It's a tragedy.'

An Estonian man interviewed in the 1990s, noted that the restoration of homeland independence in 1991 represented the end of exile for the Baltic communities in Britain: 'We are no longer refugees'. His comment summed up the significance of liberation for the communities. They were no longer exiles or refugees and were free to return to their homelands. Independence was the goal for which the communities had been striving for half a century. However, when liberation came, the implications for the Baltic communities were not as straightforward as had originally been envisaged. On their arrival in Britain, they had imagined the mass return of the diaspora to the homeland and the transplantation of cultures and identities. In 1991, the meaning of independence for the diaspora was uncertain for some time to come.

When Mikhail Gorbachev came to power as General Secretary of the Communist Party of the Soviet Union in 1985, there were few signs that his premiership would bring about any shift in the fortunes of the three Baltic Soviet Socialist Republics. However, changes did begin to occur, unexpectedly and rapidly, as a result of the introduction of the policies of *Glasnost* ('openness') and *Perestroika* ('restructuring') in 1986. Change had taken almost five decades to finally happen, but when it did, developments were brisk, leading to homeland independence just six years after the start of Gorbachev's premiership.

The first effect of *Glasnost* on the diaspora was an increased flow of accurate news emanating from the homelands. Western journalists and television crew were allowed greater access than ever before, although controls were still exercised. Increased media coverage heightened wider public awareness of the Baltic republics. *LYNES* reported in August 1989 that the high coverage of events in the Baltic States had 'had a knock-on effect in the lives of people of Estonian, Latvian and Lithuanian descent living here in Britain', due to the greater awareness of the British public. *LYNES* addressed its audience of young Lithuanians:

> *'You must have experienced it. You are asked your name and after your reply, the usual question about its origin. Then instead of the usual inane smile (as if to say "Mm, yes – I know where that is – near Romania isn't it?", you are greeted with instant comprehension and, maybe, an intelligent comment, like, "Lithuania! Isn't that where Sajūdis [Lithuanian Popular Front] recently had such a sweeping election victory?"'*

This was echoed by a Latvian woman who stated that whereas previously nobody had known where Latvia was:

> *'Not until, when this Perestroika started – Glasnost and Perestroika. Then everybody said, "I know where Latvia is now."'*

Among Latvians, Lithuanians and Estonians in Britain, the movement towards independence brought about a significant upsurge in community activities. Baltic refugees in Britain reported that members previously engrossed in work and family responsibilities reconnected with the communities and club attendance increased significantly.

In the late 1980s, the communities set about with renewed optimism to highlight the plight of the Baltic States among the British public, to apply pressure on the British Government to support the push for independence and to aid the nationalist movements in the homelands. Strategies designed to support the independence movements included the distribution of *samizdat* material and connecting with exiles and dissidents globally. The Baltic Council, originally formed in 1947 but operating on a mainly ad hoc basis, began to work with greater organisation and vigour to draw attention to the plight of the Baltic States among the general public and to educate people about the history and culture of the region. In 1987 and 1989, Baltic Focus was held in London, organised by the Baltic Council to publicise Latvia, Lithuania and Estonia to the people of Britain. Baltic Focus included a full programme of folk singing, dancing and exhibitions relating to the culture and history of the region.

In the late 1980s, while there was hope among the exile communities that homeland independence might be achieved, there was also an unease, based on anxiety over the Soviet regime's response to the growing nationalist movements in the Baltics. The author of an article in the *Sunday Telegraph* on 27 November 1988 suggested that apprehension was justified, given that 'Spring in the Soviet Union has traditionally been followed by winter'.

Not only was the diaspora uneasy, the communities did not at first expect any significant changes within their homelands. In 1988, in the introduction to *Latvia and Latvians*, Juris Sinka outlined the political and economic changes associated with *Glasnost* and *Perestroika* in the Soviet Union, before posing the following questions:

> *'And what about Latvia, Estonia, Lithuania and other captive non-Russian nations in the Soviet Union? Has their status altered in any way? Has life for their people changed in the direction of greater political freedom or even independence?*
>
> *'The bitter truth is that neither Gorbachev nor any other Kremlin leader has said or done anything to engender the hope that Latvia or any other captive nation would be allowed to secede from the Soviet Union and enjoy independent existence as a free and sovereign state.'*

However, developments continued apace, and in 1991, less than three years after Sinka's projections, Latvia, Lithuania and Estonia regained their independence. In Britain, celebrations took time to get under way, as the diaspora waited for the consolidation of independence and particularly for recognition by the United Nations and Soviet Union. A Lithuanian mother and daughter stated that when independence was declared there were no celebrations at the Manchester Club: 'Not in our club. London maybe, but we were all glued to the telly'.

Many Latvians, Lithuanians and Estonians felt rather cut off from events in the homeland and it took time for the reality of independence to sink in. Many feared that it would not last. I asked a Latvian how he felt when Latvia became independent again. He replied: 'Oh, delighted, delighted, but [it] could be short-lived'. News that the Soviet Union had recognised the independence of the three Baltic States on 6 September 1991, followed by membership of the United Nations on 17 September, provided some reassurance, although some members of the diaspora retain a concern about the permanency of independence even today.

As independence finally became a reality, the diaspora began to wonder about the consequences for the homeland. The Baltic communities in Britain felt that while independence was a happy event, it was not so much independence in itself, but what it brought, which was the most important thing. Views about the prospects for a successful transition from communism evolved over the years following independence. While most were optimistic about the future of their homeland, others felt concerned about the road ahead. One Latvian in Leeds stated bluntly: 'I don't think they will make anything out of it.' In 1992, Juris Sinka wrote in the introduction to the Australian edition of *Latvia and Latvians* that Latvia remained in a 'rather precarious situation', and that:

> '*Unfortunately, the freedom and independence for whose recovery the Latvians have fought, suffered and died are accompanied by problems which have considerably dampened the initial euphoria and must be solved if Latvia is to become viable as a state again.*'

As well as evaluating the consequences of independence for the homeland, the diaspora also began to assess the meaning for themselves both as individuals and as communities. One thing was clear – the aim of independence for which they had been working towards for so long had now been achieved, and, consequently, Latvians, Lithuanians and Estonians in Britain were no longer exiles or refugees. They were now free to return to the homeland, and, for the first time, they would be able to choose whether to live in Britain or the homeland. They would also be free to visit, meet up with family and visit childhood towns and villages. In a few cases, they would be able to visit or even return to live in their former homes, or family homes. Shortly after independence, they were also able to apply for passports from their new Embassies in London. Almost everyone who could returned to their homeland to visit during the first few years of independence, a highly emotional experience. For some, contact was made with long lost friends and relatives for the first time. Visiting experiences were mixed, but overall positive. A Latvian woman described her first visit to Riga in 1992 with her Latvian husband:

> *'It was very emotional. There were quite a few people [who] met us at the airport and they have this habit of going to meet you at the airport with flowers, and I ended up with lots of them, so I said, "Can you park me at the Freedom Monument?" and they said, "Well, if we can find a space," and I said "Right we'll go there", and I took all the flowers and laid them at the Monument because that's what people did in those days and when I got back to where we were staying with my husband's nephew she'd got all vases. She said, "I'm sure you've been given lots of flowers," and I said, "Yeah, but they're all at the Monument." Because people used to do that you know. It's like re-addressing Riga again, coming back and signing on again ...'*

A Lithuanian man living in Manchester was asked, 'How has the restoration of independence changed your life as a Lithuanian in Great Britain?'

> *'Change inside, it has changed very, very much. We were all pleased that Lithuania is free ... I went for a holiday to see my family and I felt free, going to anywhere I wanted, doing anything I wanted. When the Soviets were running the country, I went twice, but then from the radius of the hotel [you could] only go [a] radius [of] ten kilometres, so we felt like prisoners in the camp.'*

Following the restoration of independence, he travelled to Lithuania in 1992:

> *'I visited the place where I growing and I visited my relations in different towns and where I lived ...'*

The importance of opened links to family was expressed by a Lithuanian woman who stated that independence affected the Lithuanian community in Britain, 'in a sense that there was almost like a sigh of relief. You could actually feel the sigh of relief, because it opened the doors to their families...' A Lithuanian woman living in Nottingham described the importance of the freedom to travel freely without fear:

> 'You feel free, because I can speak on the road freely. I'm not frightened. Russia time if I met my relations ... I [was] frightened.'

Many of the refugees spoke about the shock they experienced upon seeing relatives for the first time in fifty years. Sisters, brothers, parents and cousins were now fifty years older, and many of the former refugees could barely recognise them nor the other way around. One Latvian man talked about his experiences upon return to the homeland in 1992:

> 'I went back, just spur of the moment I decided. There was a seat free – chartered plane. I went home and I didn't expect to meet anybody, any relations but as it happened I found some [had] been to Siberia, come back, broken mentally and physically by it. Died. Just last year, one died, two of them died. So ... sister still is okay. Shock when ... seen her before the war and when I see her now ... shock like you can't overcome. Well, that's how it is.'

Not all those who visited the homeland were shocked by what they found, particularly those who had visited with the Soviet travel agency, *Intourist* during the Soviet period, when despite the lack of freedom to travel, they were often able to invite relatives to meet them at the hotel they were staying in. Others who had communicated regularly may have sent photographs. A Latvian from Leeds, stated that:

> 'I didn't meet a great deal of people that I didn't know. I knew some of my neighbours, ex-neighbours and so on, and they were just the same as I remembered them then and with all my family I didn't have any difficulty whatever.'

179

One of the main changes experienced through visits was the dramatic alteration in the rural and urban landscapes. Most felt that industrial and urban developments had been detrimental. A Latvian man living in Leeds, Bruno, explained how his home village had changed:

> 'A lot of it is different now, I mean the village there used to be just like a little centre there. It's like a little town, with streets now. There was no streets before, there were just roads going that way and that way and that's it. But the place is there. The place is there. And that's what matters so much. That's why I said as soon as there was [a] chance to go, we went.'

Bruno first revisited Latvia with his family in 1990, even before independence had been secured:

> 'You see I said that as soon as I can go back where I like and see who I like in Latvia I'll go back, because it's been so dear to me, everything, I've grown up there as a child … it's in me. I'm part of all that. A lot of people don't want to go back because they think it will be all different. Of course, it will be different. I know when I went there I felt sad. Well you feel sad either way. But it's there. To be there. To feel it.'

The deterioration of the urban and rural landscape was stark, but some returning refugees felt that the industrial and urban developments were largely positive. One Lithuanian returnee stated:

> 'Well, I'm in a minority because when I came and when I saw how Lithuania [had] changed since I saw it last I was very pleased. I noticed electrification. I noticed the road system. I noticed improvements outside the towns, so many ships. We've now got a navy, with accepted war ships. The improvement in air travel – there was no air travel when I left. Cities [are] most probably not to my liking, because this is the pattern of the Soviet architecture but again it fulfils its function. New communities are [being] built up, so it's quite nice, and there's quite desirable residential places, so I've found many changes. Most of them are favourable, I mean I favoured.'

Many people noticed negative changes to Latvians, Lithuanians and Estonians in the homeland, particularly in terms of attitudes and character. Most of the members of the diaspora blame the years of Soviet occupation for this. One Latvian woman, asked if she felt that the mentality of Latvians had changed since the interwar period replied:

> 'Yes ... To our opinion they ... they don't care. I suppose they are improving now, but they didn't care very much about their surroundings ... I thought we were very, tidy, very clean and like the Europeans. I can explain this, that when we came, first we came to Germany during the war and we didn't feel that we were a lower class ... we felt equal and that was the same when we came here.
>
> 'But now, when we had the visitors [from the homeland], to start with they said, "Oh we're just poor people, we're just country people and we don't have anything," and they feel that they are [a] lower class than they used to be and I think it is because of the Russians.'

A final aspect noticed, particularly by Latvians and Estonians, was the presence of Russians, especially in the capital cities, and, related to this, the lingering usage of Russian, particularly during the early post-independence years, even among ethnic Latvians, Lithuanians and Estonians. One Latvian found that on his first visit to Latvia after independence, '... going into shops in Riga ... there was hardly anybody [that] wanted to speak Latvian ... and they were very obstinate ...' Although more Russians spoke Latvian when he returned in 1995, 'apart from what they had to sell me or tell me in the shop ... no further conversation was possible at all.'

Another Latvian explained how disappointed the diaspora visitors were, when they saw how Latvians in the homeland had grown accustomed to having Russians around:

> ... 'people are a bit disappointed here, because over the fifty years that they've been under the Soviet regime, they got used to having Russians around ... You go along and hear a Russian in Riga and it sends shivers down your spine.'

Although many Latvians, Lithuanians and Estonians in Britain managed to visit their homeland, sometimes as often as once a year, many were unable to, due to poor health, and a few actively chose not to. There were several reasons for this decision. Perhaps the most common was a desire to retain untainted the images of the homeland from a pre-war child-hood. Some of those without family or friends felt there was little point in returning if there was nobody to visit. There was also the fear among some that returning to the homeland would awaken painful memories. A Latvian woman living in Leeds explained her reasons for not returning to visit:

> ... 'I've never been back mostly because I haven't any relatives left, any close relatives left in Latvia. That was probably [the] main reason. And again, I was happy while I was there and they always say you should never go back where you've been happy and it's been too many years and so I've never been back really, now. That's it.'

One Latvian woman also told me that she would not return to the home-land because she felt so angry towards the Russians there and was afraid of what she might do to them if she visited Latvia.

In the decade following the restoration of independence, only a tiny minority of first generation Latvians, Lithuanians and Estonians from Great Britain returned to their homelands to live. At that time, all three communities gave very low estimates of the numbers of returnees. Precise figures are elusive. A Lithuanian returnee based in Vilnius estimated about ten Lithuanian returnees from the first generation and while the Estonian community estimated a similar number of Estonian refugees, it appeared that there were greater numbers of Latvian returnees, most likely due to the greater size of the community in Britain.

A few first generation returnees opened up shops, businesses or engaged in politics. This was much more common, however, among returning diaspora members from America, Canada, and Australia. For example, Vaira Vīķe Freiberga, who was voted in as Latvian President in June 1999, was a member of the Canadian-Latvian diaspora. Other American and Canadian Latvians also gained seats in the Latvian Parliament in 1993, as members of the 'Latvia's Way' political party.

The Lithuanian President from 1998 to 2003, and again from 2004 to 2009, was Valdas Adamkus, a member of the American Lithuanian diaspora. Adamkus had been born in Kaunas in 1926 and had joined the underground resistance against the first Soviet occupation of 1940. During the Second World War, his family fled Lithuania, in order to avoid the second Russian occupation in 1944. While living in a DP camp, he attended the University of Munich in Germany before emigrating to the United in States 1949. He returned to Lithuania in 1997.

Although they did not have such a huge impact on homeland politics, returning Latvians, Lithuanians and Estonians from Britain played important roles in the rebuilding of their homelands by setting up businesses and contributing to the economic and cultural life of the newly independent states. For example, a Latvian returnee couple from Britain opened up a hotel in Riga, the well-known '*Radi un Draugi*', owned by the DVF, and a Latvian man from Corby, Mārtiņš Rītiņš, set up a restaurant '*Vincents,*' on *Elizabetes iela*, a very successful, upmarket restaurant right in the heart of Riga. Mārtiņš was born in a DP camp in Germany in 1949 and went to Latvia to open the restaurant in the early 1990s. Among the many famous people who have dined at *Vincents* are Prince Charles, Elton John and Heston Blumenthal. In 2007, Mārtiņš was awarded the Order of the Three Stars (*Triju Zvaigžņu ordenis*), a prestigious national award for service to Latvia.

A Lithuanian man who had been very active in the British Lithuanian community returned to Lithuania from where he edited the newspaper *Europos Lietuvis* for a period, and contributed greatly to the British Lithuanian community in post-independent Lithuania. As editor of the Lithuanian newspaper *Europos Lietuvis* ('Europe's Lithuanian'), he saw an opportunity after independence had been declared, to take the paper to Lithuania and edit it from Vilnius. In doing so, he hoped to make the paper more profitable, after a period of financial difficulties while it had been published in England. He returned to Vilnius in the autumn of 1992. He described why he had come:

> '*This was a sort of homecoming because I always wanted to be in Lithuania. I saw in this a chance, not only to come, but to come as a working man.*'

Some retired returnees wanted to return to their homelands to spend their retirement years. Many had very active social lives and some earned extra money by teaching English to supplement their pensions.

A small number of second generation Latvians, Lithuanians and Estonians also migrated to the Baltic States, most frequently on a temporary basis often for educational or employment purposes. The increasing number of international firms established in the Baltic States since independence and of universities running courses geared towards foreign students stimulated this type of migration. One second generation Latvian took on the running of his parents' former farmstead whilst also being heavily engaged in agricultural politics.

A small number of Latvians, Lithuanians and Estonians from Britain returned to the homeland simply because they wanted to die there. A Lithuanian woman explained: 'I think it's probably…because they started their lives in Lithuania, they want to finish their life in Lithuania'.

A Latvian returnee in Riga summed up the main reason for his return in 1997: 'Well it's the roots. It's home you know.' However, he also talked about other considerations for his decision to return to Latvia:

> *'They're all dying out the Latvians [in Britain] … and I was getting a bit lonely and not direct family, sisters, I don't have any left, but loads of cousins and … a nephew and they're all around here [Riga] and out in the country, further up, up north from here.'*

The fact that he was single with no children gave him the flexibility to return. Many of the returnees were single or widowed, and a few Latvian, Lithuanian and Estonian couples also returned. A spouse's lack of desire to live in the Baltic States was often a significant reason for not returning. However, one Lithuanian man returned to Vilnius to live, despite his wife's opposition. His overwhelming desire to return meant that he did so, even though this meant leaving his wife in England. He explained:

> *'Family conflict became apparent, because my wife didn't want to come. Reasons? I don't know even today, but there was probably some apprehension, some … well there was something but she definitely stated that she did not want to come.'*

A few non-Baltic spouses did agree to live in the homeland, although this was rare. and often this experiment was unsuccessful. One man returned to Latvia, initially accompanied by his English wife and children, his Latvian parents and grandparents, with the intention of reclaiming the family farm and transforming it into a working farm. He explained his reasons for returning:

'It was a very difficult decision. It was a decision based on many factors and it's difficult to put it down to one factor. An import-ant factor was that because both my parents were Latvian and I lived with my grandparents in England who were also Latvian from my mother's side, brought up in a Latvian community or very close to a Latvian community, I knew a lot about Latvia. There were a lot of hopes that Latvia developed very quickly on its first declaration of independence after the First World War. It was looked upon as our hopes, opportunities to develop along with the country as one thing. For ourselves, the other thing was that we lived in a town in England and I'd always had an interest in farming and it was not possible to do in England, yet I always wanted to do farming, so I came to Latvia where I was able to have a farm.'

Unfortunately, his wife returned to England with one of the children and it was uncertain what the future held. Like many returnees, this Latvian faced a variety of challenges after the move to the homeland, including hostility from locals and burglary of farm machinery. However, he per-sisted and after joining a large farmers' association, began to integrate successfully into Latvian society. Like many members of the second gen-eration, he had a dual identity, and when asked where he belonged, would jokingly reply, 'On the Moon', a statement that nevertheless reflected the feeling that he did not fully belong either in England or in Latvia.

Many first generation returnees also felt they had 'dual identities'. One Latvian returnee who was living in Riga felt that he might, in the future, spend six months of every year in Latvia and six months in Britain, as once returning to Latvia he realised that he did not want to shed all ties with Britain. Subsequently, he decided to live indefinitely in Latvia, but to visit Britain regularly.

An Estonian in Britain told the story of an Estonian woman who returned to her homeland, having spent years looking out of her win-dow in Sheffield and longing for the homeland. Once back in the home-land, she looked out of her window and longed for Sheffield. Even for the small minority of returnees from Britain who felt certain that the homeland was their home, bonds to Britain remained. Returnees brought with them values and culture influenced by fifty years of life in Britain, and had to adapt to a very different country from that which they left half a century earlier. A Lithuanian returnee explained:

> 'I have no complaints, no regrets, and once or twice I went back to England, I went like a visitor, and after about a week or two weeks I wanted to go home. I don't miss it [England] at all.'

However, he also stated that:

> 'If for instance Britain was in some sort of danger or some sort, needed some sort of support, of course I'll be first there. It was, it gave me [a] second home, it still is a home of my family, my former family, my ... son and daughter.'

Returnees were initially treated rather cautiously, but gradually became accepted back into society, and as the countries re-orientated themselves towards Europe, the views and opinions of returnees became respected to the extent that, as already noted, some gained important positions in the political and economic spheres.

The vast majority of first generation refugees, however, did not return to their homelands to live. While some were unable to return due to poor health or financial reasons and therefore had no choice, the majority made an active decision not to return, citing a mixture of practical and identity-based considerations.

Among the practical reasons mentioned, perhaps the most important explanation provided was age, the fact that they were too old to start again. One Latvian stated simply: '[I'm] too old to go back'. Age was also the main reason cited by a Latvian lady in Derbyshire, when asked had she ever considered returning. She replied:

> 'Not really because I think if I were younger I might do because there's a lot of demand for people with English you see. You could work for a British firm or something because you'd have use of both languages ... but I mean at my age there's not much point. I think when you're in your seventies it's a bit much.'

Some of the respondents felt that they would return if they were single, including men from both intermarriages and same nationality marriages. However, after spending fifty years, that is the largest part of their life in Britain, they were too rooted to move. They had family, houses and a life in England. An elderly Latvian from Leeds described the rooting process and the role of family in the decision to stay:

'We hoped to go back to live from the beginning, but now you see we get old, we get settled here slowly. Many people married here, get children here. Our cemetery is full. Some people whose husband or wife has died don't like to leave [they] just want to stay where they are. So there it is. Some people went [have gone] back now, because you know it, from '91 it's independent again.

'I personally wanted to go back and I went several times, but my son is not going back and my wife wants to stay where the son is. How can I do it? [I am] 86 years. What will I do there? And there is no very close relatives to us, and of course if they were there, I would go back at once. Not for a better life, no, but just because that is my country and there is my people. That is only reason.'

An Estonian man also cited family as one of his main reasons for not returning.

'I never considered it [returning] seriously because of the family and I can't, it's not open, it's not an option that is open to me, but I felt that I probably could. I still feel that I probably [could] because, as long as I get income from here, then I will be reasonably all right, but I could not live with their means. If I had to exist on the pension that they are receiving, I could not.'

Another Latvian man from Leeds also felt that he would return if he was on his own:

'If I was on my own I would [return]. Because the cultural ties are stronger for me there, if I was on my own, if I didn't have a family.'

187

He even pointed out the benefits of returning to Latvia:

> *'Besides, just imagine even as a pensioner I get [a] pension about eight times more than they do. So you can imagine how well off you are.'*

Another Latvian pointed out that it cost only £2,000 to buy a house in Latvia at that time. One woman from Sheffield was reported to have built a new house in Latvia, being able to afford it due to the low prices of building materials and labour. Although the low cost of living in the homeland was cited as a benefit of returning, other factors tended to dissuade the diaspora. These included the complexities of bureaucracy, instability of banks and poor healthcare, the last factor being particularly important given the fact that the original refugees were, by then, in their late sixties or older.

Being rooted in Britain also had identity-based aspects. Although age and practical considerations have often been the most important factors in the decision to stay, others relating to identity and conceptions of home and belonging were also significant. This was summed up by the comments of a Lithuanian woman in Britain;

> *'Well, I am Lithuanian yes, but if somebody says, "Do you want to go back and live there?" I should say straight away, "No, no," because so many years gone. All the generation mostly die. The younger generation [in Lithuania] is brought up different way. It's not that way when I [was] brought up. And that make me feeling that I couldn't be there happy. I am happy here. I am very, very happy here, and yes, visit, yes, for one week, for a few days but no more.'* ·

The experience of visiting the homelands, led to shifts in identities among Latvians, Lithuanians and Estonians in Britain. One of the reasons for this was that in the homelands they were treated as foreigners. Among the characteristics distinguishing the visiting diaspora members from the locals were the different accents and for some, a loss of fluency in the homeland language. This was particularly common in the intermarried diaspora. An Estonian man described the difficulties he experienced speaking Estonian in Estonia:

... 'it does come back in a certain fashion, but you find you can't say it correct way, you kind of say things upside-down and you're looking for some word, [but] you can't get that word out, and there's certain words you just don't know; some of the trees, things like that, you just can't think of the Estonian word for it at all until you look it up in the dictionary then it comes to you.

'You see, they definitely all noticed that I had some kind of accent and you can't find the words, certain words, you have to find some other word that means the same thing

... when I go to Estonia and I listen to people, I can understand almost everything I feel like I'm Estonian, but when it comes to me to talk, to explain or to do things I find it quite difficult.'

Many of the refugees had picked up slight regional accents, for example, traces of Yorkshire or Lancashire. A Latvian man felt that when he visited Latvia he felt different from the local population there. He explained why: 'Even if I speak to them they look...You speak Latvian but it's not Latvian accent. You speak foreign accent.' Young children in Liepāja even laughed at him when he spoke: 'Yeah, they called me bloody foreigner. I spoke then in my own language like, you know in Latvian...' A Lithuanian woman had a similar experience:

'They [called] me foreigner in Lithuania now. They say, "You look foreigner." If I speak in Lithuanian, "Your accent is foreigner." I speak in Lithuanian. I am born in Lithuania. I went to high school, everything, and they [call] me foreigner still. It's upsetting.'

It was not only language or accent which singled out the visiting diaspora. A Latvian woman from Nottingham explained how the locals could tell them apart straight away:

'The Latvians in Latvia, they say they can tell us straight away because of our behaviour, how we look and how we smile, and how we talk ... we have the confidence and they don't. They could tell straight away if someone was from abroad.'

189

Visits also quashed romantic visions of pre-war homelands, which were replaced by the harsh realities of living in the Baltic States in the 1990s. Greater knowledge about standards of living along with the perceived lack of security and poor health care prompted many individuals to feel a greater sense of gratitude for their lives in Britain. One Latvian woman described her visits to the homeland:

> *'Well, the first time it was very pleasant, because we met all the relatives after so many years. But the second time, you can see behind all the scenes then. You can see what the country has become and more of their nature and I was very upset because the country was very neglected, and we travelled quite a lot, and then you realise how the people talk then as well, what their opinions are, which are quite different from ours.'*

The idea that the inhabitants of the Baltic States had in some way been *Sovietised*, and had a different way of thinking from members of the diaspora was a very common theme in the interviews. There was also an acknowledgement of how far the diaspora's own attitudes and values had changed, as a result of living in Britain. The result was an increase in feelings of difference between the local and émigré populations. Not only did many members of the diaspora hardly know their relatives when they first returned, they also realised that even relatives saw the world differently. Both these factors contributed to feelings of not belonging. One Estonian man explained:

> *'I certainly didn't feel as if I belonged in the first couple of weeks, you didn't know the people, they are relatives of mine – it was just a couple of weeks short of 40 years that I saw my brothers and sister.*
>
> *'I felt that I could live there, but that's probably deceptive, if you go as a tourist that's one thing and then you start living there is another thing, so I'm not taken as a local person by my relatives, although we are, we feel like brothers and sisters and all that, but there are differences as well. My thinking is a bit different to theirs.'*

Some members of the Latvian, Lithuanian and Estonian communities in Britain were even dissuaded from visiting the homeland through a fear of feeling 'foreign' and being regarded as foreigners. A Latvian woman from Leeds who had never returned to visit, primarily because she had no family left there, felt that she would not belong in Latvia if she returned. She linked not belonging to the fact that she felt that her Latvian identity had weakened. I asked her whether she had a stronger or weaker sense of Latvian identity than she did when she first came to Britain. She replied:

> *'Weaker, weaker, much weaker now, yes. Oh yes, I think I would probably feel an outsider if I went back to Latvia. Would feel an outsider there, definitely.*
>
> *'I don't think I would fit in anymore. No way. I've been over fifty years now in England, in Yorkshire, longer than anywhere else.'*

For some Latvians, Lithuanians and Estonians in Britain, visits further confused already contested identities. One Latvian talked about how, after visiting Latvia, he felt as if he did not belong there, but nor did he feel that he belonged in Britain:

> *'When I came [went] to Latvia, it's all different. I not fit in. We don't fit in you know. We are foreigners over there. Same as we're foreigners here. It's a tragedy in one way.'*

Another Latvian man talked about how he still felt like an 'outsider' in Britain, yet even though he felt that his identity was 'just the same' then as when he first came to Britain, he also 'felt different' when he visited Latvia.

Some Latvians, Lithuanians and Estonians felt that they belonged in both the homeland and Britain, a feeling reinforced by visits to the homeland, and were yet to reconcile the dual nature of their identities. This characteristic was described by an Estonian man living in Chesterfield, who was asked if he felt like a foreigner when he travelled to Estonia. He replied:

> *'No, I don't feel like a foreigner, but I don't particularly feel as if I belong there. That's an odd thing. If I'm in Estonia I think I'm more of a Briton than a … I think of my home, it's here, it's here. It's a very odd thing, a very odd thing. And whereas if I'm here, then I think I'm more of an Estonian than anything else.'*

A Latvian woman expressed similar views:

> *'It's rather difficult you know. You identify with the Latvian peo-*
> *ple there because you are a Latvian, but you also belong here,*
> *because you've spent, I mean I've only spent 19, hardly 19, I*
> *was just turned 19 when I left Latvia so I spent 18 years there,*
> *and I've spent 50 here, so you certainly have a sense of belong-*
> *ing here as well. I mean you've got, you know, your home and*
> *whatever you've got, you've got it here. I should say one's split*
> *sort of halfway as it were. In a way you go there and then you*
> *talk, "Oh you must go home," and at the same time, you go home*
> *and as I say, you suddenly start reckoning well, if I don't buy*
> *this and if I don't do that, then next spring I can go again, so …*
> *the pull is both ways.'*

For this woman, the presence of Russians in the homeland was one of the most important factors contributing to a feeling that she had difficulty identifying with the country in which she grew up. She explained:

> *'It's just that when you go there [Latvia], the country to which*
> *you belong doesn't quite feel the same anymore, but you still feel*
> *Latvian, it's just that you think the country's gone wrong. The*
> *country isn't quite what we left. I mean we left a country that*
> *was Latvian and you go back to Riga now and it's still Russian*
> *and a lot of the way they do things they've been made to do them*
> *the way Russians do, which we didn't do before.'*

Inevitably, the opening of links between the diaspora and the homeland engendered a shift in the goals and activities of the organised communities. The achievement of independence, the main aim of the organised community throughout exile, freed the communities to concentrate on other tasks. Independence brought the communities into a new phase of existence and led to a reassessment of their aims.

The intended role of the diaspora following the re-establishment of independence – to replant Latvian, Lithuanian and Estonian cultures and identities in the homeland – was largely defunct due to independence. Although the diaspora felt that the culture in the homeland was not as rich as it had been in interwar period, they were surprised that it had survived and had, in fact, moved on. This awareness, since independence, contributed to a belief that the residents of the homeland were quite capable of looking after themselves and that it was their responsibility to take cultures and identities forward in a way that suited them. This acknowledgement led to a reduced role for the diaspora. A Lithuanian stated that one of the effects of independence was that in part 'it closed the doors to cultural activity here. It was felt that there was no need to continue because it was already there much better and so on'. A Latvian woman expressed the post-independence realisation of the extent of the changes:

> 'There are changes [in the homeland] definitely, but then there are changes in England in fifty years. I mean there would have been changes in fifty years anywhere, because people look at things differently, but it's not quite what we left and I think it is wrong in a way to go back fifty years later and expect to find what you left isn't it?'

A Lithuanian woman also described the effect of a new awareness of culture in the homeland since independence on the communities:

> 'We thought we were the up-to-date original Lithuanians, and it was a shock to find that in fact, Lithuanians in Soviet times had moved on. There were patriotic undercurrents. They had moved on. Their culture, their ways of approaching culture were if you like, more up to date. We had actually aged. Our attitudes in that direction had aged. We were living in the past. Really that summarises it.'

Latvian, Lithuanian and Estonian cultural activities in Britain continued after homeland independence was declared, although the orientation of many of these events shifted. For example, commemorations of independence became happy, relaxed, celebrations, compared to their previous sombre, nationalist-militaristic orientation.

These events became strictly for the community in Britain, rather than a way of maintaining culture on the homeland's behalf. One change after the Soviet years was increased cultural exchange between Britain and the homeland. Dance groups, musicians and singers were invited to Britain on a regular basis to perform concerts for the diaspora and the British public. Many Latvians, Lithuanians and Estonians also attended cultural events in the homeland such as song festivals during visits. One Latvian noted that cultural activity in Britain had waned due to the popularity of such events. Speaking about the celebration of St John's Day in Britain, he noted the following:

> *'Of course there's too many old men now and the young ones are not taking part. It would have been different I think if Latvia wasn't free because everything is sort of thrown into the goings on in Latvia. They go to – next year there's a Latvian Song Festival in Riga.'*

Although the idea of the transplantation of cultures and identities back into the homeland became regarded as somewhat inappropriate, the communities did feel that they still had some role in helping to re-build their homeland. As well as individuals helping their families financially in various ways, the communities undertook important charitable work on behalf of schools and communities in the homeland, and played a minor role in the politics, economies and cultures of the homelands. The communities also increased charitable donations for the benefit of the homeland, primarily since the passage of goods became far easier. For example, the Latvian club in Leeds regularly sent parcels of clothes, shoes and other goods to Latvia. A Latvian woman talked about the over-whelming desire to help relatives and locals in the homeland:

> *'We think a lot about the people in Latvia. You want to help them. At first we used to send parcels and clothes, although we've been sending parcels all these years, but not very [often] you know, approximately twice a year because they used to be big parcels. They used to be about 44lb.*
>
> *'And the first few years we were really … you know you thought yes, we'll do this and we'll do that and now we real-ise this is going to the extremes, and no, I have to pull myself together and we do get things when we go, but we've certainly calmed down.'*

Another way of helping relatives was to hand over to them, or allow them to live in, properties reclaimed by the diaspora. Many Latvians, Lithuanians

194

and Estonians in Britain were unable or unwilling to restore and live in the properties themselves. A Latvian woman from Nottingham described how she and her Latvian husband helped relatives in Latvia. She began by talking about the reclamation of her husband's father's house:

> ... '[he] has got his father's house where his brother and the family who stayed in Latvia lived, but he didn't want to claim half of it, so he gave it to his sister-in-law. We still have to help out. They need a new roof, but we are helping because you feel sorry for them as well because now she's a pensioner, so she can't save any money, and our god-daughter who is the niece, she's our god-daughter and she's got a job locally but it doesn't pay much, so we have to help.'

Another aspect of the communities' new relationship with the homeland was the ability for all those with Latvian, Lithuanian or Estonian citizenship to vote in homeland elections and thus influence the life of the country.

Following the declarations of independence, Latvian, Lithuanian and Estonian Ambassadors and Embassies were restored in London. In addition to the traditional functions of Embassies, these undertook important work with the diaspora, including supporting social, cultural and political activities. They also carried out important campaigning work on behalf of the homelands, supporting applications for asylum in Britain and coordinating a variety of activities between the diaspora and groups and organisations in the homelands.

In addition, the Baltic Council, which was established in 1947 to undertake joint campaigning and to work towards closer political, economic, social and cultural ties between the Baltic States and Great Britain, continued, with representatives of the three Baltic communities as members. According to *LYNES*, in 1999, one of the main functions of the Baltic Council in the 1990s was to 'campaign for admission of the Baltic States into the European Union and NATO'. It also held regular commemorative services in London marking the June 1941 deportations. Other groups and associations also came into being to disseminate information about the Baltic States in the Western World and to discuss the various options for the Baltic States' political future. Examples included 'The British-Baltic Association', linked with the University of Bradford, and 'The Baltic Committee' in Bradford.

Independence not only stimulated visits and return migration from Britain to the homelands, it also led to migration from the homelands to Britain. This migration consisted of three main types: educational or cultural migration which was intended as temporary; economic migration which was an attempt find better jobs and a higher standard of living; and thirdly, there were those who came to Britain as political refugees seeking asylum. The third category was particularly numerous in the mid-to-late 1990s, as minority groups in the Baltic States sought asylum from policies which initially curtailed the rights of minority groups, particularly in Latvia and Estonia. It took several years for all three independent nations to introduce policies regarding minority groups, and of them, Lithuania's were the most tolerant. In Latvia and Estonia, governments initially introduced discriminatory policies towards the Russian-speaking minority, although these were later modified as a requirement of EU membership.

Small minority groups such as the Roma were also subject to discrimination and hostility in some areas, and in all three countries, many of the officials associated with the former Soviet authorities left the countries due to aggression and intimidation by locals. It is not clear how many of those who sought asylum were granted it, but it is likely to be a small number. Overall, during the period from 1994 to 2004, 75 per cent of all asylum applications in the UK were turned down.

The newcomers headed mainly for London and other large cities in Britain, and many approached the established communities for support. The addition of these new migrants into the established communities brought about some revitalisation, particularly in London. However, tensions also emerged. Lithuanians composed the largest number of migrants to Britain of the three Baltic countries. The Home Office cited Lithuania as one of the top 35 asylum producing countries in the United Kingdom in 1999. It was partly due to their large number that the impact of these so-called 'new migrants' on the established communities was most significant among the Lithuanian community.

UNHCR statistics state that in 1998, the monthly average of Lithuanians applying for asylum in Britain was 100. During the first eleven months of 1998, '1,170 Lithuanian asylum seekers arrived in Britain', 'second only to Turkey and the former Yugoslavia'. Numbers of Lithuanian asylum applicants dropped in 1999. In January 1999, applications for asylum numbered eighty-six, and in February 1999, only twenty-five. The decline was attributed to the implementation by the Lithuanian authorities of new measures requested by the British government at a meeting in London between the Lithuanian Minister for the Interior and the Secretary of the British Home Office on 19 January 1999. New measures included passengers on flights from Lithuania to London providing more detailed information about their travel, and their personal information being recorded by officers of the national migration service at Vilnius Airport. Border checks on buses leaving Lithuania were also stepped up.[1]

Relations between the post-war Latvian, Lithuanian and Estonian communities and the later migrants and refugees were not always amicable. During the first half of 1999, *LYNES* and *Europos Lietuvis* discussed the tensions arising between the so-called 'New Lithuanians' and the 'British Lithuanians'. *LYNES* stressed the term 'British Lithuanians' to highlight their distinctiveness and differences from the 'New Lithuanians'. In February 1999, it reported that 'New Lithuanians' in London had already established a new branch of DBLS at Lithuanian House, Freeland Road in London, with a membership of 100 and rising. The editor asked: 'Is this a take-over by the new Liths?'. His concerns were that:

> ... 'many are political asylum seekers having only a temporary license to reside in this country. They are not keen to include the British Liths in their circle of activities. Where do we British Liths stand in this encroaching foray on our community assets? There were 800 DBLS members in Gt. Britain last year. If a new branch registers with over 400 members, its representatives have the power to nominate and elect their own directors to control the British Lithuanian assets in this country. In other words, a complete takeover.'

Many British Lithuanians were aware that the community did need 'new blood' but did not want the new Lithuanians to become the dominant force in the community. In previous years, the input of new blood was regarded as a positive development.

Despite the flurry of activity in the initial years after independence, as the new millennium approached, the numbers of Latvians, Lithuanians and Estonians attending clubs and community activities in Britain continued to decline. Many of the original first generation refugees had passed away, and the majority of second generation members took limited interest in their Baltic heritage. Second and third generation members were,

197

by now, well integrated into British life, and clubs and associations were suffering a seemingly irreversible decline in participation levels.

One Latvian in Nottingham estimated that while there were over 300 Latvians in the Nottingham area, when she first arrived in 1950, there were only 100 or 150 by the end of the 1990s, suggesting that over half of the original population had passed away. A Latvian woman explained why in addition to the declining population, the number of Latvians attending the Latvian club in Nottingham had decreased: '… a lot of them don't come now. But you can understand if you are old and you don't want to travel. We live so near, but we don't go very often'.

Despite this huge decline in numbers, the Latvian community's two main organisations: *Daugavas Vanagi* and 'The Latvian National Council in Great Britain', remained very active. *Daugavas Vanagi* (DVF), also known as the Latvian Welfare Fund, continued to be a strong support for the Latvian communities in Britain, owning multiple club buildings and benefiting from international DVF backing. In 1995, the DVF bought a hotel in Riga – *Radi un Draugi*, which proved to be a very fruitful business venture, as a popular hotel among Latvians from Britain during their trips to Riga. The hotel, in the heart of the old town of Riga, has been successful both financially and in helping the DVF to bring Latvians across the world together. The hotel was later extended, modernised and refurbished, and now houses a very successful restaurant *Niklāvs*.

In addition to *Radi un Draugi*, the DVF in Britain, continued to successfully run Catthorpe Manor and the London Latvian Centre. The London Latvian Centre at 72, Queensborough Terrace, one of London's most desirable streets right next to Hyde Park, also housed a guesthouse for visiting Latvians to London, as well as the wider population. The DVF's aims and purpose were noted on its website as follows:

> *'Over the decades, the DV members perpetuated their mission to gather and unite Latvians for the preservation of the Latvian nation. For many years, this was interpreted as a tireless struggle in defence of Latvia's right to freedom, which earned DV the eternal hate of the Soviet occupiers. DV has also striven to foster the education and involvement of young Latvians in the expatriate Latvian community providing stipends to students and facilitating the work of Latvian schools, choirs, folk dance groups, theatre troupes, sports teams, and various other cultural activities.'*

Although some club branches were closed during the latter part of the twentieth century, the DVF was remarkably successful in maintaining clubhouses and branches in many areas. The booklet *Latvians in Great Britain* noted that in 1978, there were 32 branches of the DVF in Britain. In 2000, the overwhelming majority remained, including branches in South Wales, Wolverhampton, Catthorpe Manor (*Straumēni*), Carlisle, Leicester and Nottingham. In Yorkshire and Lancashire alone, six clubs with social clubs were listed by a Latvian in Leeds, in 1997, at Bolton, Bradford, Doncaster, Huddersfield, Halifax and Leeds.

The 'Latvian National Council in Great Britain' also maintained its traditional function – to extend the work done by the DVF in social, cultural and political fields and serving the interests of the British Latvian community. In addition, the Latvian Lutheran Evangelical Church continued to fulfil the religious and spiritual needs of the Latvian Lutheran community. Ministers visited various Latvian communities regularly, giving services at local churches. Rowfant House in Sussex, which had been run by the Latvian Lutheran Church since the 1950s continued to be run for the Latvian community, while earning additional income through weddings and functions. Almeley House was sold in 1999, but *Straumēni* at Catthorpe Manor, remained very active as a retirement home and hosting cultural events, as did *Mūsmājas* at Wolston near Coventry, which continued to provide retirement accommodation for Latvians in Britain for some years after independence.

The Latvian community issued several publications, including *Brīvā Latvija*, a European-wide Latvian paper published weekly from Catthorpe Manor in Leicestershire. As the internet became increasingly popular *Brīvā Latvija* as with many others, published news and information on its own website which increased readership levels particularly among second and third generation Latvians. Latvians in different localities also published their own newsletters, for example the DVF branches in the East Midlands (Chesterfield, Derby, Leicester, Mansfield, Nottingham) published a bi-monthly information bulletin: '*Mūsu Balss*' ('Our Voice').

Latvian youth organisations also remained active, including the British branch of 'The Association of Latvian Youth in Europe' and the youth section of 'The Latvian National Council in Great Britain'. Weekend language schools persisted in some areas, for example on a trip with the Latvian club in Leeds in 1995, I learned that about 12 children attended Latvian language classes in the schoolroom on Saturday mornings.

Among Latvians in Britain, St John's Day on Midsummer's Eve and Latvian National Independence Day continued to be the most important events in the annual calendar. A Latvian woman explained how Latvians in Nottingham celebrated National Independence Day on 18 November:

> *'Well, there's usually a talk and singing these days we hold it at the club and there's usually refreshments. People sit at the table and in the club we can't have concerts really, but before we used to have a dance even. We used to have a concert in one of the big halls before and either a choir or a soloist, and we had records and dance afterwards.'*

Although these events were well attended, the numbers going to the clubs to drink and chat on a regular weekly basis continued to fall.

As the middle in size of the three communities, the Lithuanian community also suffered a major decline in participation during the years leading up to the new millennium. Without the international backing that the Latvian organisation had from the DVF, the main organisation of the Lithuanian community, the DBLS, was relatively fragile. Lithuanian House Ltd. continued as before to manage the financial affairs of the Lithuanian community. It is notable that some ventures such as the newspaper *Europos Lietuvis*, were subsidised by Lithuanian House, as due to low readership levels, it was unable to be self-sustaining during this period. LYNES noted in 1998 that attempts had been made to publish the paper in Lithuania following independence, with the aim of reducing costs, but this was unsuccessful and publication was moved back to Britain. New equipment was bought to publish the paper and assistance was sought from new members of the Lithuanian community, as it was noted that: '…those times have gone where persons within the community were willing or able to give a written contribution without a fee, or for a small honorarium. The few remaining today would not be able to fill its pages on a regular basis… Consequently, assistance was sought from new Lithuanian arrivals to this country'.[2] In 1998, Lithuanian House was subsidising the paper at a cost of £10,000 per annum. Unfortunately, *Europos Lietuvis* later collapsed.

The Lithuanian Youth News-sheet, LYNES continued until 2005, when it also ceased publication. The Lithuanian Scouts' journal, *Budekimė*, also ended, although scouting remained very popular among the

Lithuanian community. However, despite growing financial issues and falling membership, the DBLS remained remarkably active. Although several branches closed during the 1980s, clubhouses or Lithuanian centres were maintained in London, Nottingham, Manchester, Bradford and Bellshill. According to LYNES, as of January 1999, there were twenty-two branches of the Lithuanian Association in Great Britain. In 1998 and 1999, the DBLS appeared to be expanding, benefiting from the post-independence migrants, with the opening of several new clubs, and the closure and re-opening of the Sodyba branch (re-named Sodas branch). Two branches, at Leicester and Northampton, re-opened after being wound up in the early 1980s. In 1999, LYNES reported that a new branch, Lithuanian House, Freeland Road in Ealing was opened, composed entirely of 'new' Lithuanian migrants. *Sodyba*, the Lithuanian retirement home and holiday centre in Hampshire, also continued to serve the Lithuanian community, hosting annual cultural events, scouting festivals and a variety of dance and music performances.

The Lithuanian community also had its own church, St Casimir's, at The Oval in London, which was very active, holding regular services and providing a venue for marriages, christenings and funerals. St Casimir's benefited from post-independence migration from Lithuania to London, during this period. In Nottingham, the Lithuanian Marian Fathers (*Židinys*) had a chapel in Hound Road, which continued to hold regular services in Lithuanian, and other events and facilities for the Lithuanian community in the area, including a library. Services were also sustained in other areas through visiting priests: apart from London and Nottingham, *LYNES* noted in 1999, that Roman Catholic Church services were held regularly in Bradford, Eccles, Manchester, Derby, Sodyba, and Bellshill, Lanark (Scotland).

LYNES estimated in January 1999 that over 80 per cent of DBLS branch members were over seventy years, so the participation of the second generation was key to the future of the organised Lithuanian community during this period. The problem of maintaining interest among younger generations can be seen by looking at the circulation figures of *LYNES*, the Lithuanian Youth Newsheet. In January 1999, the editor noted that '*LYNES* has a readership of 114'. *LYNES* also noted that 94 per cent of its' readership was over 36 years old, and half were over 51. The editor also noted that the DBLJS had only twenty-five members in 1998, but even so, described the association as 'reasonably active'. The Lithuanian youth organisation, the DBLJS (*Didžiosios Britanijos Lietuvių Jaunimo Sąjunga* – Lithuanian Youth Association in Great Britain), which was intended initially for Lithuanians between 16 and 35 years old, had many members in their thirties and forties, and few younger Lithuanians.

Due to low attendance, almost all of the clubs, including some in London, were only open at weekends and possibly one day in the week at the time of the research. For example, the Lithuanian club in Manchester was open on Saturdays, Sundays and Mondays. The Lithuanian Sports and Social Club in Victoria Park Road in London was open on Fridays, Saturdays and Sundays. At the Manchester Lithuanian Club, a medium-sized club, unless there was a special event, a Lithuanian regular attendee estimated that only about six or seven Lithuanians attended on Saturdays. Once a month, when a Lithuanian Church service was held at a local Catholic Church, St. Chad's, the numbers rose and people attended from different parts of Manchester and surrounding areas, including Rochdale. One Lithuanian woman estimated that about thirty participated in the church service. The Lithuanian Church, St Casimir's in London experienced an upturn in attendance due to the new Lithuanian migrants, and the Catholic organisation, *Židinys* in Nottingham also continued to flourish.

A leaflet produced by the Estonian Association in 1997, suggested that the Estonian community numbered 1,000. This compares to an initial number of approximately 5,000 Estonians (5,154 Estonians, with 504 dependants) migrating to Britain as part of the EVW schemes by December 1950. Despite this, at the end of the twentieth century, the 'Association of Estonians in Great Britain' (*Inglismaa Eestlaste Ühing*) remained active, and maintained three Estonian clubs, in London, Leicester and Bradford, as well as several societies in other areas, including those representing ex-servicemen and the younger generations. The Estonian Association in Great Britain described its functions on its website:

'Since 1991 Estonians have seen the re-establishment of independence as a sovereign state, have visited their homeland, have welcomed relatives and friends to these shores and continued to support the association and its member organisations in their aim to provide for the cultural welfare of the Estonian community.

'In the words of the late ambassador, August Torma, "We strove to bring together into groups the widespread Estonian

exiles in this country, in order to achieve closer co-operation and achieve an effective network between them. This was a necessary precursor to the continued existence of our culture in exile."'

Although a small community, the Estonian community in Britain benefited from a small number of dedicated and active members and active community participants. For example, the community newspaper *Eesti Hääl*, continued to be run successfully by a small team of dedicated individuals. The newsletter continued to be mainly published in Estonian, with a few smaller articles written in English, which contrasted with the largely English-language Lithuanian youth newsletter LYNES.

Tulevik (The Future), the Estonian communities' youth association, established in 1974 by second generation Estonians, continued to be very active. The aim of *Tulevik* was noted on its website: 'The purpose of the group was, and still is, to promote and preserve the Estonian language and culture'. The website noted that group met four times a year at Catthorpe Manor (the Latvian retirement home) near Rugby and organised the annual Estonian Children's Summer Camp in the UK. *Tulevik*, along with the Association of Estonians in Great Britain, also organised the *'Rahvapidu'* at Catthorpe Manor, the main Estonian gathering of the year in Britain.

Changes to the Latvian, Lithuanian and Estonian communities in Britain during the ten years after Latvian, Lithuanian and Estonian independence, were to be amplified in the subsequent decades, as Latvia, Lithuania and Estonia joined the European Union, allowing free movement of labour and people across Europe.

CHAPTER 9

'This is our home now!' –
The migration of Latvians, Lithuanians
and Estonians to Britain since 2004

'When we go on holiday to Lithuania and it's time to go back to Boston we say "we're going home." This is our home now. We have a little pain in our hearts for our country. We still dream of going back there but we have a business here and our little one is going to school and will be a proper English girl.'

(Post-EU Lithuanian migrant interviewed by Emily Dugan, Finding Home*)*

'When my Grandfather died, we discovered photographs and lots of them. As a refugee travelling from place to place you would only carry what was important, what kept you alive and these photographs survived. They were important to them. Every single one. When you look at them closely they all tell a tale, a tale that I wanted to find out about. Years have passed, it's a new generation. Maybe now is the time to start looking deeper, delving into the past. Finding out who the people are in all these old photographs, before they fade forever. You start delving deeper. These are special, the people in them are real. You want to find who they are. Suddenly they start to come alive. Things are changing!'

Alexandra Māzers, Another Country Called Home

At the end of the twentieth century, despite the initial excitement and flurry of activity around the restoration of homeland independence, Latvian, Lithuanian and Estonian clubs and associations in Britain

204

continued to face problems of falling membership. The on-going decline in attendance figures put severe financial pressure on many clubs, particularly the smaller branches, and some began to close. Although the communities continued to attract a small hardcore of participants who took part in cultural activities and celebrate days of national significance, attempts to attract and maintain second and third generation members were largely unsuccessful. At this time, it was mainly the community branches in London and other major cities that remained vibrant, benefiting from visiting students, newer migrants and important political, social and cultural events and activities.

However, just four years later in 2004, the entry of Latvia, Lithuania and Estonia into the European Union led to significant migration from these countries to Britain, and consequently, a transformation of the Baltic communities in Great Britain. The new rights given to Latvians, Lithuanians and Estonians to live and work in Britain, as a result of EU membership meant that tens of thousands chose to do so, leading to an unprecedented migration from all three countries to Britain. This led to a significant revitalisation of existing community structures as well as the establishment of new structures to serve the needs of the newly arriving immigrants. Twelve years later, as this book was being written, many have chosen to stay, to bring up children here and to plan for their futures in Britain. In short, for many Latvians, Lithuanians and Estonians, Britain was once again, *becoming home.*

Unlike the post war arrivals comprised of refugees, the newcomers were primarily economic migrants who wanted a better life, wider opportunities and a higher standard of living. They came in unprecedented numbers, especially Lithuanians, whose country was hit particularly hard by the global economic recession. The extent to which migration from the Baltic States took place as a result of EU membership, can be seen by some research from the Office for National Statistics which analysed data from the Worker Registration Scheme (WRS) for the period immediately after EU membership, from May 2004 to December 2006.

Workers from the three Baltic States and the other five countries joining the EU in 2004 (Czech Republic, Hungary, Poland, Slovakia and Slovenia), a group collectively known as the A8, were required to register on the Worker Registration Scheme to take up employment in the UK. The data shows that while Poles constituted the largest number of migrants to the UK from all A8 countries, Lithuanians were the second greatest in number. During the first few years following EU membership, they made up ten per cent of the A8 total, and headed primarily to areas in London, the South East, the North East, Northern Ireland, Eastern England and parts of Cornwall and Herefordshire. Over 50,000 Lithuanians arrived in Britain during the first three years after EU membership, a significant number.

The geographical pattern of Latvians within the UK was similar and they made up over 5 per cent (28,810 people) of the A8 total migration to the UK from 2004–06. Particular concentrations of Latvians were found to be in the Outer Hebrides of Scotland and the East Riding of Yorkshire, as well as the more traditional areas around London and the South East.

Estonians were fewer in number, amounting to under 6,000 in the three years following EU membership and only 1 per cent of the A8 total. They headed primarily for London, as well as areas of the South East, Wales, South Lanarkshire and Northamptonshire.

Over the course of subsequent years, these migration patterns broadly continued, with Lithuanians forming the highest number of migrants to the UK of the three Baltic nationalities, and Estonians the smallest. In part, this reflected the difference in population size of the three countries, with Lithuania having the highest population (approximately 3 million in 2012, and Estonia the smallest (an estimated 1.1 million in 2011), with Latvia falling between the two, at just over 2 million in 2011. Another reason cited by Helen Pidd in an article in *The Guardian* newspaper in early 2013, is that Lithuanians suffered particularly badly from the effects of the global recession, with public spending cuts of 30 per cent across the board in 2009, which led to a spike in Lithuanian migration to Britain in 2010.

Compared to the number of Poles migrating to Britain, the number of Lithuanians migrating to the UK has been relatively small. However, it is still highly significant and considerably outnumbers those who migrated in the period following the Second World War. Census data from 2011 shows the extent of Lithuanian migration, recording a figure of 97,083 Lithuanians in England and Wales, including almost 40,000 in London. The highest concentration of Lithuanians in London, was in the borough of Newham, which, according to the 2011 Census, had 8348 Lithuanian residents, compared to a 2001 population of just 360. Official census data is, however, regarded as an underestimate by the Lithuanian community which has suggested that as of 2013, there were approximately 200,000

Lithuanians in the UK (including Scotland and Northern Ireland), with 100,000 of them in London. It is argued that census figures underestimate true numbers as landlords put pressure on migrants not to complete census forms and because the census recorded place of birth rather than ethnicity, so it did not include Lithuanians born in England and Wales (i.e. second and third generation Lithuanians).

Data from National Insurance registrations (NINO's) also shows how many Latvians migrated to the UK (Great Britain and Northern Ireland) in the years following EU expansion. By March 2010, nearly 75,000 Latvians had acquired NINOs. However, as an article on the *Latvians Online* website has it, NINOs do 'not necessarily track permanent immigrants, just people who are living in the UK', and some of these may have since returned to Latvia or moved on to another country.

Estonians came to the UK in fewer numbers for several reasons. Firstly, as already stated, Estonia has a much smaller population than Latvia or Lithuania, secondly, Estonia has fared better economically principally due to its close ties with the Scandinavian countries and thirdly, because of these close ties, many Estonians chose to migrate to these Scandinavian countries. The relatively small size of the Estonian community in the UK may also have been a factor. Figures from National Insurance number registrations from 2011/12 show the difference between the number of Estonian migrants to the UK and those of Latvians and Estonians. In 2011/12, only 2,150 Estonians registered. This compares to figures in the same year (2011/12) of Latvians of 18,590 and Lithuanians of 33,190.

Migration from the Baltic States to the UK declined slightly, as the UK suffered recession during 2011–13. National insurance registrations from all three Baltic nationalities fell during this period, although numbers began rising again from 2014.

In her analysis of the motivations of post-EU Lithuanian migrants to Britain, Violetta Parutis notes that Lithuanians along with other Eastern European migrants have had a high level of job mobility, moving from one job to another fairly rapidly, 'aiming to improve their situation in the British labour market.' Initially, Lithuanians, including those with extensive qualifications, opted to get '*any* job' such as cleaning, fruit picking or factory work. However, as they became more knowledgeable about the UK job market and gained confidence and improved English language skills, they moved to '*better*' jobs, where they made fuller use of previous skills and educational qualifications. This finding has implications for migration policy in Britain, as although newly arriving migrants have been willing to do *any* job initially – usually the lowest paid unskilled work in agriculture, factories, care and hospitality sectors – they have rapidly moved on to better paid and higher skilled positions (although many have remained in the unskilled sector, albeit in slightly better positions), leaving the lowest paid and unskilled jobs lacking manpower. These positions were filled in many cases by Bulgarians and Romanians who became entitled to live and work in Britain free of restrictions from 2014.

The Worker Registration Scheme data shows that although many migrants did take low paid, low skilled work, those who headed for the higher paid South Eastern area of Britain tended to draw higher wages. The data also shows the areas of work they worked in. Over one third worked in the administration, management and business services sector, approximately twenty per cent in hospitality and catering, ten per cent in agriculture, five per cent in food processing, almost five per cent in retail and related services, as well as in health and medical services and smaller percentages in transport, the computer services industry and financial services.

Data from the Office for National Statistics suggests that there are networks pulling certain nationality groups to specific areas, where communities already existed, most obviously to London. However, although some headed for traditional areas of Latvian, Lithuanian and Estonian concentration, others did not, and compared to the post-war migration, the new migrants have been more widely dispersed throughout the UK, with significant numbers settling in areas with negligible previous Baltic migration such as Devon, Cornwall and Northern Ireland. A report by the Centre for Population Change in 2012 suggests that unlike many previous waves of immigration, the initial destinations of East and Central European migrants have been remarkably geographically dispersed as opposed to being centred on major conurbations with an existing history of receiving immigrants. This has had a major impact on local authorities which have had limited experience of immigration, and has also had implications for Latvian, Lithuanian and Estonian community structures, as new groups and organisations have been established to serve the needs of these migrants.

In contrast to the post-war migration of Latvians, Lithuanians and Estonians to Britain, the British Government put very few measures in place to help the post-EU migrants settle into life in Britain, and in the longer term, to integrate. State intervention to facilitate integration has at best been piecemeal, the process being largely left to the 'Big Society' through the provision of support by charities and community groups, particularly during the Conservative and Coalition Governments since 2010. There has been minimal and underfunded local authority help in many areas, including lack of any systematic or organised attempts to provide English language tuition. In many cases, English language classes have been provided by the companies employing the immigrants. Many charitable organisations set up to help new arrivals have only received temporary funding and have thus been unable to plan long term strategies. In some areas, especially rural areas such as the South West, provision for the newcomers has been particularly inadequate. In the east of England, measures to improve relations between the local population and the migrants from the A8 countries have been inadequate and in some places, there have been some hostilities both with locals and among different nationality groupings.

During the decade following the integration of the Baltic States into the European Union and at the time of writing in 2016, Britain had no integration policy; a 2011 Report from The Migration Observatory noted that Britain had no coherent and agreed strategy on integration, and that the term itself continues to be contested. Successive governments have failed to introduce any active policy towards recent Baltic and Eastern European migrants. This contrasts with the highly planned and strategic policies of the post-war period, when the numbers of newcomers were actually, much smaller.

In contrast to Latvians, Lithuanians and Estonians who moved to the more outlying areas of the UK, those who headed for London and the bigger cities were able to access more support services in addition to local Latvian, Lithuanian and Estonian clubs and community organisations. This led to an expansion and increase in participation in these areas. In London, establishments such as London Latvian House enjoyed a surge in participation levels and new organisations were also set up to provide the newcomers with social support and information.

Many new businesses and services have also been established to cater for the needs of the new arrivals. For example, there is now an array of food shops catering for Latvians, Lithuanians and Estonians. In 2016, there were nine branches of *Lituanica*, described on its website as 'the largest supermarket chain in the UK, specialising in Eastern European cuisine with roots firmly fixed in Lithuania'. Most British cities have at least one Baltic or East European food store or supermarket, with some towns and cities with significant Latvian, Lithuanian and Estonian populations having an assortment of bars, cafés and restaurants serving Baltic and East European food. An article in *Time* magazine dated 6 June 2016 described Wisbech in Cambridgeshire, which has a high Baltic and Eastern European population:

> *'The Fenlands, where Wisbech is located, is a flat region in east-ern England known for having the most productive farmland in Britain. It has historically relied on seasonal, foreign labor, attracting migrants from across [the] world to spend a few sum-mer and autumn months working in some of the 4,000 farms or food-packaging factories in the surrounding countryside. As a result, Wisbech has become an Eastern European enclave in the heart of rural Britain, complete with a Catholic church offering a Polish Mass, and close to a dozen Eastern European grocery stores and delicatessens selling delicacies such as pickled her-ring and frozen dumplings.'*

Like Wisbech, Boston in Lincolnshire also has a high Lithuanian and Latvian population (as well as other East European nationalities) due to its position at the heart of an agricultural based economy. In Boston, there is a Lithuanian supermarket, a Lithuanian cake shop and various East European shops selling produce from the Baltic States. Boston's Lithuanian community has its own Facebook page with over 3,000 fol-lowers. According to the site, the 'Boston Lithuanian Community' is 'a non-profit organisation, providing educational activities and cultural events for local communities in Boston'.

It is unclear how many of the new migrants will settle permanently in the UK and how many will return to the Baltic States, especially in the light of Britain's 2016 vote to leave the EU. Many are settling down and starting families with children at school, but others have stayed only for temporary periods either to study or to earn some money and then return to Latvia, Lithuania and Estonia. According to the Lithuanian Embassy, in 2012, 6,000 people returned to Lithuania from Britain. The Embassy believes that more will return as the economic situation in Lithuania improves. All three Baltic States have seen quite a serious exodus from their countries and are currently implementing strategies to attempt to halt out-migration, but much more needs to done by all EU members to help bring about economic vitality in these countries.

The effect of the recent migration on the established post-war communities has been immense. Although there have been tensions in some areas, the new migrants have brought a new vitality and vigour to the established communities, as well as establishing their own community groups and organisations. For example, post-EU Lithuanian migrants set up the flourishing British Lithuanian Basketball League, with over 500 members, and the Lithuanian City of London Club, for 'high-flying' Lithuanians working in the city and professional jobs in London. Although in some areas the recent migrants are co-existing and integrating with the post-war communities, in other areas, they are largely independent of each other. This is partly due to language barriers, with many members of the second and third generations from the post-war communities having poor Estonian, Latvian or Lithuanian language skills, but it is also due to huge cultural differences and contrasting ideas about the content and nature of social and cultural events they wish to attend.

Latvian, Lithuanian and Estonian community websites and social media pages show the energy and dynamism that many of the clubs and associations have experienced as a result of the new migrants. The result is that many of the community organisations that existed in 2000 continue, with some reporting significantly increased participation levels. Language schools have been revitalised, as the new migrants want to ensure that their children learn Latvian, Lithuanian or Estonian, and there are now scores of language schools and classes across the UK catering for different age groups and language levels. Many large-scale events and activities have been organised by the new migrants, including outdoor festivals, music concerts and a wide variety of social and cultural events covering everything from the more traditional cultural celebrations to gigs by rock bands from the Baltic States, Baltic Art events, film festivals, sporting activities and fashion shows. All three communities continue to be supported by the Latvian, Lithuanian and Estonian Embassies in the UK and by consuls which have now been set up in Scotland, Wales and Northern Ireland, as well as in some of the larger cities and regions of England, to cater for the recent migrants.

The original size disparity between the three nationalities has now shifted, with Lithuanians currently being the largest of the three Baltic communities in Britain. This has had particular implications for the established post-war Lithuanian community. Following some initial caution and friction, recent Lithuanian migrants were welcomed into the post-war Lithuanian organisation, the DBLS, and over time, began to take more high-profile positions within the organisation. As first generation post-war Lithuanians began to pass away and their children became decreasingly active in the organisation, the post EU migrants began to hold the majority power within the organisation. The DBLS was renamed as the JKLB (*Jungtinės Karalystės Lietuvių Bendruomenė*) and its function shifted gradually to primarily serve the needs of the new migrants. The JKLB has been very active in organising events and activities, but, due to the fact that most of the websites, information and activities are in Lithuanian, many second and third generation Lithuanians in Britain do not feel included or welcomed within the organisation. One second generation Lithuanian in Britain, noted in a conversation in 2016 that '… the Lithuanian Community in GB doesn't really have room for the likes of me.'

At the time of writing in 2016, due to the high costs of maintenance and debts, the Lithuanian countryside property *Sodyba* had been sold, as well as the Manchester Lithuanian Club, both of which had hugely rich histories and significance for the post-war Lithuanian communities. The cost of maintaining such large properties along with the different aims and priorities of the newcomers has also impacted on the Latvian community which also sold its Rowfant House property in 2016. One second generation Latvian in Britain, Sarah Dauksta, described her sadness at Rowfant House closing:

> '*It has been the saddest thing in recent years, we have already lost two Latvian Houses and about to say goodbye to Rowfant. It is all the memories and these places mean so much to us. They were not just buildings they were so much more. As a child and up to 1991, these places were Latvia for my father and his friends.*'

Despite the closures of these properties, other centres, such as those in London, have thrived. Among the Latvian community, the DVF has maintained its core function – existing for, and serving the post-war refugee community – yet it has also welcomed newcomers to its activities.

Latvian House in London, longtime a centre for arriving Latvian students and newcomers, continues to be a vibrant and busy place. Now with its own bar, *Balzāmbārs*, it hosts a variety of musical and social events. By presenting information in both English and Latvian, and by providing a range of events and activities for both the post-war refugee community and for recent migrants, Latvian House has been successful at linking the two communities together.

Among the Estonian community, *Inglismaa Eestlaste Ühing* has also maintained its primary function as existing to serve the needs of the post-war refugee community, while at the same time welcoming recent new-comers to its local branches. The Leicester Estonian Club notes on its website that:

> *'The Estonian House in Leicester is the home for Estonians in Leicester and in Midlands. It was established 50 years ago as a social and cultural centre for the many migrant Estonians who came to Midlands. Now the Estonian house bar is open on Friday evening and Sunday midday.*
>
> *'Estonian Cultural events and holidays are marked at the club by themed evening gatherings. These include: Estonian Independence Day, Club's anniversary, celebrations by former Estonian Airmen and soldiers, Christmas.*
>
> *'Most of our Estonian members came to the UK in the 1940s and 1950s, however, new Estonian arrivals are welcome to visit our club and apply for membership.*
>
> *'We welcome all visitors to our club, particularly those visiting the UK from Estonia, or those who have recently relocated to the UK from Estonia.'*

Due to the relatively small size of the post-war Estonian community structures, however, many new organisations and associations have been set up to serve the needs of recent migrants. For example, according to its website, the Estonian Guild was set up in London in 2009 'by a group of enthusiastic Estonians with the support of the Estonian Embassy in London and Enterprise Estonia':

> *'Its prime objective is to encourage contacts and share information and ideas about Estonia, Estonians and their activities*

through the medium of organised events and functions. Each event has a fresh up to date theme, with new speakers, and a professional outlook. Different venues are used on each occasion. In the four years of its existence, the Guild has organised more than 50 events, advertised through a mailing list of over 1,200 people, of which more than 350 have joined the Guild's online communications network.'

Londoni Eesti Selts, set up in 1921, has flourished and is now composed primarily of newcomers who organise a wide variety of activities and events in London and further afield. Many new Estonian organisations, including Estonian language schools have been set up around the UK, while established clubs in Leicester, Bradford and London continue to thrive.

In Wales, the Wales Baltic Society was formed in 1991 (initially as the Cardiff Baltic Society) as a response to the nationalist uprising in the Baltic States, to raise awareness in Wales of the situation in the Baltic States and to bring exiled Latvians, Lithuanians and Estonians in Wales together. Antra Linarte noted in the *Baltic Times* on 21 September 2000, that:

'The initial purpose of the society, which now has 60 members, was to campaign for the recognition of independence for the three Baltic countries, as well as to help them forge relations with Wales. [After independence] the Wales Baltic Society continued furthering contacts, promoting friendship and increasing awareness about the Baltic countries through research, education and publicity. In a small way, it also provides practical and financial help'.

The Cardiff Baltic Society originally consisted of members of the exiled Lithuanian, Latvian and Estonian communities in Wales and a handful of Welsh people (later to include politicians) plus other interested parties. According to Anita Šovaitė-Woronycz, in an article for the VilNews website ('Greetings from Wales!'):

'The Wales Baltic Society has seen many of its members pass away over the years, but has also welcomed new members from across the Baltics.'

In Scotland, the existing Lithuanian organisations, composed both of nineteenth/early twentieth century Lithuanian descendants and post-war Lithuanians, have benefited from post-EU migration to Scotland. The Scottish Lithuanian Club in Mossend continues to flourish and collaborates with the new organisations that have been set up in response to the new migrants, such as L.I.S.A (Lithuanians in Scotland Association). The Scottish Lithuanian Club notes on its website that, it is proud to 'announce an affiliation with the *Lithuanians In Scotland Association. L.I.S.A* is an association of community groups formed by, and for, recent Lithuanian migrants and the communities they live in'.

New organisations have been set up all over Scotland to provide social and other support to recent migrants. For example, the EULS, the Edinburgh University Lithuanian Society hosts a basketball league, social events, Lithuanian cultural events and trips to the Scottish countryside. Similar organisations have been set up in universities across Britain for Latvian, Lithuanian and Estonian students who have benefited from free movement across Europe to study, work and live since 2004. For example, Glasgow University noted in 2016 that each year 60–80 Latvians began their studies there every year.

Numbers of newcomers heading for Northern Ireland have been relatively small due to the lower number of job opportunities there and the lack of established communities. Nevertheless, according to a report by the Northern Ireland Assembly, Worker Registration Scheme data shows that from May 2004 to March 2011, 18.8 per cent of the 45,525 by A8 nationals were Lithuanian (approx. 8560), the majority being young males in their twenties and thirties. A Lithuanian Honorary Consulate was established in Northern Ireland to support Lithuanians, and organisations such as the Armagh Lithuanian Community organisation 'Amber', were also set up by Lithuanians to provide support. Charitable associations such as the 'Community Intercultural Programme' based in Portadown employed a Lithuanian Inclusion Officer to facilitate integration and community cohesion. Similar provisions have also been made for the Latvian and Estonian communities in Northern Ireland.

One of the main differences between the newer migrants and the older established communities is the ability of the new migrants to move freely between Britain and the Baltic States both through travel and via social media. For example, many migrants use email or Facebook as a way of connecting with friends and relatives all over the world, which is in stark contrast to post-war migrants who struggled to keep in touch with their homelands during the years of Soviet occupation. There are multiple Facebook and other internet pages for local Latvian, Lithuanian and Estonian communities up and down Britain, which enable easy exchange of information and correspondence among members of the communities.

The advent of social media and internet based resources has also had a positive impact on members of the post-war second generation Latvian, Lithuanian and Estonian communities, who have used the internet to connect with Latvians, Lithuanians and Estonians across the world, as well as to research their family histories. In many families, the past was barely discussed, experiences of war and displacement too traumatic to recall and talk about. Many families were unaware of what had happened to family members even ten years after independence, and set about trying to piece together family trees and family histories. During recent years, many archives have been opened in Latvia, Lithuania and Estonia, as well as relevant archives in Germany, Russia and destination countries, such as the USA and Great Britain. Archival resources have been digitized, enabling access to records and sources via the internet from across the world. Forums and social media resources allow members to post queries, questions and photographs online, allowing many links to be established across the diaspora, and many questions to be answered.

Alexandra Māzers, a second generation Latvian living in Devon, in Britain, is one of the many members of these communities who has become interested in finding out more about her Latvian family history. Alexandra had minimal involvement in the Latvian community in Birmingham where she grew up, and her father was only four when he arrived in Britain as a child dependent on the EVW schemes in 1949. Keen to trace her father's brothers and other relatives from whom they had heard nothing since the war, Alexandra set out on a journey to find answers to these and many other questions about the family's past. Through a meticulous and far-reaching search of internet-based resources, sending out letters and participating in discussions on Baltic history forums, Alexandra was finally able to trace her father's brothers, one of whom was found to be alive and living in the United States. She also found living relatives in Latvia and has met up with them in Latvia. Alexandra's journey to find family mirrors that of many other Latvians, Lithuanians and Estonians both in Britain and across the world, and shows that the past has such a huge significance for the present-day lives of so many descendants of the original EVWs, as well as of earlier refugees to Britain.

Some of the dependants of the original refugees who came to Britain, have written up their experiences into memoirs, most notably, 'Into Exile' by Elina Toona Gottschalk and 'God Give Us Wings' by Felicia Prekeris Brown. These two books are essential reading for anyone, looking to understand the experiences of the Baltic EVWs in Britain. Both Elina, an Estonian, and Felicia, a Lithuanian, were children when the war broke out, and eventually came to Britain after long and arduous displacement journeys. Both Elina and Felicia's mothers were recruited onto the Balt Cygnet Scheme and they were able to join them with some other family members later on. Both Felicia and Elina had difficult experiences when they first arrived in Britain and overcame immense challenges. Their fascinating memoirs make a significant contribution to a greater under-standing of the experiences of Baltic European Volunteer Workers and their families, who came to Britain after the war, as well as the immense contributions these families made to the British economy during this critical period.

Since 2004, the original post-war communities have been trans-formed. The arrival of tens of thousands of new migrants from the Baltic States has led to a transformation of the Baltic communities in Britain. The integration of the Baltic States into the European Union in 2004 has enabled young Latvians, Lithuanians and Estonians from the Baltic States, to turn westwards, *towards Britain* and other western European countries, to travel, study, work and live. Meanwhile, the youngest of the original EVWs and their descendants in Britain have been able to ori-entate themselves with greater ease *towards the Baltic States*, for visits, meeting long lost family, and in a few cases to study, work or live, while at the same time maintaining a solid foothold in Britain. Many second and third generation Latvians, Lithuanians and Estonians in Britain have gained a new interest in their family histories and in the countries of their ancestors, with many visiting the Baltic States for the first time. Although many of the original first generation have now passed away, the dual processes described above have brought about a re-energising of the Latvian, Lithuanian and Estonian communities in Britain, as well as significant changes in Latvian, Lithuanian and Estonian community structures and activities in Britain.

217

Rebuilding Post-War Britain – The Contribution of Latvians, Lithuanians and Estonians

Jānis, a Latvian man who came to Britain in 1947 at age 18, was initially sent to Bedford to work in a brick factory which produced 20,000 bricks a day. He described it as 'hard, dirty work', which few British people were prepared to do. He worked alongside other Latvian, Lithuanian, Ukrainian and Italian men, as one of nearly 3,000 EVW men recruited to work specifically in Britain's brick making factories. The bricks Jānis made, were used to rebuild Britain's bomb wrecked houses, schools, factories and hospitals. Yet, despite working long hours and earning low wages, locals called Jānis 'an idle and bloody foreigner'.

Juozas, a Lithuanian man who came to Britain on the Westward Ho! scheme in the spring of 1947, was sent to work in coalmining in South Wales. The severe winter of 1946–47, the harshest in three centuries, had led to critical coal shortages which had a devastating effect on industrial production and power cuts were commonplace. The crisis was caused by several factors, one of them being an underproduction of coal, which could only be addressed by additional manpower. Coal mining was not an attractive industry due to the dangerous and dirty nature of the work and the government had no choice, but to address the recruitment issue through employing foreign workers. Eleven thousand men were recruited for coal mining via the Westward Ho! scheme, of whom a significant number were Latvians, Lithuanians and Estonians.

Juozas spent his first six months in the West Midlands learning English: 'because when you're working in the mines [it is a] … very dangerous job, you have to at least minimum to speak English.' Juozas worked in the mines for twenty years before moving to the Greater Manchester area to work in the rubber industry, where he initially worked as a moulder:

'in those days you know, you had to pick among the bad jobs, all English people had the best [jobs] you know.' Juozas noted the jobs that were open to him: 'textiles, and the rubber industry, asbestos, those kinds of jobs'. The contribution made by men like Juozas and Jānis, and by the thousands of women employed on the EVW schemes, particularly in hospitals and textiles, needs to be recognised.

After the war ended, British people wanted the towns and cities of Britain to be rebuilt quickly, they were desperate for rationing to end and for life to return to normal. Yet many British people were completely unaware of the quiet contribution that thousands of Latvians, Lithuanians and Estonians were making to the British economy, working in the brickworks, iron and steel, and in factories, manufacturing clothes for them to wear, in agriculture producing food for them to eat, in hospitals caring for their sick and wounded relatives, and in coalmines, mining coal for their fires and ranges.

By 1950, several years after the first Baltic refugees began working in Britain as EVWs, Britain was making good progress on the road to recovery. Some food rationing was still in place, yet the national debt was already in steep decline, imports had been reduced and the country was finally beginning to export a significant amount of goods again. The NHS had been established and many nationalised industries were now receiving significant investment, laying strong foundations for the subsequent decades, when Britain experienced sustained economic growth. Although Britain still had huge strides to make to fully heal the wartime wounds of the country, there is no doubt that a solid base for subsequent economic prosperity was established during this period.

While the contribution to the British economy of the immigrants from the Caribbean and Indian sub-continent during the subsequent decade, the 1950s, has been recognised, the vital input of the European Volunteer Workers to rebuilding the British economy in the late 1940s and beyond, has been largely ignored and furthermore, the British public are largely unaware of it. A common misconception is that the recent movement to Britain of migrants from Latvia, Lithuania and Estonia, since these countries joined the European Union, is the first movement of these nationalities to Britain. Yet this is not the case, and particularly in an era, where resentment toward Baltic and East European migrants to Britain appears to be growing, the vital support they provided to the British economy in the post-war period needs to be emphasised.

REBUILDING POST-WAR BRITAIN

The Baltic refugees in Britain also made a valuable contribution well beyond the post-war period, through economic, social, scientific and cultural innovations and influences, and through the positive achievements of their children, the second and third generations. We have already noted such notable Baltic refugees among the pre-war refugees, such as Montague Burton, the founder of Burtons Menswear. Among the post-war generation, some of the refugees were able to pursue professional careers after fulfilling the initial labour contracts. Along with nurses, lawyers, scientists, teachers, authors, business owners and university lecturers, a number of individuals made particularly significant contributions. An Estonian, Ernst Öpik became an internationally renowned astronomer and astrophysicist who worked at Armagh Observatory in Northern Ireland. Öpik was recruited individually directly from a DP camp to work as a Professor, and won many international prizes for his outstanding contribution to astrophysics. A Latvian man, recruited on the EVW schemes, Reinhards Vitols, became a Professor at Loughborough University and designed patented innovations relating to the manufacture of textiles, which have made an important contribution to the development of the textile industry. Artists such as the Latvians, Nikolājs Sojkans, Valdemārs Tone and Laimonis Mieriņš, all EVWs, made an international impact with their works. Mieriņš was also a renowned tutor at the highly acclaimed Leeds College of Art. His influence on future generations of artists in Britain can be seen in the many enthusiastic dedications to him by former students. Writers such as Valdis Pulis, a Latvian in Britain, have also contributed through internationally recognised poetry and plays.

Their children too, have had an important influence on Britain's culture and society. For example, Olly Murs is a well-known singer of Latvian descent; Mel Giedroyc, a TV personality with Polish-Lithuanian roots; TV Chef Martin Blunos, a second generation Latvian; politician Lembit Öpik, a second generation Estonian, and Guy Martin, an internationally successful racing driver and TV personality, is the son of an EVW; and there are many, many others, including actors, writers, musicians, sportsmen and women, and scientists, in addition to teachers, filmmakers, businessmen and women.

Most of the refugees stayed in Britain their whole lives, making a quiet contribution through their work, in a wide variety of economic sectors. They were invisible to many people, calmly integrating into British society. Parallels can be drawn between the way Latvians, Lithuanians and

220

Estonians made such a valuable contribution to Britain's economy in the immediate post-war period and the positive economic impact that recent newcomers have made. Once again, they have filled jobs that British people have been unwilling to do and meant that the British economy has been able to overcome manpower shortages and flourish.

In most cases, the second generation of the original EVWs have integrated fully into British society. The fast pace at which the children of Latvian, Lithuanian and Estonian refugees and migrants integrate, can also be seen today with the young children of the post-EU arrivals – children who have been born in Britain and who are well-integrated into British life, going to school, speaking English fluently, and having British friends and hobbies.

However, there is no doubt that the measures brought in by the British Government during the post-war EVW schemes to facilitate integration (referred to at that time as 'assimilation'), helped the newcomers settle into life in Britain and aided the integration process. The lack of policies in recent years to help facilitate the integration of the post-EU newcomers contrasts markedly with the series of measures put in place to enable the rapid settling in and integration of the post-war arrivals. Much can be learned from the EVW schemes, and the work required to facilitate the integration of the newcomers. If Britain is to remain the tolerant country it has long been, relatively free of racism and division, more effort needs to be made by government to harmonise relationships between locals and newcomers. Moreover, the histories of overlooked groups of refugees and migrants to Britain's shores, and the vital and positive contributions they have made, needs to be written both into popular histories, as well as integrated into public understanding and perceptions of Britain's post-war history. This book makes a small contribution to this mammoth challenge.

Endnotes

Introduction

1. For the most comprehensive summaries of the EVW schemes to date, including discussion of Latvians, Lithuanians and Estonians, see the bibliography including: Brown; Holmes; Kay and Miles; Lane; McDowell; Paul, Tannahill; Watson, Webster.

Prologue

1. See: Holmes, Lunn, Millar, Rodgers, White.
2. Rodgers (1984), 141.
3. Holmes (1988), 49–50.
4. Džialtuvaitė.
5. Millar, 100.
6. Holmes (1988), 29.
7. Bučys, 116.
8. Holmes, 222.
9. Hindo.

Chapter 2

1. Plensners, 7–8.
2. Misiūnas and Taagapera, 70.
3. Simanis, 197.
4. Plakans, 149.
5. Milosz, 43.
6. Misiūnas and Taagapera, 60.
7. Senn (2001).
8. Hilberg, 119–121.

9. Ibid., 112–113.
10. Misiūnas and Taagapera, 56–57.
11. Plensners, 39–40.
12. Ezergailis, 32.
13. Ibid., 10.
14. Misiūnas and Taagapera, 58.
15. Ezergailis, 9.
16. Sinka, 30.
17. Ezergailis, 12.
18. Kasekamp, 133.
19. Hiden and Salmon, 118–119.
20. Kasekamp, 135.
21. Veidemanis, 121.
22. Roos, 43.
23. See Kulischer and Vernant.
24. FO371/55974.

Chapter 3

1. FO1049/414.
2. FO1049/613.
3. FO1049/414.
4. FO1049/415.
5. FO371/55977.

Chapter 4

1. LAB8/90.
2. FO945/496.
3. Ibid.
4. LAB8/90.
5. Kay and Miles, 123–124.
6. FO371/55977.

7. FO1032/846.
8. Cooper, 122.
9. McDowell (2004), 32.
10. FO1049/497.
11. FO1052/445.
12. FO1052/446.
13. FO945/497, FO945/499.
14. FO371/66709, FO945/499.
15. FO371/66709, FO945/497, FO945/499.
16. CAB14/47.
17. FO945/499.
18. LAB8/97.
19. FO371/66711, FO371/72040.
20. FO371/66711.
21. FO371/66711.
22. FO371/66713.
23. FO371/66714.
24. FO371/66711.
25. Tannahill, 49–50.
26. Kay and Miles, 43.
27. Cooper, 122.
28. FO1006/513
29. FO945/503
30. FO1006/514.

Chapter 5

1. Tannahill, 66.
2. FO371/66713.
3. FO371/66713.
4. LAB26/247.
5. Ibid.
6. Kynaston, 19.
7. LAB26/247.
8. McDowell (2004), 35.
9. Lunn (1992), 585.
10. LAB26/247.
11. Ibid.
12. Tannahill, 70.
13. Lunn (1992), 585.
14. FO1006/247.

15. LAB26/247.
16. Murphy, 91.
17. Ibid., 182–183.
18. Ibid., 187.
19. Bülbring, 108.
20. Brown, 30.
21. Grunts and Smith (ed), 462.
22. Ibid., 465.
23. FO371/66711
24. FO1006/513.
25. LAB26/247.

Chapter 6

1. Brown, 51.
2. Ibid.
3. Tannahill, 81–82.
4. Kay and Miles, 158; Tannahill, 139–40.
5. Tannahill, 69.
6. Ibid., 86.
7. Ibid., 88.
8. Ibid.
9. FO371/143521.
10. FO371/106114.
11. FO371/11379.

Chapter 7

1. BHRU interviews: see Bibliography.
2. Brown, 52.
3. Hurwitz, 299.
4. King and Wilson, 55.
5. Ibid.
6. Tannahill, 98–99.

Chapter 8

1. See UNHCR documents cited in Bibliography.
2. LYNES 30 (1998).

Abbreviations

BHRU	Bradford Heritage Recording Unit
CCG	Control Commission for Germany
DBLS	*Didžiosios Britanijos Lietuvių Sąjunga* (Lithuanian Association in Great Britain)
DBLJS	*Didžiosios Britanijos Lietuvių Jaunimo Sąjunga* (Lithuanian Youth Association in Great Britain)
DP	Displaced Person
DVF	*Daugavas Vanagi Fondas*
EVW	European Volunteer Worker
FO	Foreign Office
HO	Home Office
IRO	International Refugee Organisation
LAB	Ministry of Labour
LYNES	Lithuanian Youth News-sheet
UNHCR	United Nations High Commissioner for Refugees
UNNRA	United Nations Refugee and Rehabilitation Administration
WRVS	Womens' Royal Voluntary Service

Bibliography

Oral History Sources

Unless specified otherwise, all interview excerpts in the text are from the interviews with 25 Latvians, Lithuanians and Estonians that I carried out in the 1990s, as part of the original research project. The interviews lasted between 2–4 hours and were recorded, transcribed and analysed. 3 interviews were carried out but not recorded, with notes taken. A further interview with a second-generation Latvian in Britain was carried out in 2014.

Bradford Heritage Recording Unit Interviews (BHRU), Bradford Local Studies Library.

1. BO 060, First Generation Latvian.
2. BO 122, First Generation Latvian.
3. BO 127, First Generation Estonian.
4. BO 166, First Generation Lithuanian.

National Archive Sources

125 British Government files relating to the EVWs schemes were consulted, of which the most important were contained within the following record classes: CAB 9; PREM 9; HO 213; LAB 8; LAB 26; FO 371; FO 945; FO 1006; FO 1032; FO 1049; FO 1052; FO 1056; FO 1110.

Governmental Papers

Department for Work and Pensions, *Statistical Bulletin: National Insurance Number Allocations to Adult Overseas Nationals Entering the UK – registrations to March 2012*, Sheffield: August 2012
Home Office, Lithuania Assessment, Version 4, September 1999, Country Information and Policy Unit, 4. (http://www.homeoffice.gov.uk/ind/lit4.htm)

Office for National Statistics

Population Trends, (2007) *Migrants from Central and Eastern Europe: local geographies*, Office for National Statistics, Autumn 2007

The All-Party Parliamentary War Crimes Group

'*Report on the Entry of Nazi War Criminals. and Collaborators into the UK, 1945–50*', The All-Party Parliamentary War Crimes Group, November 1988.

UNHCR documents

'Lithuanian Asylum Applications Declined Significantly in the UK', *UNHCR Asyl Nord* No. 9, 19 April 1999. Information collated by UNHCR from: *ELTA* 31 March 1999. (http://www.immi.se/asyl/nord9.htm)
'Tighter Control on Travellers to London from Lithuania', *UNHCR Asyl Nord* No. 7, 16 February 1999. Information collated by UNHCR from: *ELTA*, 20 January 1999; *ELTA*, 26 January 1999. (http://ww.immi.se/asyl/nord7.htm)

Websites cited

Changing Identities: Latvians, Lithuanians and Estonians in Great Britain
https://changingidentities.wordpress.com/
Global True Lithuania (Lithuanian Communities and Heritage Worldwide)
www.global.truelithuania.com/category/western-europe/united-kingdom
Lituanica Supermarkets in the UK https://lituanica.co.uk/
Leicester Estonian House https://sites.google.com/site/eestimaja/
The *Baltic Times* http://www.baltictimes.com
The *Economist* http://www.economist.com
The Estonian Guild http://www.estonianguild.co.uk/
VilNews: The Voice of International Lithuania http://vilnews.com/

Books:

Andrups, J., (1995) 'A History of Latvians in Great Britain', (English translation by Andris Abakus), in Auziņa-Smita, I. (1995*) LatviešI Lielbritanijā(Latvians in Great Britain*), vol 1, London: Latvian National Council in Great Britain and Daugavas Vanagi.
Auziņa-Smita, I. et al. (ed.) (1995) *LatviešI Lielbritanijā (Latvians in Great Britain*), vol 1, London: Latvian National Council in Great Britain and Daugavas Vanagi.
Barėnas, K. (1978) *Britanijos Lietuviai, 1947–1973 (Lithuanians in Britain, 1947–1973*), London: Lithuanian Association in Great Britain.
Brown, J. (1970) *The Un-Melting Pot: An English Town and its Immigrants*, London & Basingstoke: Macmillan.
Bučys et al., Bradford Lithuanian Club "Vytis" (ed.) (1995) *Bradfordo Lietuvių Veikla Didžiojoje Britanijoje, 1947–1995 (Lithuanians in Bradford, 1947–1995*), Vilnius: 'Litfondas'.

BIBLIOGRAPHY

Bülbring, M. (1954) 'Post-war Refugees in Great Britain', *Population Studies*, viii(2): 99–112.

Cesarani, D. (1992) *Justice Delayed: How Britain became a refuge for Nazi War Criminals*, London: Heinemann.

Cooper, K. (1979) *The Uprooted: Agony and Triumph among the Debris of War*, London: Quartet Books.

Dugan, E. (2015) *Finding Home: Real Stories of Migrant Britain*, London: Icon Books.

Džialtuvaitė, J., "The role of religion in language choice and identity among Lithuanian immigrants in Scotland." In Tope Omoniyi & Joshua A. Fishman (eds.) *Explorations in the Sociology of Languages and Religion*, Roehampton/New York, 2006.

Estonian Committee in Göttingen, *Estonia: My Beautiful Land*, 1946.

Estonian Latvian National Council in Great Britain (1995) *Latvians in Great Britain*, London: Latvian National Council in Great Britain.

Ekstein, M. (1999) *Walking Since Daybreak: a story of Eastern Europe, World War II and the heart of the twentieth century*, New York: Houghton.

Ezergailis, A. (ed.) (1997) *The Latvian Legion: Heroes, Nazis or Victims? – A Collection of Documents from OSS War-Crimes investigation files, 1945–50*, Riga: The Historical Institute of Latvia.

Gilbert, E. (2013) *Changing Identities: Latvians, Lithuanians and Estonians in Great Britain*, Charleston: CreateSpace.

Gilbert, E. (2002) 'The Impact of Homeland Independence on the Latvian Community in Great Britain', *Journal of Baltic Studies*, 33(3): 280–306.

Gilbert, E. (2001) *Latvian, Lithuanian and Estonian Displaced Persons in Great Britain*, Unpublished PhD thesis: University of Sheffield.

Gottschalk, E. T., (2013) *Into Exile: A Life Story of War and Peace*, Brandon, Florida: Evershine.

Grunts, M. V. & Smith, I. A., *'In the Mirror of the Past'*, in Auziņa-Smita, I.et al. (ed.) (1995) *Latvieši Lielbritanijā (Latvians in Great Britain)*, vol 1, London: Latvian National Council in Great Britain and Daugavas Vanagi.

Hiden, J. & Salmon, P. (1991) *The Baltic Nations and Europe: Estonia, Latvia and Lithuania in the Twentieth Century*, London & NY: Longman.

Hilberg, R. (1985) *The Destruction of the European Jews*, NY: Holmes & Meier.

Hindo, N. (1968) *Eesti Organisatsioonid Inglismal, 1918–1968* (reference provided by an Estonian in Britain).

Holmes, C. (1994) *John Bull's Island: Immigration and British Society, 1871–1971*, Basingstoke and London: Macmillan.

Hurwitz, B., Greenhalgh, T., Skultans, V., (eds.) (2004) *Narrative Illness in Health and Illness*, London: Blackwell Publishing.

Kasekamp, A. (2010) *A History of the Baltic States*, London: Palgrave Macmillan.

Kay, D. & **Miles**, R. (1992) *Refugees or Migrant Workers?: European Volunteer Workers in Britain, 1946–1951*, London: Routledge.

King, V. & Wilson, R. (1988) 'Latvian Residential Homes for Retired People' in *Age in Exile: A Report on Elderly Exiles in the United Kingdom*, (Unpublished), British Refugee Council for the Age in Exile Conference, Noordwijkerhout, the Netherlands.

Kriščiūnas, R. G. (1983) 'The Emigrant Experience: The Decision of Lithuanian Refugees to Emigrate, 1945–1950', *Lituanus*, 29(2): 30–39.

Kulischer, E. M. (1948) *Europe on the Move: War and Population Changes, 1917–1947*, New York: Columbia University Press.

Kulischer, E. M. (1943) *The Displacement of Population in Europe*, Montreal.

Kynaston, D. (2007) *Austerity Britain, 1945–51*, London: Bloomsbury.

Lane, T. (2004) *Victims of Stalin and Hitler: The Exodus of Poles and Balts in Britain*, Hampshire and New York: Palgrave Macmillan.

Lunn, K. (1992) 'The Employment of Polish and European Volunteer Workers in the Scottish Coalfields, 1945–1950', in Tenfelde, K. (ed.) *Towards a Social History of Mining in the Nineteenth and Twentieth Centuries*, Munich: C. H. Beck.

Lunn, K. (1985) 'Immigrants and British Labour's Response, 1870–1950', *History Today,* November 1985: 48–52.

Lunn, K. (1980), 'Reactions to Lithuanian and Polish Immigrants in the Lanarkshire Coalfield, 1850–1914', in *Hosts, Immigrants & Minorities: Historical Responses to Newcomers in British Society, 1870–1914*, Kent: Dawson.

Lunn, K. (ed.) (1980) *Hosts, Immigrants & Minorities: Historical Responses to Newcomers in British Society, 1870–1914*, Kent: Dawson.

McCollum, D., **Cook**, L., **Chiroro**., **Platts**, A., **McLeod**, F., **Findlay**, A., (2012) *Spatial, sectoral and temporal trends in A8 migration to the UK 2004–2011: Evidence from the Worker Registration Scheme*, Centre for Population.

McDowell, L., (2016) *Migrant Women's Voices: Talking about Life and Work in the UK since 1945*, London: Bloomsbury.

McDowell. L., (2005) *Hard Labour: The Forgotten Voices of Latvian Migrant 'Volunteer' Workers,* London: UCL.

McDowell, L. (2004) Narratives of Family, Community and Waged Work: Latvian European Volunteer Worker Women in post-war Britain, *Women's History Review*, 13(1).

Millar, J. (Jonas Stepšis) (1998) *The Lithuanians in Scotland: A Personal View*, Isle of Colonsay: House of Lochar.

BIBLIOGRAPHY

Milosz, C. (1984) 'Lithuania, Latvia and Estonia 1940–1980: Similarities and Differences', *Baltic Forum*, 1(1).

Misiūnas, R. & **Taagepera**, R. (1993) *The Baltic States: Years of Dependence, 1940–1990*, 2nd Edn., London: Hurst & Co.

Murphy, H. B. M. (ed.) (1955) *Flight and Resettlement*, Switzerland: UNESCO.

O'Connor, K. (2015) *The History of the Baltic States*, Connecticut & London, Greenwood University Press.

Owen, D. *Country of Birth: Settlement Patterns, 1991 Census Statistical Paper*, National Ethnic Minority Data Archive, Warwick University.

Parutis, V., (2014) 'Economic Migrants' or 'Middling Transnationals'? East Europeans Migrants' Experiences of Work in the UK, *International Migration*, vol 52 (1).

Patterson, S. (1968) *Immigrants in Industry*, London: O.U.P.

Paul, K. (1997) *Whitewashing Britain: race and citizenship in the postwar era*, Ithaca: Cornell University Press.

Pidd, H., (2013) *Baltic Exchange: meet the Lithuanians who have made Britain their home*, The Guardian, 7 January 2013.

Plakans, A. (1995) *Latvia: A Short History*, Stanford: Hoover University Press.

Poopuu, H. (1985–86) *Remembering Pussa* (Unpublished personal memoirs).

Porat, D. (1994) 'The Holocaust in Lithuania', in Cesarani, D. *The Final Solution: Origins and Implementation*, London and New York: Routledge.

Prekeris Brown, F. (2013) *God Give Us Wings*, Charleston: CreateSpace Publishing.

Proudfoot, M. (1957) *European Refugees: 1939–52, A Study in Forced Population Movement*, London: Faber & Faber.

Rodgers, M. (1982) 'The Anglo-Russian Military Convention and the Lithuanian Immigrant Community in Lanarkshire, Scotland, 1914–20', *Immigrants and Minorities*, 1:

Rodgers, M. (1985) 'The Lithuanians', *History Today*, 35: 15–20

Rodgers, M. (1984) 'Political Developments in the Lithuanian Community in Scotland, c. 1890–1923', in Slatter, J. (ed.) *From the Other Shore: Russian Political Emigrants in Britain, 1880–1917, London: Cass.*

Senn, A. (2001) 'Reflections on the Holocaust in Lithuania: A New Book by Alfonsas Eidentas', *Lituanus*, 47 (4).

Sinka, J. (1988) *Latvia and Latvians*, Central Board "Daugavas Vanagi", London: Nida Press.

Skultans, V. (1998) 'Remembering Time and Place: A Case Study in Latvian narrative', *Oral History*, 55–63.

Skultans, V. (1998) *The Testimony of Lives: Narrative and Memory in post-Soviet Latvia*, London & New York: Routledge.

Snyder, T. (2010) *Bloodlands: Europe Between Hitler and Stalin*, London: Vintage.

Spencer, S. (2011) *Policy Primer: Integration*, The Migration Observatory, University of Oxford.

Stadulis, E. (1952) 'The Resettlement of Displaced Persons in the UK', *Population Studies*, March 1952: 207–237.

Taagepera, R. (1993) *Estonia: Return to Independence*, Westview Press: Boulder.

Tannahill, J. A. (1958) *European Volunteer Workers in Britain*, Manchester: Manchester University Press.

Vernant, J. (1953) *The Refugee in the Post-War World*, London: Allen & Unwin.

Von Rauch, G. (1995) *The Baltic States: The Years of Independence: Estonia, Latvia, Lithuania, 1917–1940*, London: Hurst & Co.

Watson, J. L. (ed.) (1977) *Between Two Cultures: Immigrants and Minorities in Britain*, Oxford: Blackwell.

Webster, W. (2000) 'Defining Boundaries: European Volunteer Worker women in Britain and narratives of community', *Women's History Review*, 9: 257–276.

White, J. D. (1975) 'Scottish Lithuanians and the Russian Revolution', *JBS*, 6(1): 1–8.

Wyman, M. (1989) *DP: Europe's Displaced Persons, 1945–1951*, Philadelphia: The Balch Institute.

Index

INDEX

INDEX

INDEX

INDEX